Black and Catholic

BLACK
and
CATHOLIC

RACISM, IDENTITY, AND RELIGION

TIA NOELLE PRATT

University of Notre Dame Press
Notre Dame, Indiana

Copyright © 2025 by the University of Notre Dame
Notre Dame, Indiana 46556
undpress.nd.edu

All Rights Reserved

Published in the United States of America

Library of Congress Control Number: 2025934553

ISBN: 978-0-268-21017-5 (Hardback)
ISBN: 978-0-268-21020-5 (WebPDF)
ISBN: 978-0-268-21019-9 (Epub3)

GPSR Compliance Inquiries:
Lightning Source France, 1 Av. Johannes Gutenberg, 78310 Maurepas, France
compliance@lightningsource.fr | Phone: +33 1 30 49 23 42

For the students of

Sociology of African American Catholicism

at Saint Joseph's University

and the students of African American Catholics

at Villanova University

CONTENTS

List of Illustrations and Table   ix
Acknowledgments   xi
Introduction: Why This Book? Why This Book Now?   1

ONE   Black Faith, White Space: Understanding the African American Catholic Experience   11

TWO   The Numbers Don't Add Up: Systemic Racism and Its Legacy in Urban Catholic Life   31

THREE   Finding a Place at the Table: Liturgy as Identity Work and an Act of Resistance   51

FOUR   Erasing a Legacy: The Price of St. Peter Claver   73

FIVE   Race, Community, and Process: Black Catholics' Experiences in Catholic Spaces   103

SIX   Losing Religion and Gaining Faith   131

Appendix   145
Notes   179
Reference List   193
Index   207

ILLUSTRATIONS AND TABLE

Figure 4.1. St. Peter Claver Parish Buildings   76

Figure 4.2. St. Peter Claver School   77

Figure 4.3. St. Peter Claver Church   78

Figure 4.4. St. Peter Claver Rectory   78

Figure 4.5. South Street Parking Garage   79

Figure 4.6. Multiuse Building in South Philadelphia   80

Figure 4.7. Seger Park   81

Figure 4.8. Rodman Street Flags   82

Table 3.1. Liturgical Styles and Their Key Features   55

ACKNOWLEDGMENTS

It is difficult to know where to begin. *Black and Catholic: Racism, Identity, and Religion* has had many champions. Three champions who have been with me, albeit in different ways, from the very beginning are my mother, Antoinette Pratt, sociologist Mark R. Warren, and the late sociologist Mary Ellen Konieczny. They deserve special thanks. As with all things I've ever attempted, my mother has been my most steadfast supporter. She has always believed in me. While still a graduate student completing coursework, Mark Warren, a faculty member at Fordham University at the time, was the first person to tell me I should and must write a book about Black Catholics. Years later, on the day I decided to write this book, while we were attending a symposium, Mary Ellen Konieczny quickly allayed all the fears I expressed about such an undertaking.

Champions of this book, in large and small ways, include thought partners who have helped me find pathways where I thought there were only obstacles. My cohorts at the American Parish Project and Generations in Dialogue, two programs from the Institute for Advanced Catholic Studies, provided invaluable critique and support. I am grateful for the generosity of scholars who are also friends, colleagues, and collaborators, including James C. Cavendish; Shannen Dee Williams; Maureen H. O'Connell; Brett Hoover; Maureen K. Day; Lauren Jade Martin; Rev. Lucas Sharma, SJ; Besheer Mohamed; Courtney Ann Irby; and Todd Nicholas Fuist. Thought partners for this book include all the students who took Sociology of African American Catholicism at Saint Joseph's University and African American Catholics at Villanova University. This book is for them.

In addition to my mother, I extend my deepest gratitude to my entire family, especially Marcel A. Pratt Jr., Tanya Walton Pratt, and Lena Pratt Sanders. There are many others whose support has made this book possible in tangible and intangible ways—including Sister Cora Marie Billings, RSM; Sister Bethany Welch, SSJ; Adrienne Andrews Harris; Daria Ward; Orlando and Phyllis Rodriguez; Monica Brady-Haggard; Eboni Martin-Dunkley; and Andrea Rychlicki Barone. I am especially indebted to Sharon Browning, Paul Eisenhauer, and Sara Ellen Kitchen, the professors who nurtured my love of sociology while I was an undergraduate student.

This book would not have been possible without the support of grants from the Society for the Scientific Study of Religion, the Louisville Institute, and Villanova University. All three institutions have my deepest thanks. I'm grateful to everyone in the Office for Mission and Ministry at Villanova for their support—particularly Rev. Kevin M. DePrinzio, OSA; Rev. Arthur Purcaro, OSA; and Maureen Piotti.

I am indebted to senior scholars who paved the way for me—sociologists of religion as well as Black Catholic scholars who study the Black experience in our church. These scholars include James R. Kelly; Nancy T. Ammerman; Cheryl Townsend Gilkes; M. Shawn Copeland; Rev. Bryan Massingale; Sister Jamie Phelps, OP; and the late Rev. Cyprian Davis, OSB. They have made my work possible.

I'd like to thank everyone at the University of Notre Dame Press and my editors, Emily R. King and C. David Carlson. Additionally, I'd like to acknowledge the anonymous reviewers whose thoughtful comments helped shape this book and the staff at the Charles L. Blockson Afro-American Collection at Temple University for their assistance in accessing documents related to St. Peter Claver Church in Philadelphia. I'd also like to thank my friend and longtime editor, Olga Marina Segura, who understands my voice and intent so clearly. I couldn't have gotten this book across the finish line without her.

Crucially, I'd like to thank everyone at the churches I visited who graciously welcomed me as I conducted research at Mass. I owe a debt I cannot repay to all those I interviewed who welcomed me into their homes and their lives, treated me like family, and spoke with me about their experiences. There truly would be no book without them.

It is not possible to name every person who offered me a word of kindness, encouragement, or support—often at a time when I needed it most. I thank all of them now.

INTRODUCTION

Why This Book? Why This Book Now?

My family is as Catholic as any one family can be. My family's Catholicism spans hundreds of years and through countless cities across the diaspora. My great-grandmother was born in New Orleans. Her great-grandparents' hometowns were in Cuba and the Dominican Republic; even farther back, our Catholic roots can be traced to Spain. Ever since I was a child, I have been what some would call "a listener." Though our Catholic history wasn't talked about often, I heard snippets of conversations about it growing up. From listening, I learned that my great-grandmother's youngest brother, Calvin Aguillard, had researched our family's history intensively. I was intrigued. Years later, I began studying Black Catholics to better understand my family's story. My undergraduate senior thesis had its genesis in the "Marriage and Family" course I took as an undergraduate. For an assigned project in this class, I decided to incorporate my family narrative into the bigger sociological themes of marriage, family life, race, and religion. By this time, the horrors of dementia meant that I couldn't ask my great-grandmother the questions that I desperately wanted answered. So my mother took me to see Elizabeth Washington, my great-grandmother's younger sister, who, luckily, lived in Philadelphia. The history Aunt Elizabeth provided was enough to complete my course project. When I decided to pursue the topic further as my senior thesis, my mother suggested that I contact

Uncle Calvin. Since this was the late 1990s and email was not ubiquitous the way it is now, I wrote him a letter. The letter led to a phone call where he told me fascinating information about our family. Uncle Calvin told me about our family's deep roots in New Orleans and our origins in Cuba and the Dominican Republic. He was even able to tell me some information about my great-grandmother's mother. Even though he and my great-grandmother had different mothers, he had some information about his oldest sister's mother to share with me. It was a blessing and exactly what I needed to get started.

Even before my own research began and before learning more of our Catholic history from my relatives, I have always known that there are countless other Black American Catholic stories, like those of my family. I grew up in Philadelphia, where there were a number of Black parishes, and at the beginning of my childhood, I attended a predominantly Black parish. I don't remember parish life as terribly exciting unless it was Easter or Christmas. I remember the large church being sparsely populated and attending Mass regularly with my mother, but that's about it. That is, until the *Lead Me, Guide Me* hymnal was published in 1987, the year I turned ten years old. With the arrival of *Lead Me, Guide Me* in each pew, I remember the music changed. It was almost as if having a hymnal specifically designed for Black Catholics gave us permission to be Black in church. There was no longer just one way to be Catholic at Mass. As a graduate student, I witnessed and studied the backlash parishes faced when they embraced the music and liturgy style that *Lead Me, Guide Me* encouraged; how these very spaces were labeled not "really Catholic"—the coded language for "not white." *Lead Me, Guide Me* initiated a new sense of Black Catholic empowerment that resulted in Black Catholics becoming increasingly dissatisfied with only receiving crumbs from the table of the U.S. Catholic Church.

In 2010, I completed my dissertation, *Finding A Place At The Table*. Through my dissertation process and in the years since, I have dedicated my professional life to rejecting crumbs in favor of a proper seat at the table. As a Black woman who has been a member of the Roman Catholic Church all of her life, it never occurred to me while growing up that being both Black and Catholic was an anomaly. It never occurred to me that my racial and religious backgrounds combined to form what is generally considered a disparate identity. I grew up believing—and still believe with every fiber of my being—that Black Catholics have offered immense contributions to how this country and our church understand themselves, from our music and worship traditions to our literary figures like Toni Morrison. Our stories are deeply tied to the very foundation of the United States and the American and global Roman Catholic Church. We have always been part of this church. Black people were practicing Catholicism at the same time St. Patrick was casting snakes out of Ireland in the fourth century.[1] Black Catholics have a long trajectory in both the United States[2] and the global Catholic Church.[3]

Debunking a Myth

Black Catholics are hardly a new phenomenon. What *is* new is white scholars recognizing that Black Catholics exist. It was not until I was an adult, in my early years as a graduate student, that I first heard the myth: "There is no such thing as Black Catholics." In other words, being Black and Catholic are anathema to one another and couldn't possibly go together; thus, they form what sociologists call a disparate identity. My life and work embody the joys, tensions, and contradictions of being a Black Catholic woman, including the conviction I feel in rejecting this myth while also writing through the varied, beautiful ways rage intersects with my faith, life, and work. Rejecting this myth requires understanding that systemic racism is real. We must understand how the church's systemic racism occurs physically—in different locations, namely parishes—yet is not isolated to explicit, physical spaces of worship. We must understand and assert that being Black and Catholic is an ancient identity that must be affirmed by the broader church.

Only during my graduate studies did I learn that conventional wisdom holds that being Black and Catholic do not dovetail. Initially, upon hearing this myth, I was curious. Curiosity gradually turned to conviction and rage, and both helped to form how my graduate school research interests would turn away from religion in the context of marriage and family life to religion in the context of systemic racism and identity. I began researching how Black Catholics combine their racial heritage with their religious heritage to form a unique identity. Even with this knowledge, I did not yet realize just how much the intellectual discourse and rank-and-file Black Catholics needed this book. I certainly didn't realize it in the middle of my graduate school training when I was taking an independent study course from one of my earliest graduate school mentors, Dr. Mark Warren. He said to me, "You're going to write a book about this stuff, aren't you? People need to read a book about this. You do realize that, don't you?" I didn't then. I do now.

One way I came to appreciate what Dr. Warren told me was by seeing how hard Black Catholics have had to work simply to justify our presence in the church when white Catholics have not. For example, in 1989, pioneering educator and scholar of Black Catholics, Sr. Thea Bowman, FSPA, PhD, famously addressed the United States Conference of Catholic Bishops:

> What does it mean to be Black and Catholic? It means that I come to my Church fully functioning. That doesn't frighten you, does it? I come to my Church fully functioning. I bring myself, my Black self, all that I am, all that I have, all that I hope to become. I bring my whole history, my traditions, my experience, my culture, my African American song and dance and gesture and movement and teaching and preaching and healing and responsibility as a gift to the Church.[4]

In 2015, I attended a symposium at the Institute for Advanced Catholic Studies in Los Angeles. During that weekend, I realized that when writing articles and book chapters, I was consistently using twenty percent of the space to explain Black Catholics' long trajectory in the church. I didn't want to do that for the rest of my career. I decided that if I wrote a book, I would address the myth one more time and wouldn't have to do it again. Officially, I've been working on this book since May 2015. As I write this, I realize, however, that in many ways, I have been writing this book since I took the "Marriage and Family" course in 1998.

I address what Bowman articulates: Being Black and Catholic encompasses the heartache of racism and discrimination, the solace and comfort that comes from drawing on the strength and coping skills passed down over generations, and the celebration that comes from combining the music and traditions of African American religious experiences with the belief and rituals of Roman Catholicism. The gifts that Dr. Bowman discusses are rooted in Black Catholics' culture and experiences and therefore, are unique to Black Catholics; however, the gifts themselves are as diverse as the Black Catholic community. This book examines those gifts as a means of filling an enormous gulf in the literature of both U.S. Catholicism and African American religion. This book is meant to finally end the myth, told among Catholics and non-Catholics alike, that there is no such thing as Black Catholics. This book will make clear that analyses of Catholicism in the U.S. and African American religion are incomplete without the inclusion of Black Catholics. The fact that in 1989, after Black Catholics had been in North America for hundreds of years, Dr. Bowman had to make such a forceful case for Black Catholics indicates the extent of Black Catholics' marginalization throughout the church's history. Claiming the centrality of Black Catholics in both of these spaces, African American religion and U.S. Catholicism, is the second reason I have written this book.

During that 2015 conference, I also had what I can only describe as an intellectual metanoia. It occurred to me that that if I spent my career writing articles and book chapters, I would always have to justify Black Catholics' role in literature, Black Catholics' place in the discourse on American Catholicism, and, it would seem, Black Catholics' very existence. Yet, if I wrote a book, I could use 20 percent of the space to demonstrate that Black Catholics are not an anomaly and really are a long-standing part of the U.S. and global Catholic Church. I decided that in a book, I could make this argument as part of a larger point of connecting the dots of systemic racism in the U.S. Catholic Church and never have to make it again. I could just refer inquiries to my book. This book is meant to end the incredulousness that surrounds the idea of being both Black and Catholic.[5]

I also articulate the systemic racism within the U.S. Catholic Church and challenges the Roman Catholic Church in the United States as an institution, including its scholars, to acknowledge this racism and work to make a Roman Catholic Church that is catholic in practice and action instead of only in name and theory. Being Catholic has always been an important part of my life, and my Catholicism is something I have thought about intently. My identity as a Roman Catholic is something I work at diligently. Being Black was something I have not thought about as much over the course of my life, which certainly does not mean that my Blackness is not important to me. My Blackness has always been incredibly important. I just did not feel the need to create a specific identity around my Blackness because it seemed that the world was inclined to do that for me and that there would not be much I could do about it.

Writing this book—and the benefit of time—has changed the way I think about my Blackness. I have come to realize how essential it is to stand in my truth as a Black woman and to create an identity as such. Doing that means actively refusing to let the structures of society—and the people that control them—do that for me. As Audre Lord said, "if I didn't define myself for myself, I'd be crunched into other people's fantasies for me and eaten alive."[6] I was eaten alive for far too long.

In defining my Blackness, I have also redefined my Catholicity. Doing so has helped me create a Black Catholic identity where the various elements of my identity overlap, creating what sociologist Nancy Ammerman calls embodying lived religion.[7] To continually stand in my truth as a Black Catholic woman means using the values of my Catholicism to actively resist the systemic racism that plagues not only my church, but also society.

Despite my decision to start writing *Black and Catholic: Racism, Identity, and Religion* in 2015, as a consequence of standing in my truth, writing this book took much longer than I had anticipated. There were the usual things of life and life as an academic that slowed progress. There were also the *un*usual things. Writing this book required me to take in the pain of others' experiences that I encountered in my research—whether vis-à-vis archival material, secondary sources, or interviews I conducted—process it, and put it back into the world as scholarship. It was not so easy. The time it took to process the pain meant it took longer to produce the scholarship.

From 2015 until now, a great deal has changed. The biggest change, which exponentially heightened the urgency for this book, occurred in the summer of 2020. The Catholic Church in the United States was not immune to the global reckoning around systemic racism that resulted from the murder of George Floyd. Up until that summer, my work was largely ignored within both sociological and Catholic intellectual spaces. My post-dissertation insistence on centering Blackness was dismissed in Catholic circles for not including enough white people. Among gatekeepers in sociological spaces, my work focused too much on religion for race scholars and too much on race for religion scholars. With the symposium in 2015 as the one notable exception, all of my best efforts to get published came to naught. Once, my application for a prestigious professional development and mentoring program for religion scholars was rejected. When I reached out to the director for feedback, I was essentially told that no one understood what I do and therefore, I would have no one to work with in the program.

In 2020, I suddenly became what might be called a "hot commodity." A family friend told me, only half-jokingly, that after ten years of post-dissertation struggle, I had become an overnight sensation. He was right. After years of drudgery, I will continue to seize on this moment of attention before it inevitably passes. And it will pass. The public scrutiny on systemic racism is too intrusive and requires too much accountability from whiteness and white people to last.[8] I need to do as much as I can for as long as I can. That urgency is why I have finished this book.

We have reached a point both within the discipline of sociology and our society for a long-overdue reckoning. Sociology is finally coming to terms with the reality that it has examined Catholic parishes through the lens of Protestant congregations[9] even though Catholic parishes are fundamentally different. While an emergent body of literature has started to remedy this problem,[10] this new literature does not sufficiently address the underlying problem of the sociology of religion's lack of engagement with race and racism. It is impossible to sufficiently tackle a sociological approach to religion in the United States without also tackling race and racism. Yet, the field has managed to do just that for decades.[11] Of the myriad of things the sociology of religion must contend with as a field,[12] racism is by far the most consequential. In the age of #MeToo, #MeTooSociology, and #BlackLivesMatter in which we find ourselves, it is more than two hundred years past time for the Roman Catholic Church in the United States to reconcile the way it centers whiteness and its systemic racism with why there are so few African American Catholics. It is also long past time for sociology and the sociology of religion, in particular, to confront its institutional isomorphism and the resulting lack of engagement with race and racism.[13]

In six chapters, I will explore systemic racism in the Roman Catholic Church as it pertains to African Americans and how African Americans use liturgy as an act of resistance to that racism. This book is meant to finally end the myth, told among Catholics and non-Catholics alike, that there is no such thing as Black Catholics. This book will make clear that analyses of Catholicism in the United States and African American Religion are incomplete without the inclusion of Black Catholics. Understanding that African Americans are not the only marginalized group in the Catholic Church, I want other groups who experience systemic oppression in the church—whether it is due to race, gender, sexual orientation, or a combination of identities—to know that tools to articulate and combat that marginalization exist.

Finally, it is necessary to have a word about nomenclature. Catholics of African descent in the United States and around the world comprise an incredibly rich and diverse community in an array of areas, including national origin, language, and ethnicity. According to a study by Pew Research Center released in early 2021, in the United States, 20 percent of African-born Blacks, 15 percent of Caribbean-born Blacks, and 5 percent of U.S.-born Blacks are Catholic.[14] Black Catholics in the United States are not a monolith. Any undertaking which attempted to incorporate the plethora of these experiences under one umbrella would not give any one community the attention that each rightly deserves. For that reason, my intention with *Black and Catholic* is to concentrate on the group often referred to as "Black American Catholics." This group has the longest history in what is now the United States, and its cultural ties are linked to the United States more so than those who have more recently emigrated from the Caribbean or the African continent. For the sake of variance, I will use the terms "Black" and "African American" interchangeably, but unless otherwise noted, I am referring to Black Americans. That said, because Black Americans have a distinct history, set of traditions, and culture that is indigenous to the United States (while Mexican and American Indian cultures are indigenous to North America more broadly), I am capitalizing Black when discussing Black Americans.[15]

Thank you for accompanying me on this journey. Now, let us begin.

ONE

Black Faith, White Space

Understanding the African American Catholic Experience

•—•—•—•—•—•

There are a number of scholars who have addressed the experiences of racial minorities who happen to belong to a religious denomination dominated by whites.[1] Such studies will examine how BIPOC members of a religious tradition are or are not similar to their white counterparts. These studies do go deeper into the attitudes, feelings, and lived experiences of being a minority in that tradition. I am taking on what it is like to *be* a racial minority—specifically, an African American—in an inherently racist church.[2]

It is not possible to understand the Catholic Church in the United States, or the religious life and experiences of African Americans more broadly, without analyzing Black Catholics. It is also long past time for sociology and sociology of religion, in particular, to confront its institutional isomorphism and the resulting lack of engagement with race and racism. We must understand the African American Catholic experience outside of just a Protestant lens. Black Catholics are not an anomaly—they have always been an integral part of our church's history. We must challenge our church to be catholic, not just in name and theory. We must challenge our church to confront its racism.

There are those reading this book that will balk at the notion of the Catholic Church being a racist institution and attempt to discredit me for identifying it as such. Yet, I am not the first scholar to unabashedly identify the U.S. Catholic Church as a racist institution. In what theologian Fr. Bryan Massingale has publicly referred to as the most quoted passage of his now-classic book, *Racial Justice in the Catholic Church*, he states:

> What makes the U.S. Catholic Church a "white racist institution," then is not the fact that the majority of its members are of European descent (especially since in many places, they no longer are), nor the fact that many of its members engage in acts of malice or bigotry. What makes it "white" and "racist" is the pervasive belief that European aesthetics, music, theology, and persons—and only these—are standard, normative, universal, and truly "Catholic."[3]

The sociological *structure* of the U.S. Catholic Church is white and racist. As discussed throughout the following chapters, the church's structure was constructed this way in order to protect and perpetuate whiteness as the fundamental core of the church. Black Catholics have moved through that racism to chart a path of inclusion in the Roman Catholic Church. *The History of Black Catholics in the United States*[4] by historian Fr. Cyprian Davis, OSB, is one of the best-known treatises on Black Catholics. In his highly-regarded work, Fr. Davis did not challenge the Roman Catholic Church in the United States to acknowledge its own racism and the consequences of that racism, but he laid the foundation for others to build upon and discuss what it means for the church to confront its racism. This book takes a multifaceted approach to challenging the Roman Catholic Church as an institution—as well as the people who run it, belong to it, and produce scholarship about it—to acknowledge, accept, and address the church's racism.

THEORY AND METHOD

I approach this sociological inquiry differently from previous texts in two key ways. First, it is a work of empirical sociological research. Empirical sociological research is generated by data collected using social scientific methodology and rooted in the scientific method. Second, it is a work of empirical sociological research that addresses race and religion in a way that generally has not been done. Historians, theologians, sociologists, and journalists have contributed vast amounts of knowledge to the intellectual understanding of Catholicism in the United States. Only a small amount of that work focuses on race while an even smaller amount focuses on systemic racism and racial justice.[5] Across disciplines, the body of intellectual thought on U.S. Catholicism focuses on a wide array of issues, including youth,[6] sexuality,[7] racial and ethnic history,[8] politics,[9] and culture and theology.[10] Yet sociologists have woefully understudied race and American Catholicism, especially when it comes to African American Catholics. Sociological work that examines race and Catholicism[11] often does so through a cultural lens rather than a racial lens. The absence of a racial lens means these works are devoid of discussions of racism and racial justice. Without these discussions, there is no way for the conversation to evolve to the essential work of anti-racism—the essential work of dismantling racist social structures and building new social structures that are rooted in justice.

Additionally, there is an emergent body of literature seeking to rectify the lack of sociological understanding of Catholic parishes. This emerging canon of Catholic Parish Studies consists of foundational works that respond to the call issued by James D. Davidson and Suzanne C. Fournier[12] to create a body of literature that focuses on Catholic parishes as distinct from Protestant congregations by highlighting the ways parishes are organizationally and liturgically unique. Tricia Colleen Bruce's *Parish and Place: Making Room for Diversity in the American Catholic Church*,[13] Brett C. Hoover's *The Shared Parish: Latinos, Anglos, and the Future of U.S. Catholicism*,[14] Alyssa Maldonado-Estrada's *Lifeblood of the Parish: Men and Catholic Devotion in Williamsburg, Brooklyn*,[15] and the edited volume, *American Parishes: Remaking Local Catholicism*[16] highlight the diversity of contemporary parish life in the United States. *Black and Catholic*, which deepens and builds on these works, is distinguished from them as a work of sociology that focuses exclusively on African Americans.

The intersection of race and religion—especially as it pertains to African American Catholics—is a largely untold story in sociology as conveyed by Michael O. Emerson, Elizabeth Korver-Glenn, and Kiara W. Douds.[17] Emerson, Korver-Glenn, and Douds' review of sociological works on race and religion asserts that "post-1998 research on ethnicity, race, and religion is promising in terms of theory building and methodological innovation, while highlighting some of the many gaps that still remain."[18] However, very little of that work involves Catholics. Emerson et al. also "argue that scholars of race and ethnicity cannot fully understand their object without considering the ways religion is both the cause and effect of that object."[19] A deeper critical sociological lens must be applied to the intersection of race and religion in order to further develop a theme from W. E. B. Du Bois that Emerson et al. highlight, namely, how Du Bois demonstrates that religion serves "to reproduce race and racial divisions rather than challenge them."[20]

My discussion of religion, racism, and identity, coupled with the lack of overlap between these topics in the sociological literature, utilizes multiple theoretical and methodological perspectives. The literature used to analyze the data collected for this project draws on the literatures of systemic racism, disparate identity formation, and religious culture production. It is imperative to situate the overall analysis within sociological theories found in these bodies of literature. These theories, including sifting,[21] owning identity,[22] and religious culture production,[23] create a framework for analyzing systemic racism and Black Catholics' identity formation as a means of resistance, which I discuss in later chapters. It is important to keep in mind that these theories are not given equal weight in the analysis. However, they all have a role to play in understanding the marginalization Black Catholics have endured in the church and what that can mean for both the Black Catholic community and the broader Roman Catholic Church in the United States.

My work addresses the impact of systemic racism on the lived experience of African American Catholics as a minority both in society and in their religious tradition. I draw on sociologist Joe R. Feagin's assertion that "each part of U.S. society—the economy, politics, education, religion, the family—reflects the fundamental reality of systemic racism."[24] Feagin also argues that "Whether in the past or the present, racism is not just about the construction of images and identities, it is centrally about the creation, development, and maintenance of white privilege, material wealth, and institutional power at the expense of racialized 'others.'"[25] In defining systemic racism, Feagin states:

> In the history of African Americans and other Americans of color, systemic racism has included: (1) the many exploitative and discriminatory practices of whites; (2) unjustly gained resources and power for whites; and (3) the maintenance of major resource inequalities by white-controlled ideological and institutional mechanisms.... (4) the prejudices and stereotyping covered by the umbrella racist ideology; (5) the racialized emotions accompanying prejudice and discrimination; and (6) the multiple and costly impacts of racism on targets and perpetrators.... By "systemic racism" I mean that core racist realities are manifested in each of society's major parts.[26]

While Feagin repeatedly makes clear that religion is one of society's "major parts," the intersection of racism and religion, especially as it pertains to African American Catholics, is a largely untold story in sociology. With *Black and Catholic,* I seek to correct this error. Throughout the chapters of this book, you will see how the exploitative and discriminatory practices of the U.S. Catholic Church toward African American Catholics reflect Feagin's definition.

While Feagin describes how systemic racism pervades society's institutions, sociologist Elijah Anderson describes how that specific racism is used to create specific spaces: the white space and the cosmopolitan canopy. In *Black in White Space: The Enduring Impact of Color in Everyday Life,*[27] he states, "White people typically avoid Black space, but Black people are required to navigate the White space as a condition of their existence."[28] There are few spaces in civil society where this is truer than the Catholic Church.

The Roman Catholic Church in the United States has reproduced race as a social construct and racial divisions by actively and systematically rejecting African Americans as members of the church through institutionalized actions, including slaveholding, disenfranchisement from ordained and vowed religious life, and maintaining segregated sanctuaries. The legacy of this systemic racism is found not only in the disproportionately low number of Black Catholics in the United States but also in the dearth of Black priests and vowed religious. Consequently, we see only a miniscule number of African Americans Catholics accessing these positions of authority in the church. Black Catholics face challenges in forming a unique ethno-religious identity while also navigating the disproportionate impacts of church closings and parish reorganizations in urban areas. Whiteness serves as the default mode of U.S. Catholicism. Black Catholics are told that their church is not actually for them in a way that moves beyond the racism of individual bad actors to a systemic racism. The church is a white space and off-limits.

While the church institutionally is a white space, there are spaces within it that we may be tempted to term a cosmopolitan canopy. Anderson defines the cosmopolitan canopy as "settings that offer a respite from the lingering tensions of urban life and an opportunity for diverse peoples to come together"[29] and "a diverse island of civility located in a virtual sea of racial segregation."[30] For instance, individual parishes and schools that are either solidly mixed-race spaces or predominantly racial minority spaces could be mistaken as cosmopolitan canopies. They are not. These spaces are not islands of civility where everyone can at least believe (for a short time) that they can approach these islands as equals. This cannot happen because the clergy, the episcopate, and school administrations—the people who manage and control these spaces—are almost always white. Therefore, African Americans and other racial minorities are always acutely aware of their marginalization, even when the space gives the impression that they are *not* being actively marginalized in the moment. This is what makes the Roman Catholic Church in the United States an ultra-white space.

Standing in my truth and the love that provides the strength to do so has forced me to acknowledge that, institutionally, the U.S. Catholic Church purports itself to be a "Cosmopolitan Canopy," yet instead, it is a white space[31] "where Black people are typically unexpected, marginalized when present, and made to feel unwelcome, a space that Blacks perceive to be informally 'off-limits' to people like them and where on occasion they encounter racialized disrespect and other forms of resistance."[32] Anderson lists many spaces in civil society that Blacks will encounter as "the White Space," saying Blacks "typically approach these spaces with care."[33] That care is necessary because as many, many recent events, such as the murder of Ahmaud Arbery and the shooting of Ralph Yarl have shown, entering such spaces can be life threatening. Many people, including those reading this book, would quickly admonish Blacks for entering such spaces at all, a chastisement that invokes paternalism and victim blaming. As Anderson succinctly points out, "Whites usually stay out of Black space, Black people cannot avoid White space."[34] In other words, Blacks don't have a choice.

According to Anderson, the white space is a layered phenomenon. He expounds on this when defining "Deep White spaces" as "settings in which Black folk are seldom if ever present and are unexpected; settings such as the rural outskirts of cities like Jackson and Atlanta, or isolated areas of upstate New York, Pennsylvania, and Maine—as well as certain colleges, universities, and firms with no Black people present."[35] The layering and nuance Anderson elucidates are found throughout civil society. On college and university campuses, it is not unusual to see African Americans working as members of the food service, custodial, and campus security staff. It is, however, unusual to see African Americans working as senior faculty members and senior administrators. Furthermore, for decades, it has not been unusual to see African Americans employed in civil service jobs in local, state, and federal government. Yet, despite eight years of the Obama Administration and the efforts of the Biden Administration to have a cabinet that reflects the country, seeing African Americans in the highest echelons of government isn't normalized. Not seeing African Americans in senior leadership across civil society as normal is evidenced by how many African American firsts society still experiences.[36] The continued African American firsts in society are why it is important to convey that the Catholic Church is an extreme version of what Anderson calls the white space, or the ultra-white space.

When Anderson says that "a particular organization—for instance, a corporation, a nonprofit, or a public sector bureaucracy—may pride itself on being egalitarian and universalistic and may not recognize its own shortcomings with respect to racial inequality,"[37] he could very easily be talking about the Catholic Church in the United States. The Roman Catholic Church purports to be a multiracial cosmopolitan canopy. It is not. The church's systemic racism makes the Catholic Church, as an institution, and often, its specific buildings, a white space. The church purports to be a cosmopolitan canopy, or catholic, despite its reality as an ultra-white space. We need not look further than the ranks of the priesthood, religious life, the episcopate, the faculties and student bodies in Catholic higher education, and scholars of American Catholicism (among other places) for evidence of the ultra-white space. I do not regard the U.S. Catholic Church as a deep white space, although such an argument could be made. Rather, I regard it as an ultra-white space because Catholic institutions exist as an intentional white space while purporting to be a cosmopolitan canopy. Catholic institutions are intentional white spaces because they have yet to truly confront the historical, overt exclusion of African Americans and other racial minorities. Consequently, the church as a contemporary white space doesn't exist in a vacuum. Rather, it exists because of historical realities. Until those realities are confronted, structurally dismantled, and rebuilt with an eye toward justice, the Catholic Church in the United States will continue to be an ultra-white space.

This ultra-white space exists throughout all Catholic institutions, including educational, professional, and especially liturgical spaces. An example of the church as an ultra-white space not existing in a vacuum is seen in theologian Maureen H. O'Connell's book, *Undoing the Knots: Five Generations of American Catholic Anti-Blackness*.[38] O'Connell examines her family narrative vis-à-vis the U.S. Catholic landscape. In doing so, she deftly illustrates how individuals' actions contributed to, perpetuated, and benefited from the racism that sought to systemically marginalize Blacks. O'Connell shows how her Irish ancestors, and other Irish immigrants around them, orchestrated and engaged in systemic anti-Blackness when they chose to racialize Blackness as a societal ill and, in doing so, racialized themselves as white in order to take advantage of the benefits of whiteness established by earlier European immigrants. O'Connell does not limit the discussion to parish life. Rather, she extends the discussion to Catholic higher education in examining the ways systemic racism not only factored into maintaining whiteness in residential neighborhoods but also within the confines of Catholic higher education. In connecting individual actions to systemic consequences, O'Connell elevates the conversation around racism in U.S. Catholicism from an individual-level race relations model to a systemic-level racial justice[39] model. It is only when this elevation occurs that the conversation on racism in the U.S. Catholic Church can reach the level of anti-racism.

Scholarship can also be an ultra-white space. Centuries of systemic racism, further explored in Chapter 2, have resulted in African Americans being "typically absent, not expected, or marginalized when present"[40] within the Catholic Church in the United States, thus making the church, the white space. A history of systemic racism has brought the church to its current landscape, including navigating what I call the Exoticism of Black Catholics, in which white scholars of Catholicism fetishize Black Catholics and Blackness, describing Black Catholics' existence and practice as something new and alluring.[41] These scholars regard Black Catholics with astonishment as newcomers to the church and perpetuate the erroneous supposition that Black Catholics only came into being during the decades of the Great Migration.[42] The Exoticism of Black Catholics demonstrates the inability of white scholars to center on anything other than whiteness. Black Catholics are othered, pushed to the margins, and worthy of remark only because we have been deemed unusual, which is the case only within the context of whiteness. As a result, what is beautiful precisely because it is ordinary is transformed into the extraordinary and exotic. When this happens, Black Catholics and the Black Catholic experience are deemed illegitimate. Only whiteness is legitimately Catholic. Thus, the white scholarly enterprise is cloaked in a racism its practitioners cannot see, yet it is of their own making. Unconscious bias is given legitimacy because it is called scholarship.

In addition to professional and educational spaces, liturgical space can also be an ultra-white space. I have walked into Mass and while nearly everyone there was civil, it was clear that some of them believed I did not belong there. For example, a family that I have known since I was a teenager invited me to join them at Mass because their family's new baby was being baptized. It is important to note that while the mother of the baby I was there to celebrate is white, the baby's father is Latino and originally from Venezuela. Three babies were baptized that Sunday morning: the baby I was there to celebrate and two white babies. Not long after I arrived and happily greeted the friends I knew well and their extended family members whom I had not seen in many years, the baby's grandmother, Lily, pointed to a section of pews and declared they were for our group. Telling myself that I was "holding the pews" for the group, I went and sat down while the various family members greeted each other. A few minutes later, the grandmother of one of the other two babies being baptized entered the pew where I was sitting with an entourage of several women. She inched closer and closer to me until I was nearly forced out of the pew. When she realized I was not leaving, she said to me, "You can't sit here. These pews are for the babies being baptized." I replied, "I know that." She continued, "Well, you're not here with one of *these* babies." I said, "Yes, I am." It was clear she thought that my Blackness did not belong in the ultra-white space of the church and the baptisms taking place that day. She only turned and left once the family I was with began to sit down all around me and interact with me.

About six months later, I told the baby's mother what happened, and her righteously indignant response was, "My baby's not white! She's got a white mother, but she's not white!" At that, I was emboldened to tell my friend, whom I had known since I was 19 and she was 17, what else happened that day. The incident I just recounted was one of two times that same day that an effort was made to chase me from the pew and the ultra-white space of the church. Moments before the other baby's grandmother attempted to chase me from my seat, another grandmother-aged white woman came up to me, looked me square in my face, and said, "You can't sit here. You're not with this family." I responded, "Oh, yes I am." To which she said, "You know Lily?" I said, "Yes, I do, *Sarah*. I've known her about as long as I've known you." Yes, the woman who tried to chase me from my seat—in church, where supposedly everyone is welcome—had no idea who I was even though we have been in each other's company many times with our mutual friend, Lily, for the better part of almost thirty years! Yet, in her eyes, there was no way *I* should be in the ultra-white space created in a church by parishioners who pride themselves on maintaining an atmosphere of welcome.

The white space is clearly defined throughout civil society, yet what is also clearly defined, by me, is that I am not going anywhere. When asked, always by white people, why I stay in the Catholic Church, I recount a memory I first wrote about in the foreword to Olga M. Segura's book, *Birth of a Movement: Black Lives Matter and the Catholic Church*. While visiting my now-deceased great-uncle, Calvin Aguillard, in New Orleans, I began telling him about my research and the work I would be doing while I was visiting New Orleans. In turn, he told me about his activism in the local Black Catholic community. He summarized his commitment to the church and his community, declaring, "Baby, this is *my* church, too. I'm not going to let them mess it up!" More recently, I've given a more piercing answer to that question: Only white people ask the question because it is unfathomable to whites that anyone would stay in a space where they are deliberately marginalized. Being unable to fathom such an experience is a privilege that comes from knowing that all social spaces whites enter were created for the benefit of white people and whiteness. Black people don't have that luxury. So I'm not going anywhere because the Catholic Church is my church, too. I also invite the white people who ask this question to consider deeply why it occurred to them in the first place.

The Process of Negotiating Identity

The above examples of the U.S. Catholic Church as an ultra-white space are just that—examples of a broader social experience. For me, these experiences, along with many others, have meant redefining both my Catholicism and my Blackness. This has allowed me to write this book. Recently, we have seen numerous examples of African Americans needing to justify their presence, in fact, their very existence, to whites who are the self-appointed arbiters of when African Americans can be in a public space and what they can do while there, like the aforementioned accounts of being in church. If they do not behave in ways deemed satisfactory by whites, their lives are often in danger. Examples of African Americans needing to justify their presence in public spaces and engaging in mundane activities while there abound. The murders of Botham Jean,[43] Breonna Taylor,[44] Philando Castile,[45] Ahmaud Arbery,[46] and George Floyd[47] are just a few of the high-profile killings of African Americans who were going about their daily lives. Sitting,[48] napping,[49] having a BBQ,[50] youth entrepreneurship,[51] and swimming[52] are just a few instances where African Americans have found themselves in potentially life-threatening situations while engaging in everyday mundane activities. The Catholic Church, its institutions, and liturgical spaces are not exempt from instances where everyday experiences can exemplify broader patterns of racism. What gives the church a higher degree or "ultra" status is how it purports to be an inclusive space but fails to truly be inclusive. I enhance this discussion with a specific focus on race and religion that does not appear in the extant work. The body of literature on disparate identity challenges the conventional wisdom that the two identities in question, in this case being Black and Catholic, are so diametrically opposed that they are fundamentally incompatible. Scholars working in disparate identity studies[53] have actively challenged this static, essentialist notion by discussing techniques individuals with a seemingly disparate identity use to bring these aspects of the self together. Two relevant discussions, Michele Dillon's "owning"[54] and Lynn Resnick Dufour's "sifting"[55] are well suited for the present study because of their focus on religion.

Dillon[56] discusses how members of the Boston chapter of Dignity/USA construct their identity as gay and lesbian Catholics upon the premise that homosexuality and Catholicism are not incompatible because all people are created in the image and likeness of God. They maintain this premise despite the Roman Catholic Church's unequivocal assertion "that homosexual acts are intrinsically disordered and can in no case be approved of."[57] By owning their identity as both homosexuals and Roman Catholics, the members of Boston's chapter of Dignity/USA construct an identity that seeks to integrate the two seemingly conflicting aspects of the self.[58]

Dillon found that the members of Boston's chapter of Dignity/USA in her study do not want to divorce their Catholic heritage and traditions from their gay and lesbian identity. On the contrary, "Dignity participants want a gay and lesbian worship community that specifically invokes Catholic identity and tradition."[59] In doing so, the members "own the identity differently."[60] They have established an identity that incorporates seemingly disparate elements. Dillon uses "owning" as an identity work technique to describe how gay and lesbian Catholics negotiate their religious and sexual identities.

Dillon offers detailed accounts of the liturgies she attended in order to illustrate how the members of Dignity/Boston incorporate their religious and sexual identities into the community's liturgical services. Dillon concentrates on liturgy because "for many other Catholics and Christians, the weekly Sunday Mass liturgy is Dignity's core communal worship event."[61] Dillon describes at length two members' commitment, or Holy Union, ceremony.[62] This ritual takes place at the point in Mass where the sacrament of marriage would occur. She observes, "I did not see this commitment ceremony as an exotic practice; what was striking, rather, was the 'normalcy' of the event, and the important symbolic role it played in affirming both the sacredness of same-sex couples and the sacramental power of communal life."[63] Dillon's analysis of this event and of the community's Pride Sunday observance shows that the members of Dignity/Boston go to great lengths to maintain distinctly Catholic rituals and symbols as part of their liturgical service. Owning identity differently does not require fundamentally altered rituals. Dillon says this is important because, "Not to maintain the Mass's distinctive characteristics could be taken as indicating tacit acknowledgment that what they are doing is 'not really' Catholic and never could be authentically Catholic, since in official church teaching their status as active gays or lesbians contradicts their Catholicism."[64] Dillon says these practices allow the members of Dignity/Boston to "own" their multiple identities and build a community where those identities can be expressed freely.[65]

Like Dillon, Lynn Resnick Dufour[66] offers a technique for negotiating seemingly conflicting identities. Dufour's discussion of Jewish feminists highlights women who create "Jewish feminist identities by making conscious decisions based on their Jewish, feminist and spiritual needs."[67] Dufour's three-fold typology of Jewish feminists consists of those who 1) seek to include women in the patriarchal structure, 2) transform the structure into one that is more egalitarian, or 3) reinterpret the existing structure without calling for large-scale change.[68] She says they sift together aspects of Judaism and feminism that meet their needs while also sifting *out* those aspects that do not.[69]

Dufour acknowledges that individuals have multiple identities that may overlap or come into conflict with one another. These conflicting identities are the result of mixed messages individuals receive from those who wish to legitimate and strengthen their patriarchal power. Dufour identifies "sifting" as an identity work technique that is used by Jewish feminists in her study to negotiate their identities. Dufour describes sifting as "the process of constructing a fairly stable, biographical identity that incorporates aspects of two or more potentially conflicted identities."[70] The use of the word "aspects" is a key element of Dufour's definition because, as she explains, the process involves individuals taking on only parts of an identity and sifting out those that are unsuitable.[71] Ultimately, Dufour offers a three-fold typology of Jewish feminist identity. She states,

"Each of the three types of Jewish identity"—"inclusionist, transformationist, and reinterpretationist—is best understood as a cluster of practices and attitudes that tend to get sifted in together."[72] Dufour explains that through sifting, the women she interviewed negotiated conflicts that exist between feminism, Judaism, and spirituality.[73] She goes on to say that the women in her study assess how various rituals and practices fit their desired level of Jewish, feminist, and spiritual needs: "The practices and attitudes which are sifted into the mix of one woman's Jewish feminist identity define what that identity means to her. The practices and attitudes with which she does not identify also help to define her identity; it may be part of her identity that she rejects certain practices and attitudes."[74] These women know what they are by what they are not. The women Dufour focuses on have made a conscious decision to include certain aspects of Judaism and modern feminism into their worldviews and everyday lives. Thus, they *sift out* principles that are unpalatable in order to create room to *sift in* those principles that are desirable. Throughout this book, I will use owning and sifting where appropriate.

In scholarly literature[75] and popular discourse,[76] being both Black and Catholic is seen as a disparate identity. I examine the ways race and religion work together to form an identity for African American Catholics because African American Catholics cannot separate being African American from their experience with Catholicism any more than they can separate being Catholic from their experience with being African American. The two work together to form a religio-racial identity.

A number of theories have examined how social actors negotiate disparate identities. Two such theories, "owning identity differently" and "sifting," have done this through the lens of religion. Using the lens of religion, scholars have identified various techniques that are used by those with disparate identities.

In Black parishes, these different routes of identity work (both owning and sifting) are aspects of parish culture produced and maintained through what Nancy Ammerman calls a community's "activities, artifacts, and accounts."[77] As such, Black Catholics' seemingly disparate identities come together through ritual. Understanding these elements of congregational life, or in the case of Catholics, parish life, allows us to see how congregations build a sense of community, document their identity, and immortalize institutional memory. In this way, a congregation's culture consists of what members do together, the things they make, and the stories they tell, with ritual as a primary focal element. Thereby, Black Catholics engage in *parish culture production*.

Both owning and sifting can happen through ritual, a process in which "our sense of who we are is shaped by what we do, what we make, and how we talk about ourselves."[78] These three constructs provide a means for understanding and articulating *what* happens at Black parishes (vis-à-vis owning and sifting) and *how* it happens (vis-à-vis parish culture production).

While owning, sifting, and parish culture production are constructs in religion that are best suited for a discussion of identity work, additional theoretical perspectives are needed to frame the discussion of systemic racism in the Roman Catholic Church. Joe R. Feagin conveys the pervasiveness of systemic racism in U.S. institutions.[79]

These theoretical principles certainly are not the only ones that could have been used here. Indeed, there are several others—including Patricia Hill Collins' matrix of domination,[80] Eduardo Bonilla-Silva's color-blind racism,[81] and W. E. B. Du Bois' the preacher, the music, the frenzy[82]—that would have fit into my analysis while also maintaining the book's sociological structure. In the end, the aforementioned theories were chosen because they were best suited for the analysis I am presenting.

Structuring the analysis in sociological theory provides foundational grounding for this book as a work of sociology rather than religious studies. In particular, Feagin's definition of systemic racism and Anderson's concept of the white space are useful in establishing the overall sociological framework of the book and are essential in the analysis for Chapter 3, which focuses on the participant observations I conducted during Mass. By using the parish as the unit of analysis in Chapter 3, my study adds to emergent literature in parish studies by drawing on participant observations conducted during liturgy.

A Word on Methodology

In addition to multiple theoretical perspectives, the analysis presented here required using multiple sociological methodologies. A mixed methodological approach was needed in order to glean the data needed to flesh out the connection between the overt discrimination of the 19th century to the less obvious—and in some ways, more insidious—discrimination of the 20th and 21st centuries. Mixed methods are required to demonstrate that over this long period of time, the same forces of anti-Blackness are at work. Only the procedures for executing anti-Blackness have changed. The following chapters address the issues discussed here by examining three key themes using methodologies appropriate to those themes: systemic racism in the church and its lingering impact on the Black Catholic community, Black Catholics' use of liturgy to form a unique identity, and Black Catholics' views on issues of race, space, and contemporary parish life.

My methodologies add to this book's ambition. I could have written a different book. I could have written a book that offered a contemporary examination of only one parish. I could have written a book that only looks at music, homily, and aesthetics in multiple Black parishes. (In other words, an entire book of what I did in Chapter 3.) Either format would have been more conventional, easier and faster to write, less ambitious, and frankly, boring. They would not have considered the broad, multifaceted scope of the Black Catholic experience that lays out the systemic nature of anti-Blackness in the U.S. Catholic Church. Instead, I've written a book that sociologically articulates how Black Catholics came to the active resistance we see in Chapter 3. Using multiple methodologies and theories was a risk worth taking.

Ultimately, Chapter 2, "The Numbers Don't Add Up: Systemic Racism and Its Legacy in Urban Catholic Life," addresses the question, "Why are there so few Black Catholics in the United States?" Chapter 2 addresses the question by refuting the notion that Roman Catholicism is too cerebral and rooted in symbols to be palatable for Black Americans. In this chapter, I assert that this is not true at all. In fact, the dearth of Black Catholics in the United States is the result of systemic racism in the church. This chapter explains how during the 19th century, the Roman Catholic Church deliberately and purposefully diverted its—admittedly limited—priestly and financial resources to the burgeoning Irish immigrant population in the Northeast. In addition, the Roman Catholic Church did not actively pursue the evangelization of recently freed Blacks during the latter part of the century. The church systematically disenfranchised what few Black Catholics it could claim by denying Black men and women access to the priesthood and religious life, denying Black Catholics access to many existing parishes, and creating segregated seating and Communion lines in the parishes to which they did have access. All of this was done in acquiescence to the prevailing racist norms of the time and therefore served to strengthen the church's then-fledgling institutional infrastructure as well as bolster its image and standing in an often hostile Protestant country. According to sociologist Peter L. Berger, the academic discipline closest to sociology is history.[83] Drawing on a number of historical monographs related to Black Catholics in the U.S. in the 19th century, I have sought to treat the monographs as qualitative data. In doing so, I have examined these works vis-à-vis a sociological lens. My analysis shows that anti-Blackness in the U.S. Catholic Church is not a series of isolated incidents perpetrated by a few bad actors. Rather, it is systemic and woven into the fabric of the U.S. Catholic Church.

To establish that the racism at work in 19th-century U.S. Catholicism was, in fact, systemic, I show that as the Catholic infrastructure in the United States grew, there was a solidification of system-wide anti-Blackness. The fact that the means changed after the Civil War did not alter the fact that the underlying anti-Blackness remained the same. Making this point in Chapter 2 required synthesizing multiple historical accounts through a sociological lens in order to see that the racism present was truly *systemic*.

Chapter 3, "Finding A Place at the Table: Liturgy as Identity Work and an Act of Resistance" begins by invoking the Black Catholic Bishops of the United States' 1984 pastoral letter, *What We Have Seen and Heard*, the Bishops' call to their fellow Black Catholics to be authentically Black and truly Catholic.[84] Chapter 3 discusses how Black Catholics answer that call through liturgy as a form of identity work. I examined how Black Catholics combine African American religious traditions and Roman Catholicism to form a unique identity via liturgy. To that end, I visited three parishes, two in the Archdiocese of Philadelphia and one in the Archdiocese of New York, to conduct participant observation fieldwork. While there, I fully participated in the Mass. I observed the music, themes, and tenor of the homily, and church aesthetics in particular. Because I did not want to be a distraction to parishioners or detract from my ability to take in what was happening around me, I took detailed notes after leaving Mass rather than during the service.

In bringing the traditions of the African American Religious experience to liturgy, Black Catholics actively resist systemic racism. This chapter identifies three distinct styles of liturgy and how predominantly Black Catholic parishes use music, the homily, and church aesthetics to create that identity. It also makes clear that there is no one way to be "authentically Black" and "truly Catholic." To show how contemporary Black Catholics use liturgy not only as a means of identity work but also as an act of resistance to the systemic racism charted in Chapter 2, it was necessary to utilize different methodologies. I visited multiple parishes and conducted participant observation research at Mass. I also conducted twenty-four wide-ranging, semi-structured interviews with Catholic faithful. I talked with three priests and twenty-one lay people. I use the resulting data to better understand the thematic intentions behind what I observed at Mass.

St. Peter Claver was the first parish in the Archdiocese of Philadelphia founded by and designated for ministry to African Americans. In 1986, the parish was suppressed by the then-Archbishop of Philadelphia, John Cardinal Krol. I examine the suppression of St. Peter Claver and its aftermath along with how the loss of predominantly Black parishes has reshaped the Catholic landscape in the Archdiocese and the city of Philadelphia, in particular, in Chapter 4, "Erasing a Legacy: The Price of St. Peter Claver." Conducting research on St. Peter Claver required an analysis of archival materials related to the history of St. Peter Claver as well as conducting interviews with those who are currently engaged in the fight to preserve the parish's legacy. I worked with Adrienne Andrews Harris of the Advocates and Descendants of St. Peter Claver, who provided me with access to her personal archives. I also worked with the staff at the Charles L. Blockson Afro-American History Collection at Temple University Library. They assisted me in accessing the documents related to St. Peter Claver that have been donated to the collection. Many of those who are involved in preserving the legacy of St. Peter Claver are themselves second- and third-generation members of the parish and have preserved the oral history of St. Peter Claver's founders and the parish's earliest days.

In Chapter 5, "Race, Community, and Process: Black Catholics' Experiences in Catholic Spaces," I ask and answer the following question: How has systemic racism impacted the lived experiences of African American Catholics? To answer this question, we must understand the experiences of everyday Black Catholics. I use semi-structured interviews to address issues of race and process in urban parishes as well as the importance of community in navigating the challenges of modern parish life. I draw on the twenty-four interviews I conducted with Black Catholics, priests and lay people, who talked with me about issues regarding contemporary parish life, including their concerns, struggles, and experiences. Interviewees were identified through snowball sampling and interviews took place either in person or over the phone. Most interviewees are residents of the Archdiocese of Philadelphia. This is a sociologically sound location for this research. Catholics have been openly practicing their faith in Philadelphia since at least 1707. Philadelphia's first Catholic Church was built in 1733 and is still in operation. In 1808, Philadelphia became a Catholic diocese in its own right and was elevated to an archdiocese in 1875. As of 2024, there are 1.5 million Catholics in the Archdiocese of Philadelphia, and Mass is offered in twenty-two languages.[85] The Archdiocese is both a historic and contemporary hub for Black Catholics in the United States. The third gathering of what was then known as the Colored Catholic Congress was held in Philadelphia in 1892.[86] The Archdiocese of Philadelphia is home to one of the few remaining Offices of Black Catholics in the country. Additionally, by living in the Philadelphia area while I conducted this research, I took advantage of this wealth of opportunity for conducting in-person interviews, all of which took place before the COVID-19 pandemic began. The president of Concerned Black Catholics of St. Thomas Aquinas and Friends, Daria Ward, provided invaluable assistance in identifying interviewees. Most of those I interviewed welcomed me, a virtual stranger, into their homes. They treated me like family, often providing me with a home-cooked meal, and spoke with me for an hour or more about deeply personal experiences.

Parishes are at the heart of Roman Catholic life in the United States. A book that focuses on racism and structure in the Black Catholic experience must discuss parish life. As discussed earlier, recent scholarship highlights the importance of a greater sociological understanding of the complexities of parishes. This need has grown even greater as both the number and configuration of parishes have changed significantly in recent years. This is especially true in urban dioceses where already marginalized Catholics are disproportionately impacted by church closings and mergers. In considering the ways Black Catholics experience parish life, I examine parishes not only as religious entities but also as organizations. In doing so, I use a distinctively Catholic lens to sociologically imagine how race, socioeconomic status, neighborhood, and conceptualization of a parish contribute to the experience of parish life.

In my concluding chapter, I highlight my hopes for future research, including my hopes for my research allowing other scholars to feel empowered and encouraged. Chapter 6 will conclude with a reflection on my own positionality as a Black Catholic woman who is a scholar of the Catholic Church in the United States.

TWO

The Numbers Don't Add Up

Systemic Racism and Its Legacy in Urban Catholic Life

• • • • • • • •

Systemic racism is woven into the fabric of almost all of society's institutions, like individual strands of hair woven into a thick braid. The Catholic Church is no exemption. Systemic racism, while related, operates independently from the person-to-person racism that receives the lion's share of attention in society. In order to contextualize later chapters on St. Peter Claver, Philadelphia's first parish for Black Catholics, liturgy as a form of identity work, and how Black Catholics experience race and space within the church, we must delineate the sociological nuances of the long-standing oppression of African Americans in the Catholic Church and recognize racism's impact on our liturgical expression, the closing of churches, and parish reorganizations. To fully understand the African American Catholic experience, including our long history within the church, we must understand, sociologically, the role the U.S. Catholic Church has played in systemic racism against African Americans, from its institutions to its parishes and its scholarship. This chapter is not intended to serve as a work of history. Rather, it is a sociological grounding of systemic racism in the U.S. Catholic Church.

Since the earliest days of my career, even going back to before I finished graduate school, I have encountered incredulousness at the idea that there is such a thing as Black Catholics. I've encountered downright disbelief that African Catholics and Catholics of African descent have existed since the church's earliest days. An urgent need I have with this book is to dispel such myths once and for all. These myths persist despite Fr. Cyprian Davis, OSB providing detail on the history of the church in Africa in the seminal *The History of Black Catholics in the United States*.[1] Therefore, it's necessary to reiterate that African Catholics date back to the church's earliest days, include Catholicism's most revered thinkers and writers,[2] and are (at the very least) the spiritual ancestors of Catholics of African descent around the world.

The Roman Catholic Church's presence on the African continent dates back to the church's earliest days.[3] St. Augustine of Hippo, one of the most well-known and revered figures in the church, was born in the mid-fourth century in present-day Algeria. Around that same time, St. Frumentius was ordained as the first bishop for Ethiopia by St. Athanasius, who himself was patriarch of Alexandria and born there at the end of the third century.[4] Blacks' affiliation with the church in North America dates back to the early sixteenth century when Spanish settlers arrived with slaves in tow and intending to import more from Africa.[5] The strongest roots of the Black Catholic presence in the United States date back to the seventeenth century. People of French-Caribbean descent, both enslaved and free, lived along the Louisiana Gulf Coast and in Maryland. Of course, until the latter part of the nineteenth century, most Blacks living in the South—as practicing Catholics or not—were enslaved. In post–Civil War and especially in post–World War II America, Blacks became the next wave of people, after Germans, the Irish, and Italians, to settle in the urban North in great numbers.

The U.S. Census Bureau, which does not collect data on religion, reports that as of July 2019, there are 43.98 million Blacks in the United States.[6] The Center for Applied Research in the Apostolate at Georgetown University (CARA) states that as of 2020 there were 72.4 million self-identified Catholics[7] in the United States. According to the U.S. Conference of Catholic Bishops' Secretariat for Cultural Diversity in the Church, there are 3 million Black Catholics in the United States, including Black Americans whose ties to the United States go back centuries as well as recent immigrants and their families.[8] The Pew Research Center reports that only 5 percent of U.S. born Blacks are Catholic.[9] Given the number of Blacks and the number of Catholics, coupled with the scope and breadth of the U.S. Catholic Church, the number of Black Catholics is disproportionately low. Systemic racism is the reason the numbers do not add up. To understand this, we must sociologically understand how racism has evolved in the Catholic Church, beginning with understanding how European Catholics became white in the United States and the creation of national parishes.

THE ASSIMILATION OF EUROPEAN CATHOLICS INTO WHITENESS

By the early nineteenth century, the Catholic Church in the United States had a distinctly Anglo-American flavor, with Baltimore, Maryland, serving as its spiritual capital. There were 100,000 Catholics residing in the United States at the time. They mingled freely among Protestants and made concerted efforts to maintain religious anonymity by keeping their Catholicism from becoming a major component in their public, or civic, identity.[10] During the 19th and early 20th centuries, the immigrant church in the United States was first dominated by German and Irish people and later by Italian people. They arrived in the United States in great numbers[11] and primarily settled in the United States' major northeastern cities, eventually moving as far west as Chicago in the latter part of the century. In their new homes, German and Irish Catholics encountered Catholics of French and English descent whose ancestors arrived in North America 200 years earlier. Initially, the newcomers co-existed in an uneasy alliance with those ethnic groups long established in the United States. Yet they encountered resistance from the already established French and English communities who took great pains to practice a Catholicism that did not distinguish them from their Protestant counterparts. The newcomers were distinctive in a variety of ways: immigrant status, rural origins, socioeconomic background, confinement to urban ghettos, and cultural expression. By their sheer numbers, unconcealable poverty, and unfamiliarity with the urban life they had been thrust into, 19th-century German and Irish Catholics could not go unnoticed like their predecessors. The more obvious distinctions between new immigrant Catholics and their more established counterparts distinguished them as "the other" and contributed to their classification as a separate race.

Theologian Maureen H. O'Connell breaks open this point in her book, *Undoing the Knots: Five Generations of American Catholic Anti-Blackness*,[12] where she places her own family's narrative in the larger context of systemic racism in the U.S. Catholic Church. O'Connell examines her family narrative vis-à-vis the U.S. Catholic landscape, deftly illustrating how individuals' actions contributed to, perpetuated, and benefited from the racism that sought to systemically marginalize Blacks. O'Connell shows how her Irish ancestors and other Irish immigrants around them, orchestrated and engaged in systemic anti-Blackness when they chose to racialize Blackness as a societal ill.

In discussing one of her ancestors, O'Connell states, "[Maurice Connell] carried with him an acute sense of what it felt like to be considered inferior and economically dependent. Irish were typically stereotyped as lazy, intellectually and morally deficient."[13] She goes on to point out that her ancestor "would have noticed that Irish arriving in Philadelphia with him not only seemed to despise Black people but also wanted their jobs and homes."[14] She asserts that "Irish Catholics in antebellum Philadelphia took Black jobs and pushed freed Black people out of the neighborhoods to which they had been relegated."[15] O'Connell points out that her ancestor received conflicting messages. He had clear messages from an Irishman whom he revered that his integrity would be questioned if he did not advocate for the emancipation of and liberty for people.[16] On the other hand, he heard from some Catholic leaders that strident abolition and even the emancipation of enslaved Black people could further fracture the Union and therefore jeopardize the future he had left Lisgoold in search of.[17] O'Connell states that hearing these conflicting messages, her ancestor took the path of anti-Blackness. It posed less risk and promised more rewards.

O'Connell clarifies that Irish immigrants in this period opted to racialize themselves as white to take advantage of the benefits of whiteness established by earlier white Europeans. They accepted the risk of opting to align themselves with whiteness and the power that would come with acceptance into its structures, even though it would mean enduring discrimination that would last for their and their children's lifetimes at a minimum. In doing so, they opted not to align themselves with Blacks in pursuit of mutual liberation. This is yet another way that whiteness protects itself—by showing certain newcomers the benefits of whiteness and a path from the margins to the center at the price of the continued marginalization or "othering" of another, often more oppressed, community. Irish Catholics and other Europeans were literally becoming white at Black folks' expense.

THE EVOLUTION OF NATIONAL CATHOLIC PARISHES

Immigrants new to the United States during the middle decades of the 19th century, having arrived mainly from rural areas, also felt dwarfed by the enormity and complexity of American cities. Consequently, they established an intense connection with the Catholic Church since it was, usually, the only institution they recognized.[18] These divergent groups were determined to have their worship experience serve as a distinct cultural expression. Inevitably, these various groups would come into conflict with each other as they intermingled in a church trying to accommodate the needs of all its members. Germans could not understand services conducted in English, and the Irish could not grasp the subtleties of French-American priests' homilies. Ethnic diversity and conflict intensified with each new wave of immigration.[19]

Immigrants in the United States began to petition their local bishop—or the Vatican itself, if necessary—for parishes with priests from their country of origin. Immigrant Catholics wanted churches and parishes that looked like their worship spaces back home and centered around their particular ethnic needs. These national parishes, which grew over time, reflected the intimate connections between national identity and ethnic identity and served as vehicles for preserving and perpetuating their own culture.

At their height, national parishes flourished because of support from the institutional church embodied in the local bishop, but there are indications that support for European ethnic parishes was far from widespread. James Quigley, Chicago's second archbishop from 1903–1915, understood the fine line between preserving ethnicity and fostering assimilation. He "cautiously encouraged Americanization while courageously defending ethnic rights."[20] He saw the ethnic communities as road stops on the journey toward full participation in U.S. life. During his episcopate, which began in 1903, Archbishop Quigley supported existing national parishes and opened many more, including twenty new Italian parishes by the time of his death in 1915.[21] Italians did not fare as well in other major U.S. cities during the 19th century. For example, in New York, Italians existed on the fringes of the Catholic community.[22] New York's Archbishop John Hughes did not share the vision of Chicago's Archbishop Quigley of ethnic parishes serving as a vehicle for Americanization. Unless the group in question was New York's Irish community, Hughes was indifferent to the intersection of religion, ethnicity, and nationality, as well as how preserving those bonds could benefit the church.[23]

As the Irish and German Catholics had encountered hostility in the church of the early to mid-nineteenth century, they in turn, created hostility for Italian and Black Catholics arriving in the United States' major northern cities in the late nineteenth and early twentieth centuries. Since they were unwelcome in established ethnic parishes, Italians wanted their own parishes to maintain their cultural heritage and their affection for their homeland. Institutional church support for Italian national parishes signaled the church's acknowledgment of Italians' potential to contribute to the growth of the church in the United States and the Italians' move inward from the fringes of the U.S. Catholic community. Thus, national parishes did more than provide a site for worship. They served as an incubator for the creation of a distinctly U.S. Catholic culture. Additionally, they helped maintain an identity that remained rooted in white ethnic group's European homelands. All of this happened in the midst of immigrant communities' transition from the racialized "other" to ethnicity-based whiteness within a nearly all-Catholic environment that has been referred to as a "state-within-a-state" atmosphere.[24] These parishes helped their members both to embrace Americanization and to maintain affection for their country of origin. This affection remained deep and intense for many years. For example, in the mid to late nineteenth century, one could not have an affinity for and a desire to preserve German culture if one did not have direct ties to Germany. This affinity for German culture waned after the two World Wars. The national bonds with Germany and Italy weakened, and this had severe ramifications for the continued viability of national parishes. Having gone from being German and Italian Catholics living in the United States to German American and Italian American Catholics, these ethnic groups did not want such an intense affiliation with countries the United States defeated in war.

National parishes' simultaneous religious and ethnic expression created an emulsified ethno-religious identity that made it nearly impossible for these Catholics to distinguish their religious expression from their ethnic expression. Catholics of white ethnic groups created an identity that intertwined religion and ethnicity so completely that the two were indistinguishable. They engaged in religious identity formation yet failed to acknowledge they were engaging in such a process. Instead of seeing their culture production and identity formation as a combination of ethnicity, religion, and whiteness, they only saw it as being Catholic. As a result, when Black Catholics began to create a similarly emulsified identity decades later, white ethnic Catholics spurned the nascent expression of Black Catholics' ethno-religious identity grounded in Blackness as being too authentically Black and, therefore, not truly Catholic. In reality, Black Catholics were creating an identity that co-mingled Catholicism with racial and ethnic expression in such a way as to be authentically Black and truly Catholic. As sociologist Korie Little Edwards points out, "religious space is not just about practicing one's religion; it is also about living out one's ethno-racial identity. People do not quite realize how much of their religious practice is also a way of doing ethnicity—until they have to share their religious space with people who do not share their ethno-racial identity."[25] In the case of white Catholics, their ethnicity, whiteness, or (depending on the group and the time) aspirational whiteness, and religion were so profoundly intertwined that they could not, or *would not,* see that Black Catholics were engaging in a similar process of identity formation that extolled ethno-racial identity and expression while remaining deeply rooted in Catholicism. White Catholics only saw Blackness as a threat to their burgeoning acceptance in broader U.S. society. Their response, like Catholic slaveholders before them, was anti-Blackness as "a form of racism, informed by white supremacist ideologies, centered on the particular devaluation and exploitation of Black persons," one that is "embedded in institutions, organizations, cultures, and so on."[26]

Throughout Catholicism's history in the United States, dating back to the seventeenth century even before the nation was formed, its Catholic white ethnic groups traversed strikingly similar paths. They began by holding steadfastly to the culture they brought from their country of origin. Eventually, they assimilated into Irish U.S. Catholicism, the dominant form since the nineteenth century.[27] Variations on the assimilationist model produced Catholic parishes that were eerily similar in terms of pastoral work, evangelization, homiletics, and liturgical styles. Divergent explanations exist concerning the distinguishing features and goals of national parishes. One explanation has the emergence of this model of parish life rooted in shared language, not geography, since national parish boundaries often overlapped.[28] On the other hand, geography may have been the distinguishing feature of national parishes since newly arrived immigrants tended to cluster in one area.[29] The overlapping of geographic parish boundaries came later as social mobility took immigrants and their descendants out of their ethnic enclaves, which in turn made room for new waves of immigration. While new immigrants clung relentlessly to an overt sense of nominal and cultural Catholicism, priests at the newly formed national parishes found them grossly uninformed about the intricacies of the tradition.[30] In some locales, particularly New York, national parishes worked to preserve the faith and create a cohesive Catholic community. Chicago's national parishes worked to perpetuate ethnic identity past the immigrant generation while fostering Americanization.[31] Since the church was often the only institution in the United States familiar to these newcomers, it also served as a privileged place for acclimating immigrants to other aspects of American life. The church's support of various fraternal organizations and societies provided parishioners with job training, employment services, and educational opportunities, which fostered assimilation and upward social mobility.[32] As successive generations became further ingrained in American society, the need for weekly Mass in the same style as in the country of origin waned.

Ultimately, the decline of national parishes among the immigrant populations they served directly correlates with their success at meeting their assimilationist goals—goals that the church did not extend to African Americans. African Americans were not allowed to assimilate into religious and other social institutions.[33] The job training and educational programs available at national parishes helped parishioners become upwardly mobile and move out of poverty, yet these programs fostering upward mobility were not made available to Black Catholics. Black Catholics struggled just to have parishes. So, due to anti-Blackness, Black Catholics did not have parish-based anti-poverty programs. The upward mobility white ethnic groups experienced was most notably signaled by national parish constituents moving out of the traditional neighborhoods and eventually marrying people from other ethnic groups. With intermarriage, those who were once seen as separate and distinct racial and ethnic groups easily identified as "the other" became collectively classified as white.[34] This restructuring of American ethno-racial dynamics became evident as formerly disparate cultures were blended through marriage and family life. When distinct cultures are brought together, elements of each get lost. As families moved beyond the immigrant generation, language was one of the first elements of culture to fall by the wayside. As the dominance of national parishes among white ethnic groups faded in the post–World War II United States, the notion of "the other," especially in the urban North, was redefined when the racialized language and systemic othering that white ethnic groups had reserved for each other would be used for Blacks. The consequences of this process for both the group in power and the group classified as "the other" are still being felt in the U.S. Catholic Church today.

HOW THE CHURCH MADE SURE BLACK CATHOLICS STAYED BLACK

Slavery is at the very beginning of Catholicism's story in what is now the United States. In 1536, three Spanish explorers traveled across what is now the southern United States. The fourth member of the group was Esteban, a slave who was born in Morocco. Historian, Fr. Cyprian Davis, OSB, describes Esteban thusly: "For us, he is a reminder that the first black man to traverse what is now the territory of the United States was Spanish-speaking and a Catholic."[35] Additionally, Esteban is the origin story of Catholicism's anti-Blackness and intimate connection with chattel slavery in the United States. Internalizing anti-Blackness was a way for the Catholics to, over time, move away from the margins of U.S. society. Even after abolition, successor forms of anti-Blackness allowed Catholics from white ethnic groups to take on the benefits of whiteness.

Many Black Catholics who migrated to the urban North came to the church indirectly via slavery. Many Black Catholics (or, depending on the year, their immediate ancestors) had already experienced anti-Blackness by the Catholic Church in its harshest form. Adopting prevailing societal norms, like slaveholding, was just one way the nascent church in the United States sought to move away from the margins of society to the center. The Catholic Church in the United States acquiesced to the times in an effort to fit into the larger society. Individuals within the church hierarchy—such as Archbishop John Carroll of Baltimore, Bishop Richard Kendrick of St. Louis, Bishop Benedict Joseph Flaget of Bardstown and Louisville, and Bishop Patrick Lynch of Charleston—owned slaves.[36] Others, such as Bishop Francis Kendrick (the brother of Richard Kendrick), extolled slavery a year before becoming Bishop of Philadelphia in 1842. Kendrick stated that "nothing should be attempted against the laws nor anything be done or said that would make them [slaves] bear their yoke unwillingly."[37] Catholic slaveholders used the sacraments, particularly Baptism, as a means to justify slavery. By foisting Baptism onto slaves, Catholic slaveholders were able to bring more bodies into the church—bodies that they controlled. In doing so, Catholic slaveholders did not have to recognize those bodies as people, let alone as their brothers and sisters in Christ. This would have subsequent ramifications for Blacks wishing to enter the priesthood or religious life.

Religious congregations, including the Jesuits and Sulpicians in Maryland and Jesuits and Vincentians in Missouri, owned slaves in large numbers.[38] Others, including the Sisters of the Blessed Sacrament and the Missionary Sisters Servants of the Holy Spirit, expressly forbade Blacks from entering their orders for many years.[39] St. Katharine Drexel founded the Sisters of the Blessed Sacrament in 1891 to minister to African Americans and Native Americans. In 1893, members of the congregation, under St. Katharine Drexel's leadership, voted not to admit Black and Native American women. The Sisters of the Blessed Sacrament only reversed course in 1949 under pressure from white priests.[40] Operating on a similar timeline, the Missionary Sisters Servants of the Holy Spirit were founded in Holland in 1889. They began working in the United States in 1901 with a focus on ministry in the African American community yet did not begin admitting Blacks until 1946.[41]

In 1838, the Jesuits sold the 272 slaves held in Maryland en masse to financially stabilize Georgetown University as well as other institutions along the East Coast. In addition to their financial incentive, the Jesuits realized they were ineffective farmers.[42] They were also beginning to realize that if Catholicism was really going to become a force in the United States, it was going to happen in cities, specifically in the cities where German and Irish immigrants were making their homes. The church was the only institution familiar to these immigrants. The 1838 sale allowed the Jesuits to not only financially fortify Georgetown University but also divest from unproductive farming operations and reallocate resources in urban ministries directed at German and Irish immigrants. Because of these financial and societal pressures, the church deliberately chose white immigrants at the equally deliberate expense of evangelizing African Americans.

Georgetown University owes its continued existence to the financial largess provided by the 1838 sale. Even though there was already academic literature on Jesuit slaveholding[43] (much of it written by Jesuits),[44] Georgetown's public reckoning with this history began after a series of articles published by *The New York Times*, starting in 2016.[45] As part of the ongoing reckoning with this history, Georgetown now offers preferential or legacy admissions to the documented descendants of any slaves held by the Jesuit Community in Maryland, not just the 272 sold in 1838.[46] On the surface, this sounds like a legitimate act of reparation to those whose ancestors secured Georgetown's financial solvency through their slave labor. According to Georgetown's website, one must provide or obtain documentation of descendancy, yet it is extremely difficult to document those family connections. This presents a major obstacle to accessing legacy admission. An institution puts its money behind what it values. Georgetown has not valued any of the slaves whose labor fortified it, including the aforementioned 272 men, women, and children. As a way of rectifying this, over the last few years, multiple descendants' organizations and memory projects have been founded to preserve this history and hold Georgetown and the Jesuits accountable.[47]

Records related to the Jesuits' 1838 slave sale indicate that a portion of the money raised from the sale was also used to support Old St. Joseph's Church in Philadelphia.[48] Old St. Joe's, as the parish is known, was the first site of St. Joseph's University. Without Old St. Joe's, there would be no Saint Joseph's University. I was a contingent faculty member at Saint Joseph's University from January 2010 through the summer of 2018. Currently, Saint Joseph's University is located in Wynnefield, a predominantly African American section of Philadelphia. In the fall of 2016, I spoke at a panel Saint Joseph's University held on Jesuit slaveholding. I pointed out that according to information available on the university's website, as of fall 2015, only 3.8 percent of traditional-age students were African American. Less than 14 percent of traditional-age students were people of color. In addition, as of fall 2013 (the most recent data that was available to me), there were 656 full-time faculty members at SJU. I cannot say how many are people of color because that information is not publicly available; however, I can tell you that I could have counted the number of African American full-time faculty on my fingers. These realities of the minuscule numbers of African American students and faculty do not exist in a vacuum.

BLACKS' THWARTED CALL TO THE PRIESTHOOD AND RELIGIOUS LIFE

During the 19th century, many Black Catholics (either personally or through their immediate ancestors) had experienced slavery as anti-Blackness in its most vile form. Nevertheless, as practicing Catholics, African Americans demanded that the church hierarchy recognize how their unique heritage, culture, and range of experience contributed to their expression of Catholicism. Like the Irish, Germans, and Italians before them, Black Catholics arrived in the urban North from mostly rural areas, knowing very little about the intricacies of urban life and their religious tradition. However, specific evangelization efforts were not made to bring Blacks in from the fringes of the church.[49] The national parish model, which had such success with newly arrived Europeans, did not fare as well with Blacks.

When Blacks petitioned the Archdiocese for their own parish in post–Civil War New York, those requests were denied until 1883. Even when Blacks had a parish devoted specifically to their needs, they received, at best, token support from the church hierarchy and were denied the basic elements of white ethnic parish life. Black children, for example, could not attend Catholic schools, which were free to European-American children.[50] Instead, they had to pay to attend a school sponsored by New York's St. Vincent de Paul Society.[51] For the national parish model to succeed, Black parishes using the model needed priests and vowed religious men and women who could identify with the constituent community. Assigning appropriate priests and religious men and women to a parish designated for Black Catholics was particularly difficult given the racism that limited the access Blacks had to the priesthood and vowed religious life.[52] Usually, the founding of Black parishes in the urban North was a concerted effort to keep Black Catholics out of white parishes—not an effort to support Black culture.

Significantly, even as late as the nineteenth century, hundreds of years after white Catholics arrived in the United States in large numbers, the church was still far from the massive institution it is today. The U.S. Catholic Church was not a major Pre-K to PhD educator or a major provider of social services. Rather, the Catholic Church was still classified as a mission church by the Holy See. More to the point, it was a fledgling institution that needed to grow its membership if it was not only going to survive but also thrive in the United States. Those working in the institutional church who could see this were few and far between. One such visionary who saw both this need and the disconnect between how the Catholic Church treated white ethnic groups and African Americans was Fr. John Slattery, SSJ, originally a Mill Hill Father who became the founder and first superior general of the Society of St. Joseph or the Josephites.

In 1871, the first group of priests from the St. Joseph's Society of the Sacred Heart for the Foreign Missions or Mill Hill Fathers arrived in the United States from Mill Hill, England. They found a Catholic Church that could claim fewer than 100,000 of the 4 million African Americans in the United States and had, therefore, "failed in its mission"[53] to evangelize African Americans. They also found a church that, due to its relatively small size and lack of cultural and political capital, was unwilling to challenge pervasive, racist norms of the time, especially in the Southern states where that capital was minuscule at best. The Mill Hill Fathers understood that if the church was to grow in the United States, it needed people in the pews. They saw that African Americans, many recently freed and unchurched, could help grow Catholicism in the United States. The Mill Hill Fathers also saw that for the church to stop hemorrhaging the few Black Catholics it had and evangelize and retain more African Americans, the church would need Black priests who were born, trained, and ordained in the United States.

Father Slattery was a visionary who saw that the U.S. Church needed to attract African Americans if it was to grow and thrive. That could only happen with U.S.-born and trained Black priests. Historian Stephen J. Ochs says of Fr. Slattery, "During the last two decades of the nineteenth century, the cause of black priests in the Catholic church had no greater champion than the Reverend John R. Slattery."[54] Fr. Slattery initially joined the aforementioned Mill Hill Fathers in the early 1870s and was ordained in 1877. It was Father Slattery's visionary mindset that led him to break away from the missionary Mill Hill Fathers and found the Society of St. Joseph.

Given Slattery's upbringing, his work with African American Catholics was not a foregone conclusion. His parents were immigrants from Ireland and found financial prosperity in Boss Tweed's New York City.[55] After experiencing a metanoia on the streets of Manhattan in 1872, Slattery joined the Mill Hill community. His decision to become a priest delighted his mother but left his father dejected since the elder Slattery had dreamt of even greater financial prosperity for his only surviving child.

Two years into Slattery's seminary training, his parents learned he planned to evangelize African Americans and grow the church through greater African American participation. His parents, who were New York Irish Catholics ensconced in the culture of Archbishop John Hughes, were vehemently opposed to this plan. They demanded he abandon his training and return home. He did not.[56] Instead, he took up the mantle of providing African American Catholics with Black priests to minister to them. Slattery knew for that to happen, newly ordained Black priests could not belong to the Mill Hill Fathers. As a missionary order, any priest ordained in the United States for the Mill Hill Fathers could immediately be sent far away, perhaps never to return. Because this type of movement would defeat the purpose to which Slattery had dedicated himself, he spearheaded the Mill Hill Fathers in the United States' complete disassociation from the Mill Hill Fathers in the United Kingdom. In 1893, the U.S. Mill Hill Fathers became an independent order: the Society of St. Joseph of the Sacred Heart. As an independent order, the Society of St. Joseph of the Sacred Heart, or the Josephites, could train and ordain men born in the United States and ensure that they would carry out their priestly ministry in the United States as well. In a society and a church that was entrenched in Jim Crow laws and other forms of systemic racism, this was easier said than done. The United States did not ordain its first Black priest until 1891 when Charles Randolph Uncles was ordained a member of the Society of Saint Joseph in Baltimore.

Filling the need for Black priests and vowed religious men and women in the United States would prove a Herculean task. In the nineteenth century, Black men and women felt a religious vocation or call to the Catholic priesthood and vowed religious life, even before the Civil War.[57] However, systemic racism within the church often thwarted them in their efforts to pursue these vocations.[58] In the 1850s, for example, New York's Archbishop John Hughes, leader of a large and consequential archdiocese, found himself combating charges that the Catholic Church in the United States was not fully American because it deviated from the white Anglo-Saxon Protestant roots of the country.[59] Combating these charges required Archbishop Hughes to advocate a U.S. American Catholicism that placed its emphasis on being American. Thus, he was pressured to create and perpetuate a U.S. Catholicism that was synonymous with whiteness. In fact, his detractors wanted him to advocate a particular form of whiteness that dovetailed with the standard from which Hughes was accused of deviating.[60] Hughes was called on to advocate anti-Blackness whenever possible. Consequently, Archbishop Hughes did not lend the weight of his office to supporting the vocations of Blacks to the priesthood or vowed religious life. For a nineteenth-century Black man to become a priest, he had to study abroad in the seminaries of Canada and Europe. William Augustine Williams was an early Black seminarian who entered Urban College in Rome in 1855. At that time, "canon law required all seminarians to have a bishop or religious congregation as a sponsor who would then assume responsibility for them upon ordination."[61] Archbishop Hughes refused to sponsor Williams, asserting that "the American public would be violently opposed to Black priests."[62] Williams received initial sponsorship from Bishop Louis A. Rappe of Cleveland and Archbishop Francis Kendrick of Baltimore. Three years later, both Bishop Rappe and Archbishop Kendrick would withdraw their sponsorship of Williams. According to historian Stephen J. Ochs, "Neither bishop was willing to risk the ire of whites by introducing a black priest into his diocese."[63] As we will see with Augustus Tolton and Charles Randolph Uncles, even those Black men who did manage to become ordained were not always received warmly by parishioners or their fellow priests when exercising their priestly vocations.[64]

The first Catholic priest of African American origin was James Augustine Healy, the oldest of ten children born to Eliza Healy, a slave, and Georgia plantation owner, Michael Morris Healy. The Healy children led noteworthy lives and, with the help of their father, transcended the fate imposed on them by having been born slaves. James Augustine Healy studied in seminaries in Montreal and Paris and was ordained in the latter city in 1854. He became the first bishop of African American origin in the United States. He served in the diocese of Portland, Maine, eventually becoming the Bishop of Portland.[65] Bishop Healy's brother, Alexander Sherwood Healy, studied in Rome and was ordained there in 1858. The third Healy brother to become a priest, Patrick Francis, was ordained a Jesuit in Belgium in 1864. A decade later, he became the first president of Georgetown University.[66] Ironically, Georgetown University—an institution built on the backs of slaves—had as its first president a Jesuit who had himself been born a slave. The pièce-de-résistance is that today, Georgetown's flagship building is named Healy Hall. What might have happened if he had been born on a Jesuit plantation in Maryland instead of the plantation owned by his father in Georgia?

Despite this, the Healys are omitted from the discussion of Black priests. They did not identify as members of the Black Catholic community.[67] Augustus Tolton of Quincy, Illinois, is regarded as the pioneering Black priest of the nineteenth century. Tolton, the second of three children, was born a slave in Missouri in 1854 and baptized Catholic soon after. His mother, Martha Jane, had been baptized Catholic soon after her birth on a plantation in Kentucky. At age 16, she was separated from her parents and younger brother and taken to Missouri as part of a wedding dowry. Tolton's father, Peter Paul, was baptized Catholic after being purchased at auction in Missouri.⁶⁸ At the outbreak of the Civil War, Peter Paul Tolton ran away and vowed to his wife that he would earn money and secure freedom for her and their three children. As the Civil War raged on, and with no word from her husband for over a year, Martha Jane Tolton gathered her children—ages 8, 7, and 20 months—and ran away. The family narrowly escaped capture by Confederate soldiers, thanks in part to the aid they received from "sympathetic field slaves" they encountered.⁶⁹ Union soldiers led the family to the edge of the Mississippi River, where Martha Jane Tolton gathered her children in a decrepit rowboat and paddled to Illinois. The Toltons made their way to Quincy, which had become a hub for former slaves.⁷⁰ After the Civil War ended, the Toltons learned that Peter Paul Tolton died while serving in the Union Army.

Augustus Tolton began battling systemic racism in the church early. At age 11, his mother enrolled him in the school attached to their parish, the German-speaking St. Boniface. Parishioners threatened to withdraw their children from the school, withhold financial support for the parish, and abandon the parish entirely if Augustus Tolton remained enrolled. Children mocked him and addressed him with racial slurs. In the end, the Toltons left the parish.⁷¹ Eventually, the family joined St. Peter's, an Irish parish, where the pastor Fr. Peter McGirr played a pivotal role in Tolton's life. Fr. McGirr encouraged Tolton's priestly vocation and made inquiries to every seminary in the country on Tolton's behalf. Saying "they are not ready for that," each seminary would refuse to admit Tolton.⁷²

After a series of fits and starts, Tolton left Quincy for Rome in 1880 to begin his seminary studies. Upon his ordination in 1886, Tolton knew he may be sent to serve as a missionary priest in Africa. Instead, he returned to the United States and was warmly received by Black Catholics in his hometown. However, he found the town of Quincy unbearable due to the overt racism of other priests.⁷³ Archbishop Patrick Feehan and the Archdiocese of Chicago welcomed Tolton in 1889. Deeply affected by what happened in Quincy, Father Tolton reflected on his new position in a letter to Father John R. Slattery, SSJ, superior general of the Josephites. He wrote, "If any jealousies arise here among the priests at my success . . . I will put all of my books in the trunk and come right there to Baltimore."⁷⁴ Although embraced by Black Catholics, Father Tolton felt cut off from his fellow priests. His hesitancy to build relationships with other priests was largely due to the lingering feelings of distrust caused by his experiences in Quincy.

Father Tolton was the founding pastor of St. Monica's parish in Chicago. As per canon law, the parish consisted of the people in his charge. It was up to him to get a church built for his parish. While donors provided the funds to start building the church, there wasn't enough money to finish it. During the final years of nineteenth-century Chicago, Father Tolton saw churches that were "magnificent edifices with immense spires, even twin spires, and lofty towers with chimes and bells"[75] rise around him. All of them were meant for white Catholics. St. Monica's remained an "unfinished, flat-roofed church—the [B]lack center of worship."[76] He felt defeated due to futile efforts to complete the construction of the church for St. Monica's parish. Father Tolton's biographer, Caroline Hemesath, OSF, says, "The sight of those edifices—tokens of white people's faith—awakened a longing which threatened to drown his courage. He lamented the fact that he and his people had only this humble abode for the King of Kings."[77] The trauma of constant rejection from a church he only wanted to serve wore on Father Tolton. Having experienced declining health for some time, Father Tolton collapsed from heat stroke after disembarking from a train in 105-degree heat upon returning to Chicago from a retreat. He died on July 9, 1897, at the age of 43.

As of July 2023, Father Tolton is one of six African Americans with open causes for sainthood. His cause is increasingly gaining traction. "Tolton Ambassador" groups are organized in a number of dioceses, including Chicago and Philadelphia. In June 2019, Pope Francis declared that Father Tolton "lived a life of historic virtue" and advanced his canonization cause by bestowing the title "The Venerable Father Augustus Tolton."[78] As of May 2024, there is no Black saint who was born in the United States. Given the propensity for white supremacy in the Catholic Church,[79] the importance and magnitude of a U.S.-born Black saint cannot be overstated.

Father John Slattery's connection to Father Tolton was mentioned above. Father Slattery's view of having African American Catholics in significant numbers being predicated on having African American clergy to minister was nothing short of visionary and still is not widespread all these years later. Yet his vision was clouded by the deeply internalized racism that was seen in his treatment of Charles Randolph Uncles, the first Black man ordained to the priesthood in the United States.

Charles Randolph Uncles has come to exemplify the efforts of Blacks to gain access to the priesthood.[80] However, the struggle for access to the priesthood extends far beyond Uncles and the Society of St. Joseph. Uncles' quest to join the priesthood was filled with nearly insurmountable hurdles. His difficulties reflected the church's racist and paternalistic tendencies toward African Americans, as well as those same tendencies in the larger society. Even Uncles' staunchest supporter, Father Slattery, questioned his ability to complete a course of study in philosophy during his seminary training.[81] Uncles also constantly battled with Slattery over money. As a Josephite, Uncles took a vow of poverty and was unable to earn money and hold property. Yet, as an only child, he felt a responsibility to aid his parents financially as they aged, especially since it was difficult for his father, a mechanic, to secure work because of racist practices in trade unions dominated by white Catholics.[82] The financial support of Uncles' parents would be a recurring issue and source of tension between Uncles and Slattery for many years.

In the eyes of white priests, Uncles had the temerity to see himself as their equal after his ordination in 1891. For his trouble, Uncles was accused of being "conceited as a peacock" and having a "lack of prayer and zeal."[83] Slattery, in turn, was criticized for permitting Uncles "to do as he pleased since his ordination."[84] Uncles' path was hampered by systemic roadblocks set up to keep him and other African Americans out of the priesthood, which is the gateway to positions of leadership—and therefore, the nucleus of power—in the Roman Catholic Church. The expectations placed on Uncles by Slattery, as well as others, left no room for error. Uncles was expected to be the proverbial poster child for morality, intellect, and piety as well as single-handedly combat every existing stereotype about African Americans, in particular, African American men. Slattery was personally affronted when Uncles wanted a career as a seminary teacher. Uncles refused to be paraded around the country in the name of raising money and showing white Catholics that African American men were capable of serving as priests.

These roadblocks mimicked those in the larger society put in place to keep Blacks from being upwardly mobile. Ironically, the Roman Catholic

Church regards itself as an institution that champions the voiceless and powerless. Yet, the church's treatment of African Americans was in strict accordance with the prevailing racist norms of the time.

Black Catholics were systematically excluded from the priesthood for several reasons. Because the Catholic Church was still gaining a foothold in the United States in the early nineteenth century, the church had limited resources. It deliberately dispersed those resources to the benefit of some groups and the detriment of others. At the time, most Blacks still lived in the South, an area teeming with white Protestants suspicious of and hostile toward Catholics and the religion they practiced.[85] With the exception of visionaries like Slattery, the church did not want to tread upon prevailing sensibilities and challenge the racist status quo by openly evangelizing Blacks. Consequently, the church and its leaders acquiesced to the prevailing racist ideology and practices of the time that regarded Blacks as morally and intellectually inferior. Church leaders and white lay Catholics regarded Blacks as children in need of protection and care instead of as brothers and sisters in Christ. This paternalism included the belief that Blacks were incapable of completing rigorous academic seminary training and leading a celibate lifestyle. Thus, the church both accepted and contributed to the lingering stereotype of the dumb, hypersexual Black male.[86] This rationale continues to persist, in part, because scholars of both the Black Church and U.S. Catholicism have justified the conventional wisdom of the fundamental incompatibility between Black culture and Catholicism by describing Catholicism as so symbolic, ritualistic, and stoic that it could not appeal to African Americans' need for unbridled exuberance and emotionality.[87]

This chapter has demonstrated the prevalence of anti-Blackness throughout the history of the U.S. Catholic Church. Rooted in slaveowning, it is seen across sectors of Catholicism including priestly congregations and dioceses. The Jesuit community's ongoing reckoning with its slaveholding past is just one example of how systemic racism is woven into the braid and fabric of the church. The church still wears that braid, and therefore, the consequences of that earliest Catholic racism in the United States are still with us today.

THREE

Finding a Place at the Table

Liturgy as Identity Work and an Act of Resistance

•••••••

Incorporating Blackness into Mass is essential. As the principal worship experience for Roman Catholics, liturgy is unifying. The ubiquity of its core elements, the scripture readings, the recitation of the Nicene Creed, the Eucharist, are key to the Roman Catholic Church being catholic. Around these core elements, whether through music or the homily, there is room for expression that is unique to an individual community. That individuality is expressed within the broader ritual of Mass. In the 2021 study, "Faith Among Black Americans," the Pew Research Center found that 82 percent of Black Catholics reported that "being Black is very or somewhat important to how they think of themselves."[1] African American Catholics use different tools to combine cultural expression and Roman Catholic tradition through liturgy, asserting their Blackness despite the whiteness of the Catholic Church, and engaging in African American parish culture production. In doing so, Black Catholics celebrate and amplify the part of their "selves" that has been suppressed, thus actively and intentionally resisting racism.

Music, the homily, rituals, and church aesthetics give shape to Black Catholics' identity as Black Catholics. Their identity is distinct from that of Catholics from other racial and ethnic groups, as well as from Blacks who are not Catholic. The ongoing identity work of Black Catholics may be interpreted as "owning,"[2] whereby individuals holding seemingly disparate identities "own" their multiple identities and build a community where those identities can be expressed freely. *Owning* happens when community building occurs through participation in rituals. The use of symbols brings multiple, seemingly disparate, identities together cohesively through liturgy. The use of symbols is important: "Not to maintain the Mass's distinctive characteristics could be taken as indicating tacit acknowledgment that what they are doing is 'not really' Catholic and never could be authentically Catholic."[3]

Alternatively, this identity work can be thought of as "sifting,"[4] or "the process of constructing a fairly stable, biographical identity that incorporates aspects of two or more potentially conflicted identities."[5] The process of *sifting* involves individuals taking on only parts of an identity and sifting out those that are unsuitable.[6] Sifting happens when "practices and attitudes which are sifted into the mix of . . . identity define what that identity means."[7]

In Black parishes, owning and sifting are aspects of a congregational culture that is produced and maintained through a congregation's "activities, artifacts, and accounts."[8] Black Catholics' seemingly disparate identities come together through ritual. Understanding these elements of congregational life (or in the case of Catholics, parish life) allows us to see how congregations build a sense of community, document their identity, and immortalize institutional memory. In this way, a congregation's culture consists of what members do together, the things they make, and the stories they tell, with ritual as a primary focal element. Black Catholics engage in parish culture production.

Both owning and sifting can happen through ritual, a process in which "our sense of who we are is shaped by what we do, what we make, and how we talk about ourselves."[9] There is no rote means or single ritual whereby this is accomplished. The following section describes some of the myriad ways this can happen.

UNDERSTANDING LITURGICAL STYLES IN BLACK CATHOLIC PARISHES

Black Catholics' identity work through liturgy is a dynamic process that uses sifting to bring together elements of Roman Catholic tradition and the African American religious experience in the parish setting. Scholars have asserted the centrality of liturgy as well as cultural expression *through* liturgy in the Black Catholic community.[10] For Black Catholics who have both the freedom and desire to bring cultural tools into liturgy, Mass is more than just a weekly ritual required of all Roman Catholics. It is a means of forming and expressing a specific, parish-based identity. Different parishes and even different Masses within each parish have their own tenor and flavor based on the atmosphere of the parish and the constituency of each Mass.

Here, I identify three liturgical styles, *Traditionalist*, *Spirited*, and *Gospel*, to articulate how sifting occurs in parishes and how sifting results in parish culture production. All three styles incorporate music, homilies, and church aesthetics to achieve a level of sifting appropriate for the respective communities and a cultural expression that leaves parishioners satisfied in their worship experience.

The *Traditionalist Liturgy Style* is so named because it is the most dominant liturgical form in the United States and is closely associated with Catholics of European descent. Because of the Traditionalist Liturgy Style's dominance in the United States, it has transcended its European origins and can be found in parishes whose members are not of European descent. Hallmarks of this style include rather short homilies and songs from the missalette, a book commonly found in Catholic churches that contains scripture readings for the liturgical year and a selection of often-used hymns.

The Traditionalist style is most likely to appeal to Catholics with conservative liturgical preferences. In predominantly Black parishes, this style is more likely to be found at Saturday vigil Masses and/or at Masses very early on Sunday morning. Attendance at these Masses is often dominated by senior citizens, a group less likely to want a worship experience that is noticeably different from what they have known throughout their lives.

Masses in the *Spirited Liturgy Style* bear similarity to the Traditionalist Liturgy Style, but incorporate a livelier means of expression. This livelier expression manifests itself most concretely in the music used during liturgy and style of preaching, which is more animated. Masses in this style frequently incorporate songs from the *Lead Me, Guide Me* hymnal,[11] which has played a pivotal role in incorporating Black culture into liturgy since it was first introduced nearly forty years ago. The

Spirited Liturgy Style seeks a deeper and more palpable engagement with parishioners than is found in the Traditionalist Liturgy Style.

Finally, the *Gospel Liturgy Style* invokes the style of worship most often associated with congregations in the Black Church. It specifically targets the African American experience by using preaching, music, and church aesthetics to invoke African American history and a clear African American heritage while connecting that history and heritage to Catholicism. Masses in the Gospel Liturgy Style are more likely to use gospel hymns not found in the missalette or any hymnal. The homilies at these Masses use a lengthier and more animated preaching style that engages the parishioners through the "call and response" technique. According to the Pew Research Center, 66 percent of Black Catholics who attend Mass at least a few times a year report encountering "call and response" at Mass.[12] Priests often deliver their homily from the center aisle rather than from an ambo. This liturgy style offers the most overt example of how sifting and parish culture production occurs within the realm of Black Catholics. It is also the most direct means of using liturgy as an act of resistance to racism. In *Racial Justice and the Catholic Church*,[13] theologian Bryan Massingale articulates the criticism unleashed when Catholics from marginalized groups incorporate cultural expressions into Mass: "So often, one hears complaints such as, 'Why do we have to sing in Spanish?' 'Don't they have their own church?' 'Gospel music isn't really Catholic, is it?'" White-ethnic Catholicism is built on intertwining ethnicity and religion so that they become almost indistinguishable from one another. Yet, when African Americans do the same thing, the white Catholics who have been intertwining ethnic and religious identity for generations criticize African Americans for not being truly Catholic. And it is in such spaces where whiteness becomes synonymous with being Catholic.[14]

No one liturgical style is more authentically Black or truly Catholic than another. Each meets the mandate from the Black Catholic Bishops of the United States to be "authentically Black" and "truly Catholic."[15] Each works for those who attend these liturgies and belong to these parishes. These descriptions are not intended to be rigid boxes, either, with every Mass fitting into one box or another. Rather, these descriptions of liturgy styles are best understood as a continuum: the categories Traditionalist, Spirited, and Gospel serve as benchmarks along a spectrum. Music and homilies differ across categories. Aesthetics, on the other hand, remain constant in parishes offering more than one style. It would be impractical to alter aesthetic features between Masses.

The synopsis provided in Table 3.1 shows the three liturgical styles, which together I call Liturgical Designations and their key features, not as a means of compartmentalizing liturgical expression but as a way of succinctly summarizing each category. In the following section, I describe the liturgical styles observed in three parishes: St. John Vianney in the Archdiocese of New York and St. Bernadette Soubirous and St. Catherine of Alexandria in the Archdiocese of Philadelphia.[16] I focus on how each

Table 3.1. Liturgical Styles and Their Key Features

	Music	Homily	Aesthetics
Traditionalist	• Standard hymns usually found in missalette • More likely a Saturday vigil or early Sunday morning Mass	• Generally short—less than 10 minutes • Done from an ambo	• Emphasis on African American events such as Kwanzaa and Black History Month • Images of Jesus and Mary depicted as Black • Emphasis on Black Saints • Depictions of Jesus, Mary, and Black saints are present side-by-side with white depictions
Spirited	• Standard hymns in a more upbeat style • Songs from the *Lead Me, Guide Me* hymnal	• Not as short as a Traditionalist homily • Up to 15 minutes • More engagement • Done from the center aisle or an ambo	• Emphasis on African American events such as Kwanzaa and Black History Month • Images of Jesus and Mary depicted as Black • Emphasis on Black Saints • Depictions of Jesus, Mary, and Black saints are present side-by-side with white depictions
Gospel	• Gospel songs not in a hymn book or missalette	• Can last as long as 25 minutes • Animated presence • Uses the "call and response" technique • Done from the center aisle	• Emphasis on African American events such as Kwanzaa and Black History Month • Images of Jesus and Mary depicted as Black • Emphasis on Black Saints • Depictions of Jesus, Mary, and Black saints are present side-by-side with white depictions

provides a different way of sifting Black Catholic identity that is appropriate to a parish's history and internal diversity, as reflected by the demographic profiles linked to different Mass times.

BLACK CATHOLIC IDENTITY IN THREE PARISHES

St. John Vianney

St. John Vianney sits in the Central Harlem section of Manhattan. The parish is well known throughout the archdiocese, most notably for Msgr. Jones, the charismatic pastor during the time of my data collection in 2005 and 2006. Because of the parish's notoriety, it draws parishioners not only from within parish boundaries but also from outside of New York City, including northern New Jersey. During my visits to St. John Vianney, I observed clear distinctions between the styles of liturgy at the 9:30 a.m. and 11:30 a.m. Masses.

The general tone of St. John Vianney's 9:30 a.m. Mass foregoes the notion that exuberant expression is either incompatible with Catholicism or must be limited to the Black Church. The 9:30 a.m. Mass is a Gospel Liturgy Style, its tone set primarily by the music and the homily. The parish's gospel choir provides the music. The members of the gospel choir wear robes that are typically found in Protestant congregations. They are floor-length red-and-white robes, with large bell-style sleeves. The choir's songs do not come from the *Lead Me, Guide Me* hymnal; instead, the selections invoke an expressiveness and level of emotion that is not readily identified with Catholicism. Choir members sway to the music, and the parishioners clap and join them in song. A number of parishioners stand during these selections. The use of choir robes commonly found in Protestant churches and gospel songs exemplify sifting: more traditional songs and choir attire are sifted out to make room to sift in elements that are more in line with worship seen in churches in the Black Protestant traditions. By using emotive music in the liturgy, parishioners sift out more traditional songs to make room for those that are more culturally relevant. This is a distinct means of parish culture production. Through music ministry, the choir engages the parish community and helps to create a specific parish identity.

Some of the rituals performed during the 9:30 a.m. Mass would be recognizable to Catholics accustomed to attending another style Mass. For example, the Baptismal Rite begins with a renewal of baptismal vows by those present and concludes with the officiating priest gently sprinkling holy water on the parishioners to remind those present of their baptism. To those familiar with the Roman Catholic Mass, a Baptismal Rite would not be viewed as foreign or in any way unusual. What makes it unusual at St. John Vianney is having it *every* Sunday. The parish replaces the Penitential Rite with a Baptismal Rite. During the Penitential Rite, parishioners communally acknowledge their sins and sinfulness in preparation for receiving the Body of Christ in the form of Holy Communion. Generally, the Penitential Rite is performed by having those present recite one of two commonly used prayers. On special occasions, such as Easter Sunday, the Penitential Rite is replaced by a Baptismal Rite. But at St. John Vianney, it is replaced weekly. The 9:30 a.m. Mass reimagines an unabashedly Catholic ritual. The parish makes this ritual its own, thus distinguishing St. John Vianney from other parishes.

Because this ritual lies within the structure of Mass, the parish community does not run the risk of incurring episcopal admonition by performing it every Sunday. The ritual would be easily recognizable to any Roman Catholic; however, its conventional use is sifted out to sift in a use that fits the parish's needs. This Mass clearly borrows from the Black Church's cultural playbook. The choir robes, gospel songs, and ritual adaptation are symbols of the African American religious experience that are used to incorporate Black culture into the Roman Catholic Mass. By doing so, the parish produces a specific Black Catholic cultural identity.

The celebration of the 9:30 a.m. Mass at St. John Vianney lasts almost two hours. The extra time, compared to the one hour more typical of Masses in the Traditionalist Liturgy Style, can be accounted for by a number of components. For example, in addition to the aforementioned Baptismal Rite, the homily can last anywhere from twenty to thirty minutes. The recitation of the Nicene Creed, also known as the Profession of Faith, is sung. This lengthens Mass considerably. Furthermore, parishioners recite the Hail Mary after the General Intercessions. While the Hail Mary is a well-known prayer to Roman Catholics, it is not usually recited during Mass. This is another distinctly Catholic practice that is reimagined by St. John Vianney's parishioners as a means of distinguishing this Mass from a more traditional one.

Another component that can account for the length of the 9:30 a.m. Mass is the Offertory. During the Offertory, the gifts of bread and wine that will be used for Holy Communion are presented to the priest. The Offertory also includes parishioners making monetary offerings to support the parish. In most Catholic parishes in the United States, ushers collect the money donated by parishioners. However, at St. John Vianney, each person present walks up the center aisle to leave his or her envelope in a common basket.

None of these practices are contradictory to practices commonly found at other Roman Catholic Masses. While the recitation of the Hail Mary may give some staunch traditionalists pause, reciting it during Mass is not tantamount to a disavowal of Roman Catholic doctrine. In each of these instances, the parish is sifting out standard uses of practices to have room to sift in reimagined practices that both distinguish this Mass and produce unique cultural elements.

Another illustration of sifting and cultural production in the Gospel Liturgy Style occurs during the homily. During St. John Vianney's 9:30 a.m. Mass, the Gospel reading and homily, whether given by Msgr. Jones or another priest, typically uses techniques that are closely identified with the Black Church. The priest proclaims the Gospel from the center aisle and remains there to offer the homily. Msgr. Jones uses the "call and response" technique that is generally associated with Black Protestant congregations.

During one of my visits to St. John Vianney's 9:30 a.m. Mass, Msgr. Jones used the call and response technique effectively as a means of connecting with parishioners and connecting scripture readings to parishioners' lived experience. He used his homily to ask parishioners "Who does God's will?" After asking those in attendance if the tax collectors and prostitutes mentioned in the Gospel reading were doing God's will, he heard a resounding "NO!" from parishioners. He connected this point to his parishioners' lived experience by emphasizing that doing the will of God involves not blaming others for one's own failings, including issues related to work, family life, and other personal relationships. Msgr. Jones then deftly managed to connect this message to the parish's mandatory capital campaign held in conjunction with the Archdiocese of New York's bicentennial. Msgr. Jones connected these two seemingly unrelated topics by articulating the parish's needs—such as an elevator to accommodate disabled and elderly parishioners—then emphasizing parishioners' duty to contribute to the campaign so that the parish's needs could be met. The implication was that otherwise, members of the parish were not doing God's will and would have no one else to blame for their failings.

Through his homilies, Msgr. Jones instills in parishioners an appreciation for Black history and Catholic history alike. This was especially evident during a Mass celebrating the feast of the parish's patron. Msgr. Jones went to great lengths to provide those in attendance with an understanding of St. John Vianney's life and how he used his ministry to serve God. The pastor described how St. John Vianney used his personal wealth to minister to the community and did not abandon those he served when a plague began to envelop the community. In doing this, Msgr. Jones carves space for his parishioners within larger Catholic history and makes the life of a sixteenth-century Italian saint resonate for twenty-first century African Americans in Harlem. Establishing a connection between the parishioners and the parish's patron saint generates a concrete identity for members of the parish. Parishioners can see themselves in relation to a long-dead saint and, thus, can develop a broader sense of what it means to be a Roman Catholic.

These techniques associated with the homily demonstrate combining elements that identified Catholicism with elements firmly ensconced in the Black Church. All examples above show how elements from both the African American and U.S. Catholic traditions are sifted into liturgy to create a worship experience that meets the needs of parishioners and creates a uniquely Black Catholic culture.

The 11:30 a.m. Mass in the Spirited Liturgy Style contrasts with the 9:30 a.m. Gospel Liturgy Style in several ways. The most notable difference is in the music. The music at the later Mass is provided by the men's chorus instead of the gospel choir, which consists entirely of women. During my visits, the 11:30 a.m. chorus had approximately eight members while the 9:30 a.m. choir had nearly twenty participants. The songs selected for the 11:30 a.m. liturgy came from the *Lead Me, Guide Me*[17] hymnal and consisted of both hymns, such as "Let There Be Peace on

Earth," and more African American–oriented songs, such as "We've Come This Far By Faith." The style of the men's chorus is much more reserved than that of the gospel choir. They do not wear robes, sway with the music, or clap in the same way as the gospel choir. This could be because of the chorus' smaller number; however, it is more likely a result of the muted tenor and flavor of the 11:30 a.m. liturgy.

The duration of the 11:30 a.m. Mass is noticeably shorter than the 9:30 a.m. liturgy. The service does not regularly replace the more traditional Penitential Rite with the longer Baptismal Rite. Music selections and homily length are also among the reasons that account for Mass lasting approximately thirty minutes less than the 9:30 a.m. Mass. There is some measure of sifting, as the music sifts out an abundance of traditional Catholic hymns to make room for more African American-oriented songs from the *Lead Me, Guide Me* hymnal. The muted tone of the 11:30 a.m. Spirited Mass is just as indicative of the production of a unique Black Catholic cultural identity as the Gospel Mass. Both styles reflect the depth and diversity of the community that produces them.

The only exception to the general tone of the 11:30 a.m. Mass that I observed was during an 11:30 a.m. Mass celebrating the feast of the parish's patron saint. On this occasion, the 9:30 a.m. gospel choir stayed to lead the processional for the 11:30 a.m. Mass. The processional included multiple verses of a hymn that was not found in any hymnal present in the church. The parishioners stood while clapping and singing along with the gospel choir, who stood along the altar railing instead of at their usual place on the altar. The men's chorus occupied that area since the 11:30 a.m. Mass is their usual venue. The processional turned toward the theatrical, as altar servers carrying crosses began dancing up the main aisle. The dance was in a style that is best described as a combination of hopping and marching in time to the music that is often found in the African American tradition. Initially, the altar servers made their way approximately halfway up the aisle then returned to the back of the church. The Eucharistic Ministers, then lectors, and finally the priests followed in a procession—a march in time to the music and less of a dance—to the altar. The entire procession lasted twenty minutes.

This display set a palpable tone for the occasion that celebrated the parish, its members, and its patron saint. Having attended Roman Catholic

Masses regularly for my entire life, I had never seen the feast of a parish's patron—or any other feast for that matter—celebrated with such fervor and gusto. It invoked the character of music and frenzy that W. E. B. Du Bois offered more than one hundred years ago when describing the Black worship experience.[18] Of the music, Du Bois said, "The Music of Negro religion . . . still remains the most original and beautiful expression of human life and ongoing yet born on American soil."[19] In describing the frenzy, Du Bois said, "It varied in expression from the silent rapt countenance or the low murmur and moan to the mad abandon of physical fervor." The difference between a standard Sunday and this special occasion shows how expression can move along the continuum Du Bois described.

Unequivocally, the 11:30 a.m. Mass celebration included a sifting in of practices borrowed from the Black Church, such as the dancing and long processional to begin the liturgy, and a sifting out of a more straightforward and, frankly, bland opening to the liturgy. Once Mass began, there was no ambiguity regarding what type of service was taking place. During the homily, Msgr. Jones spoke at length about St. John Vianney's personal narrative and how his life experiences influenced his actions. In doing this, Msgr. Jones called the parishioners to look to the parish's patron for inspiration on how to live their lives, to help others, and not abandon those in need during difficult times.

At both the 9:30 a.m. and 11:30 a.m. Masses at St. John Vianney, the music and the homily emphasize Jesus as "Lord and Savior." Parishioners are compelled to follow the high example set by Jesus' life on earth and to ask for Jesus' help in facing the problems and concerns of everyday life. There is much less emphasis placed on God as Creator and the Holy Spirit as Sanctifier. This emphasis on Jesus as Savior is more commonly found in the Black Protestant Church than in the Roman Catholic Church.[20] There are certain characteristics of Jesus—his humanity, poverty, and earthly suffering—that could make this aspect (or person) of the Trinity more tangible and palatable to an African American audience. This worldview is an example of how liturgy can be adapted to serve the needs of a constituency by sifting out one commonly used image, God the Creator, to create room to sift in another, Jesus the Savior.

St. Bernadette Soubirous

The parish of St. Bernadette Soubirous is located in an overwhelmingly African American and economically depressed section of Philadelphia. Having been raised in the Archdiocese of Philadelphia, I have known about the parish for some time.

St. Bernadette Soubirous is known for its numerous social programs, including a prison re-entry program and an outreach to the homeless. Because of its social programs and openness to gay and lesbian Catholics, it carries a reputation as a "last stop" for disaffected Catholics who would otherwise cease to practice Catholicism. For this reason, the parish has for many years drawn parishioners from within traditional parish boundaries and from neighborhoods outside of the immediate area.

In 2013, the year prior to my field observation at the parish, St. Bernadette Soubirous' parish boundaries were reorganized as a result of two nearby churches closing. The shuttered churches were located approximately one mile away from St. Bernadette though in different directions. Mergers of this sort have occurred throughout the Archdiocese of Philadelphia in recent years. This type of parish reorganization has especially impacted parishes within the city of Philadelphia. Many affected parishes within city limits are the remnants of the former national parish model that dominated a number of urban dioceses from the middle of the 19th century to the middle of the 20th century, as discussed in Chapter 2.[21] Over the last twenty years, similar reorganizations of parishes and/or Catholic schools have also occurred in the Archdioceses of Boston, New York, and Chicago.[22] These, reorganizations, often painful, have occurred frequently of late and disproportionately impact already marginalized Catholics, including African American Catholics. This context shapes any consideration of parish life therein.

St. Bernadette Soubirous currently operates a prison re-entry program among its social ministries. It also partners with local organizations, renting space in its former school building to a local non-profit with a soup kitchen and other services for the homeless. These outreach efforts are of particular relevance to both the neighborhood where the parish is and the African American community more broadly. These are ways in which the parish works as a parish to connect the social justice teachings of the Roman Catholic Church and the social issues of specific concern to the African American community.

Liturgy is a form of identity work and parish cultural production. Here again, the homily, music, and church aesthetics combine the Roman Catholic tradition and the African American religious experience. St. Bernadette Soubirous has three regularly scheduled weekend liturgies: a 4:00 p.m. vigil Mass on Saturday and morning Masses at 9:00 a.m. and 11:00 a.m. on Sunday. While the parish is now predominantly African American due to the recent merger, African Americans form the majority of attendees only at the 11:00 a.m. Mass. I draw from my field observations of this 11:00 a.m. Mass here.

Like the 9:30 a.m. Mass at St. John Vianney, the 11:00 a.m. Mass at St. Bernadette Soubirous is in the Gospel Liturgy Style. Music is facilitated by the gospel choir, which is led by two of the parish's three ministers of music. One leads the choir while the other provides musical accompaniment on the piano. Both have come over to St. Bernadette as a result of the merger. While the group is called a gospel choir, it does not reach the depths and breadths of exuberance found with the choir at St. John Vianney. St. Bernadette's choir uses songs that are not found in either the missalette or the *Lead Me, Guide Me* hymnal. The repetition of the lyrics makes the songs easy for the parishioners to follow and join in the singing. St. Bernadette's choir does not present a unified appearance by wearing choir robes. On only one occasion did I see the choir members dressed in a coordinated color scheme, which occurred when the choir was leaving directly from Mass to sing at a concert event at another church. While the choir is sifting in music akin to the Black Church tradition, it is not sifting in more visual aesthetics. Nevertheless, the parishioners' engagement with the music is apparent not only in the abundant singing but also in parishioners' clapping and occasionally standing in the pews. It appeared that the choir leader, in particular, desired even more exuberance from the parishioners. However, the parishioners may not find a full-on Gospel style palatable. As such, the choir leader may be trying to force something the parishioners are not ready to accept.

St. Bernadette has two priests on staff: the pastor, Fr. Peters, and the parochial vicar, Fr. Wolfe. The two priests have noticeably different, but related, styles pertaining to preaching and connecting with the parishioners during Mass. Fr. Wolfe delivers his homily from the podium while Fr. Peters uses a hand-held microphone to deliver his homily from the center aisle. Both priests tap into the lived experience of the parishioners to connect them to the teachings of the Roman Catholic Church.

On my first visit to the parish, Fr. Wolfe used his homily to deliver a fairly standard message of moving from darkness into light. He invoked the well-known image of Jesus as the Light of the World and, therefore, the path out of darkness. Fr. Wolfe discussed how, in order for the light of the world to enter our lives, we must first be in darkness. He went on to describe several contemporary forms of darkness, including the deaths of Michael Brown in Ferguson, Missouri, and Eric Garner in New York City at the hands of police officers and the societal disaffection these incidents have caused, particularly in the African American community. He went on to describe the "darkness of prison and addiction." Fr. Wolfe connected the struggle of having a loved one in prison or in the throes of addiction to darkness, saying that "it is a special grace to see the light of Jesus" come into one's life.

He went on to discuss an incident from his work in prison ministry. He said that when he arrived at the prison, he was instructed to put his belongings in a locker. The locker could only be accessed by first paying a quarter; yet, he did not have one. He feared that his entire trip would be wasted for want of a quarter until a woman standing behind him offered him one. Fr. Wolfe described the appearance of this woman and the aid she offered him at the exact moment he needed it as "Jesus' light in the darkness." Fr. Wolfe spoke heavily about addiction and prison as a darkness that impacts not only those directly affected but also their loved ones. In this example, Fr. Wolfe was sifting in relatable events from the parishioners' lived experience with a standard teaching about Jesus. By doing so, his homily worked to make the parish a space where African American Catholics feel comfortable and the experience of liturgy felt relatable.

The following week, Fr. Peters' homily focused on the importance of prayer. Whereas Fr. Wolfe's homily had been animated, Fr. Peters' was downright zealous. At the beginning of his homily, Fr. Peters called on the parishioners to rejoice, telling them that "the family that prays together, stays together." He used a variation of the "call and response" technique by asking parishioners to repeat the aforementioned statement after him. Fr. Peters also called on parishioners to turn to the person nearest to them and say, "This homily is about you." He then moved on to several statements that began with the phrase "We REJOICE . . . ," such as "We REJOICE in the love of God!" and "We REJOICE in the gift of another day!" He implored the parishioners to be in relationship with God through prayer. Parishioners applauded at key moments in the homily, such as when he said, "Our brothers and sisters in the Muslim community put us to shame by stopping to pray five times a day!"

As Fr. Peters delivered this message, he did so with vocal inflections more reminiscent of a Black Protestant preacher than a white Catholic priest. He began at the podium with the rhythmic cadence of the "We rejoice" statements. He eventually picked up a wireless hand-held microphone and moved into the center aisle to deliver the second half of the homily. His style includes boisterous, even flamboyant, arm gestures. At times, the music minister will begin to play the piano softly while Fr. Peters speaks. On occasion, Fr. Peters will call on the choir to sing as a means of reiterating his message. All of this is meant to energize and excite the parishioners while, consciously or unconsciously, invoking the preaching, music, and frenzy made famous by Du Bois. The liturgy exemplifies the process of sifting in practices commonly associated with the Black Church experience.

In addition to the homily, St. Bernadette's uses aesthetics to sift in elements of African American and Roman Catholic culture. A stunning, but likely unintended, example is the use of a cross carried by an altar server during the entrance and recessional processions. The cross depicts a Black crucified Jesus. During Mass, the cross rests on a stand in the front of the church, where Black Jesus is positioned directly in front of a painting on the wall, behind the altar, of a crucified white Jesus. The juxtaposition of these two images of the crucifixion is a powerful, unequivocal example of how a parish can use artifacts to sift African American aesthetics into liturgical practice.

During the holiday season, the church decorations included an Advent wreath with one pink candle and three purple candles, which is typical of churches in the Roman Catholic tradition and other Christian denominations. However, within inches of the Advent wreath was a kinara holding seven candles representing the principles of the African American celebration, Kwanzaa. Posters adorned the walls of the church explaining principles that are the hallmarks of Kwanzaa. The two sets of candles are potent, tangible examples of an identity that exists as the outcome of sifting. One is readily identified with the Roman Catholic tradition while the other is uniquely associated with African Americans. Putting them side-by-side shows how Black American Catholics use artifacts to produce a distinctly African American Catholic cultural identity. It also identifies the parish as a space where this identity is celebrated and perpetuated.

I observed another notable use of aesthetics in identity work when I visited St. Bernadette Soubirous on the first Sunday in February. I immediately noticed that the church was decorated for Black History Month. The posters used to decorate the church were those commonly found in elementary schools and depicted key people and moments in African American history, including Rosa Parks, Barack Obama, Jackie Robinson, and the Harlem Renaissance. Other posters depicted values such as courage, creativity, hope, and citizenship. None of the people depicted are Catholic, and none of the depicted values are uniquely identified with Catholicism. Yet having them in church as part of the celebration of Black History Month indicates that the parish is a place where the sifting of cultural, racial, and civic identities with religious identity occurs. Interestingly, I did not observe a specific sifting out of God the Creator at St. Bernadette in favor of concentrating on Jesus the Savior. St. Bernadette Soubirous made room for both.

St. Catherine of Alexandria

St. Catherine of Alexandria is a parish in West Philadelphia. I attended the 10:00 a.m. Mass at St. Catherine's for several weeks in the Spring of 2016, 2017, and 2018. Each time I visited, I was there with students from my Sociology of African American Catholicism course. What you are reading is, in essence, that course in book form. I chose this parish because of its proximity to the university where I was employed at the time, which made it convenient for students. I have been familiar with St. Catherine's for some time as I grew up in West Philadelphia. I have family friends who belong to the parish and a now-deceased relative who belonged to St. Catherine's for many years.

I took students to Mass at St. Catherine's because I wanted them to see that the themes we discussed in class do not happen in a vacuum. I wanted them to know that these themes exist in the lived experiences of African American Catholics. An example of the course themes "jumping off the page" for my students occurred when we visited in the Spring of 2017. In Chapter 2, I discussed the overt racism faced by African American men who wished to become priests in the 19th century and the ultimate result being the low number of African American priests today, which was also a major theme of the course. During that Spring visit, students stated that even after all we had talked about in class concerning Black priests, they were still startled to see a white priest leading Mass at a Black parish. Msgr. Mosby, the pastor of St. Catherine's at the time, served as pastor of predominantly Black parishes in West Philadelphia for more than forty years before his retirement in 2023. The students who found this jarring did so for varying reasons. African American students who are not Catholic, but are accustomed to going to church, are used to seeing a Black minister lead the service at a predominantly Black church. My white Catholic students, who are generally unaccustomed to being in the minority in social spaces, realized, for the first time, the value of having a priest leading Mass who looks like his parishioners.

St. Catherine's 10:00 a.m. Mass is a Spirited Mass that can last anywhere from one hour and fifteen minutes to almost two hours. The choir's selections are taken from the *Lead Me, Guide Me* hymnal and the missalette. The first time I visited this Mass, the choir projected a unified look by wearing matching kente cloth stoles with the initials of the parish. They were seated haphazardly in a cramped space along the side of the sanctuary. At that time, work was underway to create a more spacious, but by no means elaborate, auditorium-style choir section in the front of the church. By the following year, the choir space had been completed and the members now wear matching robes in the same flowing, bell-sleeved style seen at St. John Vianney. This change gives the choir a more distinct presence at Mass.

Msgr. Mosby was pastor of the now-closed St. Teresa's church. Then, he was pastor of both St. Teresa's and St. Catherine's when the two parishes were "twinned" in the 1990s. Twinned parishes maintained their church buildings and parish boundaries but shared one priest who served as the pastor of both parishes. When St. Teresa's closed, its parish territory was absorbed by St. Catherine's with Msgr. Mosby continuing to serve as the pastor. He knows the community well, and this knowledge is reflected in his homilies. He will often spend time at the beginning of the homily informing parishioners of the illnesses, hospitalizations, or deaths of parishioners. In addition, he often mentions a specific parishioner at Mass or refers to an incident from many years ago while making his point during the homily.

During my visits to St. Catherine's, the homilies and music stood out just as they had at the other parishes I visited. Frequent use was made of the *Lead Me, Guide Me* hymnal and the missalette. During the Prayer of the Faithful, also known as the Petitions, prewritten prayers are read by the lector. St. Catherine's reimagines this prayer seen throughout Catholicism by inviting parishioners to extemporaneously offer their own petitions from their seats. This can add considerable length to the Prayer of the Faithful, much like the weekly Baptismal Rite at St. John Vianney. Since music, the homily, and reimagined prayers are in line with observations at St. John Vianney and St. Bernadette Soubirous, I will not dwell on these things here. Instead, I want to turn to something I saw at St. Catherine's but did not see at the other parishes.

During a visit to St. Catherine's, I had an opportunity to observe a baptism. St. Catherine's constructs this ritual to be distinctively and specifically Black *and* Catholic, thus providing elements of sifting and parish culture production. The Sacrament of Baptism is the ritual that welcomes new members to the Catholic Church. Some parishes perform this Sacrament outside of Mass, often early on a Sunday afternoon, while others celebrate it during Mass. St. Catherine's is one of the latter parishes. By having baptisms take place during Mass, new members are welcomed into the community of the local parish and the global Catholic Church during the principal gathering and worship experience. The actual sacrament took place in between the Liturgy of the Word and the Liturgy of the Eucharist. At this point of the Mass, Msgr. Mosby invited the baby, parents, and godparents, along with additional family members, the choir, and any member of the parish community so inclined, to gather around the baptismal font in the back of the church.

As part of the ritual, the choir sang the "Litany of the Saints." Hearing the "Litany of the Saints" is not at all unfamiliar to anyone accustomed to attending a Catholic Mass. However, the litany sung by St. Catherine's choir stood out to me because of its inclusion of African saints, like the Martyrs of Uganda, St. Josephine Bakhita, Sts. Perpetua and Felicity, St. Augustine, and St. Athanasius, as well as saints with close ties to the African American community like Philadelphia-native St. Katherine Drexel. As of 2023, there are no saints of African descent who were born in the United States, which gives these aforementioned saints added importance. To that end, there is a large portrait of St. Josephine Bakhita at St. Bernadette Soubirous, and I remember there was a shrine to the Ugandan Martyrs in the now-closed church I belonged to during the early part of my childhood. Including these saints in the litany was a specific act of inclusion on the part of the St. Catherine's community. They proclaimed that Black saints are part of the Church, too. In order to do this, some of the more often-heard white saints were sifted out. By doing this, the litany, a beautiful and ancient prayer, becomes an act of resistance to racism. It rejects the notion that the Catholic Church is an ultra-white space by asserting that people of African descent are, indeed, among the most revered individuals in Catholicism. These saints belong to the whole church, not just its Black members. Yet, it is unlikely to hear these names in parishes that are not predominantly African American. The inclusion of these saints allows the St. Catherine's parishioners to claim saints of African descent as their own. This embrace of Catholic Blackness resists the notion that only white saints are worth mentioning, making the "Litany of the Saints" an act of resistance to racism and toward racial justice. Because it is unlikely to hear these saints mentioned, especially all of them at once, outside of a predominately Black Church, racial justice in the Church becomes something white Catholics do not have to partake in because minorities are doing all of the work.

At the conclusion of the baptism ritual, the baby—the newest member of the St. Catherine of Alexandria parish community—is lifted high and carried around the church so that each parishioner in attendance can see the baby and extend a hand of blessing. This final part of the baptism can extend an already long ritual for an additional eight to ten minutes. Yet, its symbolism and beauty are unparalleled. The presentation of the baby brings together the role of Mass and the Sacrament of Baptism as a means of creating and perpetuating community as an act of parish culture production.

The 10:00 a.m. Mass at St. Catherine's exhibits Lynn Resnick Dufour's sifting and Nancy Ammerman's use of activities, artifacts, and accounts in parish culture production. Through the kente cloth and later choir robes as well as the music, the Mass sifts in elements of African American culture into liturgy as we have seen at St. John Vianney and St. Bernadette Soubirous. Through the baptism ritual, the parishioners of St. Catherine's engage in parish culture production by asserting the place of *Blackness* within the Church through the emphasis of Black saints and the emotive welcome of newly baptized parishioners.

St. John Vianney, St. Bernadette Soubirous, and St. Catherine of Alexandria are three of the 516 predominantly African American parishes in the United States.[23] These parishes, each in their own way, exemplify the pronouncement by the Black Bishops of the United States in their only pastoral letter to date, *What We Have Seen and Heard*.[24] The Black Bishops declared that Black Catholics' liturgy was both authentically Black and truly Catholic. Mass at these three parishes exemplifies liturgy as a rich, dynamic process. There is more than one way to be authentically Black and truly Catholic. More recently, Pope Francis expressed a complementary point: "Unity . . . does not mean uniformity of . . . cultural life, or ways of thinking."[25] To this end, we have seen how these three parishes produce a unique Black Catholic cultural identity.

At St. John Vianney, standard Mass rituals have been reimagined to incorporate song and communal activity, thus creating specific Black Catholic rituals. St. John Vianney's focus on Jesus the Savior over the other two persons of the Trinity draws on the Black Church's emphasis on Jesus without sacrificing Catholicism's depiction of God. St. Bernadette Soubirous's side-by-side placement of the Kwanzaa kinara and the Advent wreath create a tangible symbol of how Black Catholics' dual heritages are not disparate at all. Rather, they exist as parts of a larger cultural tradition. In addition, the parish's use of secular Black History Month posters offers a way to integrate civic, racial, and religious identity. This integrated identity is further advanced by the parish's emphasis on social justice, borrowed from both Catholic Social Teaching and the long tradition of civic engagement by leaders in the Black Church. St. Catherine's deliberately brings unabashed Blackness into an unequivocally Catholic prayer by including multiple Black saints in the "Litany of the Saints." All three parishes use music and the homily—in content and delivery—and aesthetics to sift in elements of Roman Catholic tradition and the African American religious experience. Doing so produces a distinct Black Catholic cultural identity. Black Catholics actively produce Black Catholic parish culture while also engaging these tools as acts of resistance to systemic racism. These three parishes exemplify how—through sifting and parish culture production—Black Catholics own their identity as Black Catholics.

Black Catholics must face the lingering ramifications of an often painful history with the Church in the United States, including implicit and explicit support of slavery, segregated communion lines, and systematic exclusion from the priesthood. They must negotiate their own membership in the Roman Catholic Church with this painful history. Black Catholics do so, in part, by sifting in elements of the African American religious experience and Roman Catholic tradition to produce a unique Black Catholic cultural identity. Black Catholics' sifting through liturgy challenges the idea that all Catholics must either acquiesce to or vocally reject conventional Roman Catholic practices. Sifting can have a deep emotional resonance for the social actors engaged in it. Understanding Black Catholic identity work in parishes is essential if African American Catholics are to claim, and not just find, a place at the table of U.S. Catholicism.

During a 1998 television interview, Nobel Laureate Toni Morrison reflected on her vast acclaim, readership, and centering of people and experiences that are often ignored in literature: "I can't tell you how satisfying it is to know that I have *earned* a readership that is that large. I stood at the border, stood at the edge, and claimed it as central. *Claimed* it as central and let the rest of the world move over to where I was."[26] Similarly, we see that African American Catholics, which Toni Morrison was, have claimed as central the emotive liturgical expression that interweaves Blackness with Catholicism. The fact that the rest of the church in the United States has yet to move over to where Black Catholics stand is an indicator of how much work remains.

FOUR

Erasing a Legacy

The Price of St. Peter Claver

•‑•‑•‑•‑•‑•‑•‑•‑•

St. Peter Claver is a story of racism, lies, betrayal, false heroes, and erased heroes. This reality is woven throughout St. Peter Claver's entire history. The parish was founded in 1886, the church was consecrated in 1892, and the parish was suppressed in 1985 with activities ceasing completely in 2014.[1] These milestone events are markers in the story of St. Peter Claver's erasure. Historian Shannen Dee Williams captures the story of St. Peter Claver in her essay in *American Catholic Studies*, titled "The Color of Christ's Brides." Williams writes, "The most dangerous weapon of white supremacy has always been its ability to erase the history of its violence *and* its victims."[2] The suppression triggered a battle to save St. Peter Claver that is ongoing. The civil court case ended in Philadelphia's Orphans' Court in 2017. As of 2024, the battle in the community, the press, and under Canon Law continues.

St. Peter Claver was the first parish founded by and for Black Catholics in Philadelphia. Located at the southwest corner of 12th and Lombard Streets in South Philadelphia, the story of this parish encapsulates the larger story of African American Catholics in the 19th, 20th, and 21st centuries.[3] St. Peter Claver was founded because Black Catholics encountered roadblocks to the practice of their Catholicism. They were not welcome at territorial parishes and faced pew fees and segregated communion lines. St. Peter Claver and other parishes like it were distinct from their counterparts founded for European American Catholics. In European American national parishes, a first generation's racialization and ethnic exclusion gave way to socially constructed whiteness by the second and third generations. Consequently, any kind of exclusion or unwelcomeness that the founding families of the aforementioned white ethnic parishes encountered had given way to inclusion, a sense of welcome, and power by the time their grandchildren were born. The same did not hold true for Black Catholics. Furthermore, when white ethnic communities did experience exclusion in parish life, hierarchical leadership supported them and affirmed their ethnic identity and Catholicism through the founding of national parishes. Black parishes had to do that work themselves while battling the church's hierarchical leadership just to have the tiniest acknowledgment of their race, ethnicity, Catholicism, and humanity.[4] Consequently, Black Catholics would only see their racialization, marginalization, and exclusion intensify in successive generations.

Throughout *Black and Catholic,* I have used pseudonyms for the churches I've visited and the people I've interviewed. I will continue to use pseudonyms for all the people I interviewed. However, using a pseudonym for this church is not possible. There is no church in Philadelphia with a story like St. Peter Claver. Anyone even slightly familiar with the parish's story would recognize it immediately, and those who aren't would only need a few seconds with Google to find out the parish's identity. In using St. Peter Claver as a lens, we will begin to look at how the plethora of church closings and parish reorganizations found in so many cities—especially in the Northeast and in midwestern cities like Chicago—impact African American Catholics' feeling of belonging to the church. By understanding St. Peter Claver's history, including its resistance in the face of church and societal oppression and suppression, we can better understand the depth and breadth of systemic racism in the U.S. Catholic Church and how it is directly connected to the short and long-term impact of church closings and parish reorganizations. The national parish model and its plethora of churches in the Northeast and Midwest were founded to minister to white ethnic groups. Over time, with white flight, smaller families, and a strong ethnic identity giving way to symbolic ethnicity[5] or generic whiteness, there were not enough Catholics in those cities to populate all of those churches. St. Peter Claver was founded in 1886[6] under the national parish model to serve the African American Catholics of Philadelphia. Yet, it wasn't a "national parish" in the same way as other parishes founded around the same time in Philadelphia, including St. Aloysius (German, 1894), St. Laurentius (Polish, 1882), St. Casimir (Lithuanian, 1893), Sacred Heart (Hungarian, 1913), and St. Donato (Italian, 1910). Unlike St. Peter Claver, these parishes were founded in an effort to affirm the identities of white ethnic groups and support the melding of those identities with Catholicism to create an ethno-religious identity separate from the territorial parish model.[7]

How did St. Peter Claver come to be closed? What was the institutional process for making the decision? How did that process impact believers and their futures as members of the Catholic Church?

A TRIP TO 12TH AND LOMBARD

On Monday, March 4, 2019, the Archdiocese of Philadelphia made known via its digital newspaper, CatholicPhilly.com,[8] that the canonical status of the long-shuttered St. Peter Claver was changed from "sacred to profane but not sordid use" by then-Archbishop Charles Chaput, O.F.M., Cap., in accordance with Canon 1222 of the Code of Canon Law, the internal legal code that governs the global operations of the Roman Catholic Church (see Appendix, Document 4.1). This move, which essentially deconsecrated the church, was necessary before the three-building corner property could be sold. That decree would be withdrawn in May 2019, only to be reinstituted in December 2022 (see Appendix, Document 4.2).

The three buildings are the rectory at 502 South 12th Street, the adjacent church at 1200 Lombard Street, and the school that is next door to the church (but not adjacent) at 1212 Lombard Street (see Figure 4.1). I have seen this property many times while driving, but I had never really *looked* at it. On Wednesday, March 6, 2019, two days after the original decree was issued, I drove to the neighborhood to look around and take in St. Peter Claver while it was still there. Unlike most Catholic churches

Figure 4.1. St. Peter Claver Parish Buildings, courtesy of Tia Noelle Pratt.

in the northeastern United States, St. Peter Claver Church is not an imposing stone edifice. Rather, it is made of made of stucco. This is not incredibly surprising since the structure was not built as a Catholic Church. Prior to becoming St. Peter Claver, the building was the Fourth Presbyterian Church of Philadelphia.

Time and lack of care have damaged the church's paint; trash is strewn around the building. The school building at 1212 Lombard Street was built as St. Peter Claver School and has a decidedly different aesthetic than the church (see Figure 4.2). The school is a large, three-story stone building that is reminiscent of many Catholic elementary schools in Philadelphia as well as other cities. There are other signs that the school building has lost its former glory. The front door facing Lombard Street is sealed shut with sheet metal painted an oxblood red to match the window trim. Incidentally, this paint also matches the trim and front doors of the church as well as the front door of the rectory. Despite appearing like an abandoned building, the school was actually in use by Catholic Social Services. The March 2019 decree stated that the Catholic Social Services programs would continue; however, programs would cease at that location.

Figure 4.2. St. Peter Claver School, courtesy of Tia Noelle Pratt.

Adjacent to the church building is the rectory at 502 South 12th Street. The shared wall between the two buildings likely allows access between the rectory and the church without needing to venture outside. The four-story-brick rectory building is large in comparison to the historic buildings that remain in the area, but the style is in keeping with what one would expect for buildings that are historic, but of a later time period than colonial buildings found closer to Independence Hall and Penn's Landing. Like the church, the rectory appears in disrepair. Tattered paint around the windows, discolored bricks, old curtains discolored from the sun in the first-floor windows, and stagnant water on the top step that has frozen in the cold temperatures all belie a building that has been neglected for many years. As the dispute between parishioners and the archdiocese regarding the future of the building and whether or not the archdiocese has the legal authority to sell St. Peter Claver continues, the archdiocese let the property fall into disrepair (see Figures 4.3, 4.4).

Figure 4.3. St. Peter Claver Church, courtesy of Tia Noelle Pratt.

Figure 4.4. St. Peter Claver Rectory, courtesy of Tia Noelle Pratt.

This active neglect of the buildings has a two-fold consequence. In the short term, funds do not have to be expended to maintain the buildings. In the long term, as a court battle wages over decades, the archdiocese can find itself in a position to argue that the property is not worth saving because it is in such disrepair—a state of disrepair of the archdiocese's own making. In accordance with Canon 1222 of the Code of Canon Law,[9] such disrepair is a reason to relegate the church to profane but not sordid use.

The neighborhood around 12th and Lombard is like many in Philadelphia. It is an area rich in history and experiencing rapid change. The area was experiencing major change at the time St. Peter Claver was founded, and the 1980s ushered in a new era of change for the neighborhood. It became more desirable as evidenced by the construction of a large parking garage at the corner of South 11th Street and South Street (see Figure 4.5).[10]

Figure 4.5. South Street Parking Garage, courtesy of Tia Noelle Pratt.

The location is just one block south and one block east of St. Peter Claver. Like much of South Philadelphia, the area around St. Peter Claver is notorious for its limited parking. Limited parking was not necessarily a problem in a time when residents had modest financial means, didn't have cars, and, therefore, depended on public transportation to get around. A key marker of the neighborhood's transformation into what it is today is the parking garage. Today, it looks like the nearly forty-year-old structure that it is. When it was first built, it was a state of the art marvel and a harbinger of the mixed-use construction that is seen throughout South Philadelphia and elsewhere in the city (see Figure 4.6). The structure runs the length of the block along South Street from South 11th Street east to South 10th Street and extends approximately half a block north to the border of Seger Park.

Figure 4.6. Multiuse building with retail and residential space in South Philadelphia, courtesy of Tia Noelle Pratt.

Two retail spaces are on the ground level: a CVS on the South 11th Street side and a supermarket on the South 10th Street side. The three-story parking garage is accessible from South 11th Street. It's hard to say if the construction of the parking garage ushered in gentrification or if it was a response to gentrification. As the neighborhood changed, or more accurately, changed again, parking became a necessity. Having a clear answer requires research that is beyond the scope of this book. What is certainly within the scope of this book is to say that the two are connected.

The day I went to look at St. Peter Claver, I paid attention to what the neighborhood looked like. Seger Park is a lovely playground with new equipment (see Figure 4.7). The 1100 and 1200 blocks of Rodman Street are just a half block from the church. Both blocks are decorated with flags from nearby universities such as Temple University, Villanova University, and the University of Pennsylvania. It gave the impression that university

Figure 4.7. Seger Park, courtesy of Tia Noelle Pratt.

flags were playing the role of the white picket fence. It gives the appearance of a quaint, close-knit community reminiscent of what one may find in the suburbs—except that it's in South Philly (see Figure 4.8).

Even though it was the middle of a weekday, I saw a number of people walking around the neighborhood. All of them were white. Most of them had dogs. The parking garage, the pristine playground, the flags that take the place of white-picket fences all came together to make one thing clear: This was no longer a neighborhood for working-class and poor Black people.

St. Peter Claver also sits in what can be called a gateway location. Only two blocks west along South Broad Street is the Avenue of the Arts, home to major cultural and artistic venues in Philadelphia. Only three blocks north of St. Peter Claver is Philadelphia's major LGBTQ+ neighborhood colloquially and affectionately known as the "Gayborhood" which has become a major retail and dining destination since the turn of the 21st century. Just one block south of the church is South Street. For many years, South Street was a destination not because of gentrification, but because it was a haven for artists; a magnet for late night eating, drinking, and cavorting; and the place to be seen. Gentrification has managed

Figure 4.8. Rodman Street Flags, courtesy of Tia Noelle Pratt.

to deftly maintain some of this culture while bringing in many trendy, high-end shops, bars, and restaurants to South Street. All of this has made the surrounding area a highly desirable residential neighborhood. Because of the extraordinary potential for redevelopment at 12th and Lombard due to gentrification, the St. Peter Claver property is poised to sell for millions of dollars.

St. Peter Claver Church was badly in need of repair when it was officially relegated to profane but not sordid use in 2019. However, it was decades of neglect by the Archdiocese that led to the repair being so desperately needed. Closing St. Peter Claver so that it could be sold, thus allowing the archdiocese to take advantage of the real estate market, was a solution in need of a problem. The problem was a dilapidated church that the Archdiocese allowed to deteriorate over close to thirty-five years. In recent years, townhomes[11] built right across the street sold for more than one million dollars each. This reality strengthens the supposition that the St. Peter Claver property will likely sell for millions of dollars. It is important to note that the church has had historic designation since April 1984. Consequently, "its exterior cannot be altered without the approval of the city historical commission."[12]

St. Peter Claver was once an anchor in this neighborhood. The neighborhood has changed. And St. Peter Claver, in turn, has become a ghost. It's important to know how this happened. It's even more important to make clear that it didn't happen because the parishioners of St. Peter Claver abandoned it. Rather, it happened because, similar to how so many other Black parishes have been treated, the Archdiocese of Philadelphia abandoned the parishioners of St. Peter Claver in order to cash in on rising property values in a rapidly changing area.

WHAT IS A PARISH?

It is important to pause for a moment and clarify what it means when a parish is suppressed. In Catholic parlance, we tend to use the words "church" and "parish" interchangeably because in much of Catholic discourse, they are. As we discuss the suppression of St. Peter Claver, it is essential to make clear the distinction between a parish and a church in canon law. In previous work,[13] I posed the question, "What is a parish?"

and offered several points for discussion: a semi-autonomous organization, an administrative unit, a community of believers, or a combination. While thinking about and living in a parish encompasses all of these elements, the Code of Canon Law has a specific definition of a parish. According to Canon 515:

> A parish is a certain community of the Christian faithful stably constituted in a particular church, whose pastoral care is entrusted to a pastor (*parochus*) as its proper pastor (*pastor*) under the authority of the diocesan bishop. It is only for the diocesan bishop to erect, suppress, or alter parishes. He is neither to erect, suppress, nor alter notably parishes, unless he has heard the presbyteral council. A legitimately erected parish possesses juridic personality by the law itself.[14]

A church is a place while a parish is a *community* of faithful from a certain geographic territory or those bound together through shared language, nationality, ethnicity, or adherence to a rite. Canon Law states that a parish requires a pastor who acts under the authority of the diocesan bishop. Typically, when a church is closed, the parish is reorganized. Bishops, understandably, are generally reluctant to close, or suppress, a parish because it would mean telling a community that it has ceased to exist. Instead, when a bishop closes a church, the parish is absorbed by nearby parishes to gather for worship in their churches. It is for this reason that throughout *Black and Catholic*, I have used the somewhat clumsy phrase "church closings and parish reorganizations" intentionally.

Canon law professor, Fr. Pat Lagges states in *U.S. Catholic*[15] that "the parish is really a perpetual entity, because it is people. It is a community, and a community of people doesn't just cease to exist." Except, of course, when it does. Any episcopal reluctance to suppress parishes, that is, for a bishop to tell a community of Catholic faithful that it has ceased to exist, did not stop John Cardinal Krol when he suppressed St. Peter Claver in the spring of 1985.

According to Canon Law,[16] the local bishop must hear from the parishioners and receive input from his priest council before deciding something as monumental as suppressing a parish. According to the parishioners of St. Peter Claver, however, they had no prior knowledge they were even in danger of completely losing their parish. They did not know this decision was even under consideration until a letter dated May 26, 1985, was read at Mass on that same day. They had no warning and no time to prepare.

A HOME CHURCH BECOMES A CORNERSTONE

In the last decades of the 19th century, the general vicinity around 12th and Lombard Streets began to change, becoming heavily African American. Yet, in this area just outside the area immortalized by W. E. B. Du Bois in *The Philadelphia Negro*,[17] the Black Catholics of South Philadelphia did not have a church home that provided them with the racially affirming safe space white ethnic groups had. As discussed in Chapter 2, the notion of creating and performing ethnicity had become so intertwined with religion for Catholics of European descent that they often failed to realize that they were doing two distinct things simultaneously. As a result, the creation and performance of ethnicity became synonymous with the creation and performance of religion, which they regarded as just one thing—religion. When African American Catholics began creating their own ethno-religious identity, white ethnic groups regarded such identity work as not being "Catholic," when in fact it was perfectly Catholic—it just wasn't Italian, Polish, Irish, Lithuanian, or Hungarian.

According to St. Peter Claver's own documented history,[18] the parish began in the late 19th century as a home church akin to the tradition set forth by the earliest Christian communities in the years immediately following the Crucifixion. In this case, it wasn't persecution by the Romans, but systemic racism and white supremacy engineered by their fellow Catholics that kept this community from practicing their faith in a public forum. At that time, Black Catholics had very few options to worship and practice their faith without the encumbrances of pew fees, segregated communion lines, and other forms of marginalization within the church. They organized themselves under the name Peter Claver Union. Prior to the parish's founding in 1886, the members of Peter Claver Union had an almost nomadic existence worshiping at different churches in the area, including Old St. Joseph's, Old St. Mary's, St. Augustine, and Holy Trinity.[19] According to the historical sketch prepared for the parish's

Diamond Jubilee, the members of Peter Claver Union "had no church of their own, though there was a considerable number of them."[20] It's clear from the historical sketch that the members of Peter Claver Union were not able to join the aforementioned parishes despite living in the vicinity. Holy Trinity remains classified as a national parish for Germans, which explains why it wasn't possible for them to worship there long-term.

As for the other parishes, the nomadic existence of Peter Claver Union corroborates the recollections provided by second- and third-generation parishioners who said their family members weren't welcome in existing parishes. If they had been welcome, they would have stayed. Instead, the members of Peter Claver Union, as a community of believers, moved from church to church, prior to the founding of the parish in 1886. Additionally, the nomadic existence of Peter Claver Union affirms sociologist Elijah Anderson's assertion that "certain White spaces were routinely declared off limits to Blacks."[21] Prior to the parish's founding, Peter Claver Union remained anchored by the gatherings held in the members' homes. Like their early Christian forebearers and white ethnic brethren, the people of Peter Claver Union desired a public space of their own for worship. Initially, the parishioners found support in priests from three local parishes: Holy Trinity, Old St. Mary's, and Old St. Joseph's.[22] From the parish's founding in 1886 through the summer of 1889, they held their new parish together on their own. According to the Diamond Jubilee history, "Its members were most desirous and anxious to have their own church and their own priests." During this time, they repeatedly petitioned then-Archbishop Patrick Ryan for a church and priest to minister to them, but "he had no priest to take up this work." Now, it is essential to remember that Archbishop Ryan was the local ordinary for all Catholics in the Archdiocese of Philadelphia. If he wanted a priest to minister to the members of St. Peter Claver, all he would have had to do is assign one.

St. Katharine Drexel, then a young woman who had not entered religious life, offered her support by connecting the members of Peter Claver Union to the priests of the Congregation of the Holy Spirit, commonly known as the Holy Ghost Fathers. It was because of this introduction that Rev. Patrick McDermott, C.S.Sp. became the pastor of St. Peter Claver, which was still a parish without a church, on July 29, 1889. After

Fr. McDermott's arrival, St. Katharine Drexel offered the parishioners of St. Peter Claver the use of a three-story building her family owned at 832 Pine Street in South Philadelphia. Mass and other services were held in a cramped space on the second floor. However, this solution could not facilitate the growth and long-term sustainability of the parish. As a community of modest means, the members of Peter Claver Union did not have the financial resources on hand to build a church or purchase an existing one outright. So, they began fundraising. In 1891, the Fourth Presbyterian Church of Philadelphia[23] relocated to West Philadelphia trailing the movement, i.e., white flight, of its members. Consequently, its former church at 12th and Lombard was for sale. Instead of waiting for the archdiocese to hand them a church, the members of St. Peter Claver went out and secured one for themselves. They secured the bulk of the funds for the purchase of the 12th and Lombard church themselves. Through modest entrepreneurship, like selling fish fry dinners, and savings from even more modest incomes that barely provided for their families, the people of Peter Claver Union raised $20,000 ($610,883.33 in 2019) toward the purchase of the church at 12th and Lombard. Despite this success, they found themselves short of the funds needed to secure purchase of the property.

St. Katharine Drexel, by then superior general of the Sisters of the Blessed Sacrament and known as Mother Katharine Drexel, provided funds from her considerable fortune to aid the people of Peter Claver Union. These funds, along with funds provided by the estate of Patrick Quinn, an executive at the then-Beneficial Savings Bank, which counts St. John Neumann, the fourth bishop of Philadelphia as its founder, allowed for the purchase of the 12th and Lombard property. Yet, this barely receives even scant mention in the official history. The Diamond Jubilee history states that a group of donors, a loan, and fundraisers enabled the purchase of the former Fourth Presbyterian Church and only in the dedication of the document gives paltry acknowledgment to "The Faithful Colored Catholics of Philadelphia Whose Loyalty and Sacrifice Made Possible The Foundation and Continuance of This Parish."[24] The parishioners' efforts were completely erased from the story itself! By the time St. Peter Claver was founded, the lay trusteeism, or lay ownership of church properties, championed by Archbishop John Carroll[25] during his episcopate as the first Catholic archbishop in the United States, had been curtailed to the point of elimination. In its place was a practice, which continues to this day, and it had the local ordinary serving as the owner of church property. Consequently, Peter Claver Union having ownership of St. Peter Claver Church was never a viable option. Yet, this doesn't change the overall issue: Patrick Quinn and St. Katherine Drexel received copious praise both contemporaneously and historically for their financial contributions while the financial sacrifice of Peter Claver Union has been all but erased.

Those descended from those first parishioners of St. Peter Claver maintain that this narrative erases the contributions of their family members, gives credit only to white Catholics, and thus further centers whiteness in U.S. Catholicism. Ann, a third-generation member of St. Peter Claver described the founding of the parish to me:

> St. Peter Claver was built on a graveyard on [what was then] the outskirts of Philadelphia. It was the Fourth Presbyterian Church. Ultimately as that neighborhood grew it was poor white people, but then they moved out and the neighborhood became Black people. As more and more Black people moved into the neighborhood, the Fourth Presbyterian Church decided to move to the suburbs of Philadelphia, which [was then] 47th and Springfield. When the building became empty, the Black people who had organized under the name of the Peter Claver Union started saving their money and they purchased the church. [The members of Peter Claver Union purchased the church] because they had suffered so much discrimination when they worshiped at the original four churches [Holy Trinity, Old St. Mary's, Old St. Joe's, and St. John the Evangelist]. They were welcomed at first, but as their numbers became larger, the white congregations grew more unwelcoming to them where they had to sit at the back and receive communion last. They decided to have a church where everybody would be welcomed all the time. So, St. Peter Claver was always an inclusive parish. Everybody was welcomed, didn't matter what your race, sexual situation, or any of that was. Everybody was welcomed at St. Peter Claver.

Ann's description corresponds with the narrative from the Diamond Jubilee history, but also fills in gaps. For example, the Jubilee history says the founding parishioners were welcomed at various churches in the area. If they were truly welcomed, it would have been expected that they would have stayed, even as their numbers began to grow. After all, what church doesn't want more people? Ann describes the members of Peter Claver Union being turned out of established churches. As the group got larger, they did not want to be marginalized and treated as second-class citizens at Mass. These circumstances align with a desire to establish their own church.

However, securing a building was not enough. In order for it to be used as a Catholic Church, it would need to be consecrated by then-Archbishop of Philadelphia, Patrick John Ryan. With the commitment of the Holy Ghost Fathers and the aforementioned donors, Archbishop Ryan's hands were tied. He finally relented and agreed to consecrate the building as St. Peter Claver Roman Catholic Church. However, there was a catch. In order for this to happen, his name, not the name of Peter Claver Union, would go on the deed to the property. It is standard in the Archdiocese of Philadelphia for the archbishop to be named on property records. The difference here is that the archdiocese didn't contribute the funds. When the Holy Ghost Fathers learned of Archbishop Ryan's demands, they, in turn, demanded that the name of their order also be included on the deed as a condition of their service to the parish.[26]

The erasure of Peter Claver Union's legacy resulted in the loss of power. Losing their power would have dire consequences in the years that followed. Peter Claver Union would receive consolation in the form of protective language that would be at the heart of a court battle years later. The protective language included in the deed stated that St. Peter Claver's "premises are to be used as Church for colored people, parsonage and school attached thereto, white people, however, being permitted to attend."[27] Having their legacy erased was the steep price the members of Peter Claver Union paid to have a church they could call their own. With all of these pieces in place, including the erasure of the members of Peter Claver Union, Archbishop Ryan agreed to consecrate the church, which occurred on January 3, 1892.

CHANGE COMES AGAIN

African American Catholics in Philadelphia were not welcome at existing parishes, yet steeled by their faith they worshiped privately in homes until they had the means to purchase a church building on their own. When they were able to do that, however, the local ordinary refused to send priests to minister to them and to consecrate the building they bought. Only when two false heroes providing minimal funds were centered, and with one of them securing the services of a group of priests not under the archbishop's jurisdiction, did the archbishop relent and decide to consecrate the building. The price for St. Peter Claver finally having a church home to call their own was the erasure of Peter Claver Union's contribution to securing their church. Having something that was truly theirs could only be possible if the white supremacy in the Catholic Church maintained control of the narrative. Blackness couldn't be centered even in a church for Black Catholics. Racism, specifically the particularly insidious anti-Black racism, and a need to maintain white supremacist organizational structures were at the root of the erasure of Peter Claver Union.

As the years progressed, the St. Peter Claver parish property grew to include the aforementioned large school building next door to the church on Lombard Street, staffed principally by the Sisters of the Blessed Sacrament and a three-story rectory building adjacent to the church on South 12th Street. I talked to members of the St. Peter Claver community about the education they personally received and the role of St. Peter Claver School in their families. They also spoke to me about the role of St. Peter Claver School in providing Catholic education to Black children at a time when that was not possible in all Catholic elementary schools. Eventually, St. Peter Claver School would close as fewer and fewer African American Catholics lived in that part of South Philadelphia.

By the 1980s, change was afoot in South Philadelphia again. Even though gentrification would not become a widely used term for some time, John Cardinal Krol used the term to describe the changes in the Washington Square West neighborhood around St. Peter Claver. Hindsight makes it obvious that's what was happening. Ann, a long-time member of St. Peter Claver, described the change in the neighborhood during the years leading up to the suppression:

> As other neighborhoods changed and went from white to Black, churches that hadn't welcomed Black people before suddenly found room because they needed to keep their churches open. So, they accepted Black people when there were no more white people. But as Black people were forced out of the neighborhood of St. Peter Claver, this church that had always been inclusive, continued to welcome the new people that moved into the neighborhood. St. Peter Claver, which always had been integrated, became more integrated.

Julia, another long-time member of St. Peter Claver echoed this conclusion:

> The reason why I think [St. Peter Claver was suppressed] is because . . . people could go anywhere now, and they needed us [African Americans] because the white folks were not going to church. They [white Catholics] were moving out of the neighborhood. So they had to find some kind of way [to keep the churches open].

Because churches that had formerly excluded African Americans began accepting them out of the necessity of self-preservation, St. Peter Claver as a national parish for the African Americans of the Archdiocese of Philadelphia was no longer needed and thus was expendable.

With the demographic shifts in the Washington Square West area and parishes in other areas of the archdiocese accepting African Americans as members, Auxiliary Bishop Martin Lohmuller directed the archdiocese's Commission for Parish Sites and Boundaries to conduct a study of St. Peter Claver Parish. According to the final report, the study was ordered on February 3, 1984, and the final report is dated April 2, 1984. Known to the parishioners of St. Peter Claver as the "Sites and Boundaries Report" (see Appendix, Document 4.3), the document provides data on St. Peter Claver and recommendations on the future of the parish. The Commission's final report "recommends that the Parish should remain as it is" and offers five reasons why. The first reason is that "the Parish would be financially viable now that the school has been closed." The report went on to say that because of St. Peter Claver's significance to the archdiocese's Black Catholic community, closing it may be problematic for the archdiocese and may thwart the archdiocese's own outreach efforts to Black Catholics. Specifically, reasons three through five read:

> 3. The historical background, in fact the site is historically certified, has a real symbolic significance to the black Catholics of Philadelphia. This factor is considered especially important during these times when the Church is making a concentrated effort toward evangelization of the black community.
> 4. There is a possible chance that the blacks might defect feeling that they have been abandoned.
> 5. Many years ago, the question of Title of St. Peter Claver was subject to a review of legal staff who in turn discussed its findings with the Archdiocese. The Commission does not know whether this question has been resolved or not. Also, in the deciding of the future of St. Peter Claver Parish this fact should be resolved to avoid *unpleasant complications* [emphasis added].

Nevertheless, the suppression of the parish was announced by Cardinal Krol in a letter to parishioners dated May 26, 1985 (See Appendix, Document 4.4).[28]

Ann described that day thusly:

> When the suppression happened, I was there that Sunday and Father [McAndrew, the pastor at the time] read the letter from the archdiocese, from Cardinal Krol. And then the priest, the pastor, Father McAndrew told the congregation who was in shock and dismay and total sadness, "This is the right thing to do. It's the best thing to do. I think it's for your own good." And then he finished the mass and as Father was leaving the mass, one in the congregation, Edith Collins Stevens, stepped on the altar and took to the pulpit and she said, "This is wrong. This shouldn't happen. St. Peter Claver is a special church. There is no reason for this suppression. Some of the things that are said here is wrong. This is just totally wrong." She was in tears. After the mass finished . . . everybody was out on the steps. I

went up to her because we're like family. I said, "Edith, what can we do?" And several of us approached her. "What can we do?" That's where I got involved. The archdiocese said we could no longer call ourselves a parish because the parish was suppressed and I termed suppress means to strangle. If you won't die, then I'm going to strangle the life out of you. So, they started to strangle the church by saying nobody could be baptized. Nobody could receive their First Communion or receive the death benefits, the last rites of the church, and nobody could be married there. Baptism, marriage, and the last rites are the lifeblood of the church and so they said, "You can't do that anymore."

Thirty-five years after the suppression, both Ann and Julia continue to dispute the reasons given for suppressing St. Peter Claver and cite the "Sites and Boundaries Report" as evidence.

In Cardinal Krol's letter announcing the suppression, he says, St. Peter Claver was founded "as a national parish to serve the needs of Black Catholics in the City of Philadelphia." He went on to say that because Black Catholics had moved into territorial parishes, something that wasn't possible when St. Peter Claver was founded, and because of demographic changes in the area around the church, "it is evident that the reason for the founding and existence of Saint Peter Claver parish no longer exists." Recalling the reasons for the suppression that Cardinal Krol gave in his letter, Ann said, "But the cardinal said that a Black parish was no longer necessary. Then he talked about the financial burden. But there was no financial burden." In fact, page 3 of the "Sites and Boundaries Report" explicitly says that "The Parish is not in debt." Julia echoed both Ann's assessment and the Commission's report recalling, "We owed them nothing . . . The Archdiocese. We never owed them a nickel or dime." The battle to save St. Peter Claver in the decades since the suppression and the closure of so many predominantly Black churches in the archdiocese over those same years refute Cardinal Krol's claim that the need for St. Peter Claver no longer exists.

After the suppression of St. Peter Claver, the fight to save it began. Due to the immediate outcry by the parishioners, some activities remained. During this time, the fight was waged, by the *parish,* the community of faithful, for years in civil court and has, more recently, moved to Canonical court. Throughout all these years, the community and parish of St. Peter Claver was "strangled," denied access to the sacraments, funerals, and other key rites of Catholicism.

St. Peter Claver parishioners sought the help of the predominantly Black parishes that had developed in Philadelphia in the decades after St. Peter Claver was founded to help fight back against suppression. These efforts did not bear fruit. Ann recounts that period saying,

> I felt the power of God and the ancestors telling me in my heart, "Fight for it. You go stand up for it." We all sort of felt that we were being empowered, that this is worth fighting for. What eventually happened was that we got very little support in Philadelphia although we begged the other churches. . . . we had sent letters to every congregation, every parish council, in Philadelphia. Maybe four out of the parishes in Philadelphia responded. Those that met with us were so nervous about us even being there.

Julia, a second-generation member of St. Peter Claver, recounted the same time period: "When we were being suppressed and we told them [other parishes], we could use your help . . . they said, 'well, if your church is closing, what problem is it of ours?' I said, because it could happen to you." Now, more than thirty years after St. Peter Claver was suppressed, many of the churches the parishioners went to and asked for help, are, in fact, no longer part of Philadelphia's Catholic landscape.

During the initial stages of the fight to save St. Peter Claver, after other Philadelphia parishes rebuffed them, parishioners turned to dioceses in other cities for help. They found support from St. Augustine in the Archdiocese of Washington. They visited the parish and worked with parishioners and leaders in the area to develop a strategy for protecting and preserving St. Peter Claver. Julia says of this visit:

> And when they closed our church down and we got in solidarity, St. Augustine became involved with us and I went down there and I learned. . . . My sister and I, we got up on that Sunday morning and I said, "Oh, Bernadette are you ready?" They [the parishioners at St.

Augustine] said go and teach to people what we have [at St. Peter Claver].

Ann expounded on that trip:

> Their parish council sat down and talked with us. . . . They said, "You need to find your history. You need to search and find out who you are." They didn't bash the archdiocese or anybody else. They said, "You will know what to do when you know who you are and your mission will be clear to you."

Ann went on to add that the main takeaway from that visit to St. Augustine was the need for Black Catholics to preserve and write our own history:

> Why can't the direction come from within us? We . . . have the talent. We certainly have been educated in the Catholic school system. Later, I found out how much Black Catholics did do, provide leadership and self-determination. But it was never written because the history that was written was not written by Black Catholics. It was written by others who told the story their way. So that's when I decided that if you want your story told or you want to be educated correctly, you have to look at yourself, look within, and find out who you are and where you came from and it'll be different.

DOCUMENTING PARISH HISTORY

The work of the founding parishioners of St. Peter Claver to have their own church was erased because they did not write their own story. Despite the difficulties of writing and sitting with this history, sitting with the joys and pains of parishioners like Julia and Ann, I choose to write this chapter—and all of *Black and Catholic*—to rectify that. I want, need, and must do justice to the ancestors who sacrificed so much in order for St. Peter Claver to be their church home and their descendants who have trusted me to share this story.

There is a flurry of correspondence sent over five decades, throughout the 1980s, 1990s, 2000s, 2010s, and 2020s, to members of the archdiocese's curia, the Black bishops,[29] and others (see Appendix, Documents 4.5 and 4.6). Much of it was initiated by Ann, on behalf of St. Peter Claver and its parishioners. Through all of this, the parishioners were never advised to hire a canon lawyer. Canons 1734 and 1737 of the Code of Canon Law provide only a brief window for aggrieved parishioners to appeal suppression. By the time they sought the advice of a Canon Lawyer,[30] it was many years too late to seek recourse against the suppression of the parish (see Appendix, Document 4.7). That is why the fight centers around preserving the church building.

Ann especially took to heart the admonition from St. Augustine's parishioners to document and preserve the history of St. Peter Claver. She donated eight banker's boxes worth of papers related to St. Peter Claver to the Blockson Collection at Temple University's library in Philadelphia. She also generously assisted me in accessing additional documents from the personal archives of members of St. Peter Claver. It is because of that level of documentation that this chapter is essentially an epistolary chapter. Much of the data comes from the archival materials at the Blockson collection and Ann's personal papers.

The St. Peter Claver property became the St. Peter Claver Evangelization Center[31] in 1986 and, for a time, was the headquarters of the Office of Black Catholics. During that time, the fight was working its way through civil court in Philadelphia. Access to the sacraments and rites of the church was limited, at best. Ann spoke of this time:

> Two women that had been St. Peter Claver's members their entire life were in the hospital on their deathbeds. One lady, I can remember her son, Mr. Ellis, came to ask the priest to come and give the last rites to his mother who was dying. The two priests in the rectory, Holy Ghost Fathers, who knew Mrs. Ellis, refused to go and give her the last rites because the archdiocese said they should go to St. John's and do it because of the suppression.
>
> Mr. Ellis said, "My mother was never welcomed at St. John's [another church a few blocks away]. They told her to go to the quote-unquote 'n****r church' and she never forgot that." So, she did

not want anybody from St. John's. She wanted her priest from St. Peter Claver and they refused to go. He said, "I will never set foot in a Catholic church again." Alan Stevens who was training to become a deacon at the time, he was frantic and he was trying to talk to Mr. Ellis. "We will find something." And he went about finding a priest who turned out to be Father Benz, who went and gave Mrs. Ellis the last rites. and he spoke at her funeral since the Holy Ghost Fathers refused to let her have her funeral at St. Peter Claver.

The Evangelization Center was closed in 2014. At that time, the church was completely shuttered, with Masses eliminated and the Office of Black Catholics relocating to the archdiocese's chancery building. Yet, the fight for St. Peter Claver continued. The legal basis for the fight in civil court hinged on the aforementioned protective language in the original deed and the argument that Black Catholics no longer needed a parish of their own. Following a detailed description of the property lines, the original deed states:

> The premises are to be used as a Church for Colored People, parsonage, and school attached thereto; white people, however, being permitted to attend all religious services [and] to receive the sacraments of Penance & Eucharist in the said church and the use of the said three described premises shall not be changed nor diverted from such purpose, nor shall the said three described premises or any part thereof be sold or encumbered, except with the consent of the ordinary [archbishop] of the Archdiocese.[32]

In other words, since the property must be used for Philadelphia's Black Catholics, were Archbishop Ryan or his episcopal successors to sell it, the community it served, the parish, could no longer exist. Hence, the *parish* of St. Peter Claver needed to be suppressed. The buildings couldn't be used to serve a community if that community no longer existed, thus the property could be sold.

The parishioners argued that the protective language necessitated that the church remain open and available for the Black Catholics of Philadelphia. In December 2017, Philadelphia's Orphans' Court, which has jurisdiction over such matters, cleared the way for the property to be sold and ordered that one-third of the proceeds[33] from the sale be used for the benefit of the archdiocese's Black Catholic community. The court's decision paved the way for then-Philadelphia Archbishop Charles Chaput to issue a decree changing the church's status. However, the decree was withdrawn only a few weeks later in April 2019. In the interim, a New England–based Canon lawyer, who specializes in helping parishioners reopen their shuttered churches, contacted the parishioners. This attorney successfully helped the parishioners of a historically Polish parish[34] in the Archdiocese of Philadelphia. The canon lawyer advised the parishioners to file an appeal under Canon Law and the decree was withdrawn shortly thereafter.

At this point, it's about saving the church, not the parish as a community of the faithful because the deadline for that appeal passed decades ago. Organized as the Advocates and Descendants of St. Peter Claver, the parishioners are continuing to work with the New England–based Canon Lawyer. The Advocates and Descendants have submitted a proposal to the Archdiocese for what they would like to see happen. When I asked Julia what she wanted to see come out of this process, she said, "A Christian community that helps people increase their faith and educates." I clarified by asking, "More of a community center than a parish?" Her response was, "Yes." If the church is saved and the Advocates and Descendants' vision does not come to fruition, perhaps a new parish can be formed there. This is not unprecedented, as it happened in Pittsburgh with the establishment of St. Benedict the Moor parish.[35]

As of April 2024, the final outcome of St. Peter Claver is still unknown. What is known is that the parishioners have worked diligently to make sure that they are not erased from the story of St. Peter Claver. In addition to parishioners speaking with me for this book, they have produced a short documentary film, participated in another,[36] and conducted speaking engagements. They have also made the continuation of the Our Lady of Victories Shrine—first established soon after St. Peter Claver Church opened—a central part of their plans for the church.

The story of St. Peter Claver is a story of race and money. A parish founded to serve African Americans was suppressed without warning and against the advice of the commission empaneled by Cardinal Krol. Thirty-five years later, the parish's shuttered buildings sit in one of Philadelphia's most coveted neighborhoods. The large corner property is ripe for development and could easily sell for millions of dollars. If the Advocates and Descendants are not successful and the buildings are sold, what will happen with the money? What does the deed's protective language mean without the buildings? Will the Archdiocese abide by the court order to use one-third of the proceeds for Black Catholics? If not, will that trigger yet another protracted court battle? What are the ramifications for the Black Catholic community in Philadelphia, especially in other parishes that don't have the same protections? What kind of example will the Archdiocese of Philadelphia set for the treatment of Black Catholics across the country?

What is happening and what has happened at St. Peter Claver is not unique in the country.[37] It's not even unique to Philadelphia. At another historically Black parish, parishioners are leaning into this point of history to declare that Parish Lives Matter.[38] This conflict is about African Americans being liturgically marginalized in their own parish. Simultaneously, it is about one of the parish buildings being sold for millions of dollars and the money from the sale being unaccounted for to the people of the parish. Leaders who aren't Black are not holding themselves accountable to Black parishioners. Again, it's a story of race and money. It's a story of sacred spaces that are lost to Black Catholics for a financial gain in which African Americans do not participate. As I wrote in the foreword to *Birth of a Movement: Black Lives Matter and the Catholic Church*, "An institution cannot continue to marginalize people . . . and still expect those same people to remain active in the institution." According to the Pew Research[39] Center, approximately 40 percent of Catholics in the United States are Black, Latino, Asian American, and Native American. More so among younger Catholics. As we will see in Chapter 5, there is much work to be done if the Catholic Church is going to hold on to its younger generation, thereby securing its own future.

Through all these years of struggle, the parishioners of St. Peter Claver have remained steadfast in their dedication to preserving the legacy of their parish. Some have remained active, practicing Catholics while others have stopped practicing. Ann explained:

> My heart has always been at St. Peter Claver and if that doesn't exist, I feel that I have learned enough in my lifetime. I know good from evil. I know how to do right. But I will never join another Catholic church.

She went on to say that the pain of seeing members of St. Peter Claver die and denied funerals at the church made her decide that she didn't want a church funeral. She told me that she doesn't even identify as Catholic anymore: "I say that I was raised Catholic."

Conversely, Julia is still an active, practicing Catholic. At the conclusion of our conversation, I asked Julia how this battle for St. Peter Claver has impacted her faith and her relationship with the Catholic Church. She responded, "My faith is strong. I know God loves me and I talk to him. And I know that I'm on the right path. I've served him and I'm still serving him. And I would die for my faith." The title of this book was inspired by something Julia said during our interview. Julia described Black Catholics as "good, faithful, devoted," and how those qualities are manifested because of and in spite of racism. The years of struggle and dedication have been borne out of faithfulness, devotion, and love. As we see in Ann and Julia, those qualities can manifest themselves differently, but they are there.

In February 2020, Archbishop Charles Chaput retired and Archbishop Nelson Perez was installed as the leader of the Archdiocese of Philadelphia. Having a new archbishop merits a new round of conversations around ongoing issues in the archdiocese, including the legacy of St. Peter Claver. On December 9, 2022, Archbishop Perez issued a decree relegating St. Peter Claver to "Profane But Not Sordid Use," which took effect on January 23, 2023 (see Appendix, Document 4.8).

The decree would, once again, allow for the deconsecration of the church and make way for the property to be sold. Less than a week after the latest decree was issued, on December 15, 2022, members of the Advocates and Descendants of St. Peter Claver filed a "petition for hierarchical recourse"[40] against the decree in accordance with Canon 1734, Section 2 of the Code of Canon Law (see Appendix, Document 4.9). The appeal is still in process. The final outcome of St. Peter Claver is unsettled.

Just a few months after Archbishop Perez was installed, in May 2020, police in Minneapolis murdered George Floyd. The global witnessing of his murder in a nearly nine-minute video sparked a global reckoning against systemic racism across multiple sectors of society. This reckoning has led to long-overdue conversations about whether existing systems can even be fixed or if they are so destructive, so harmful, so deeply entrenched with racism that they are beyond repair. The Catholic Church is not immune from these discussions. As I asserted in lectures throughout the summer of 2020, "The Call Is Coming From Inside The House." Systemic racism is not limited to organizations and systems separate from those where we live our lives every day. We have to look at the institutions in which we live our lives in order to ascertain the depth and breadth of systemic racism and how to eradicate that racism in favor of building a better, just world. We've seen that in the protests and calls to action that sprung from George Floyd's murder. They have not been limited to just specific institutions. Many of those who engaged in direct social action in 2020 may not have felt called to do so just a year earlier. The battle at St. Charles Borromeo parish in South Philadelphia is an example of that. As of this writing, it remains to be seen how the events of the last few years will impact whatever future St. Peter Claver will have. The year 2025 is poised to be a watershed moment for the United States, the world, and the universal Church.

CONCLUSION

As mentioned above, there is precedent both in the Archdiocese in Philadelphia and elsewhere for St. Peter Claver to reopen as a working church—though not the original parish. Personal parishes[41] have received robust attention in the last few years and are affirmed in Canon Law. I'm deeply conflicted, as a scholar and a practicing Catholic, about personal parishes for Black Catholics. The point of personal parishes is to affirm the specific Catholic affinity that led to its creation, such as racial group, ethnic group, language group, or liturgical rite. That would certainly hold true in personal parishes for Black Catholics. Yet, parishes such as these harken to the earlier need for Black Catholics to have their own sacred spaces, like St. Peter Claver, because they were not welcome at existing parishes. Additionally, during the 19th and early 20th centuries, when Black Catholics worshiped at parishes like St. Peter Claver, white Catholics were not forced to confront their own racism and the church's systemic racism. Consequently, racism festered, thus creating the circumstances we find today. My fear is that if Black Catholics leave territorial parishes for personal parishes, like St. Benedict the Moor in Pittsburgh, white Catholics won't have to confront racism and anti-Blackness—out of sight, out of mind. Yet I also deeply understand, as a scholar and a practicing Catholic, the need for Black Catholics to have sacred spaces that are safe—where they can feel at peace and don't have to be on guard all the time.

The issues of race and racism surrounding St. Peter Claver are among the clearest examples of the U.S. Catholic Church as a white space[42] where Blacks are unwelcomed and often not found, all while the church purports itself to be a cosmopolitan canopy or "an island of civility in a sea of racial segregation."[43] Thus, the U.S. Catholic Church is an ultra-white space.

From the very beginning, we saw parish culture production at St. Peter Claver as the parishioners built community through the things they did, what they made, and the stories they told. Creatively coming together as a home church community, staying together after being pushed out of existing churches, and finding the money to purchase the church building are just a few of the activities the founding members of St. Peter Claver did to create their parish culture. When the parishioners were trying to maintain a semblance of parish life despite the suppression, they incorporated African ritual into the community through a Naming and Blessing ceremony because they could not have baptisms.

Most importantly, the parishioners who have fought to protect St. Peter Claver's legacy for so many years have both created and preserved parish culture through their accounts. Speaking with me, participating in documentary films, and participating in speaking engagements ensures that the people of St. Peter Claver will no longer be erased from their own history. As Ann declared, "St. Peter Claver became everything that the ancestors wanted it to become." With their story preserved by their fellow Black Catholics, those ancestors are erased no more.

FIVE

Race, Community, and Process

Black Catholics' Experiences in Catholic Spaces

•—•—•—•—•—•—•—•

The parishioners of St. Peter Claver in Philadelphia have encountered many struggles in their work to preserve the legacy of their church and parish community. The story of St. Peter Claver and its people can serve as an exemplar of what so many Black parishes have endured. As sociologist Korie Little Edwards argues, "When it comes to racial trauma, any trauma really, churches are often the least safe places for people to go. For sure, churches have often been the perpetrators of racial trauma. This is a tragic truth, one that is counter to the gospel, and must be faced and addressed if healing and freedom are to occur."[1] In this chapter, we will examine the racial traumas Black Catholics have experienced principally, but not exclusively, in their churches, how that has formed their perception of parish life and Catholicism, and their thoughts on the future of the church.

Societal systems, whether religious or secular, are organized to create, maintain, and perpetuate the power structures of their founders and successors of the same ilk. Those systems are designed to intentionally harm those who do not fit into the image conceptualized by the systems' founders or their successors. Since the founding group defines what "fit in" means, these systems are self-sustaining and self-perpetuating. The creation, perpetuation, and maintenance of white supremacy are foundational to systems both in society and in the U.S. Catholic Church. Over time, this results in religious and secular institutions that are so beholden to doing things the way they have always been done that creating any real change may seem impossible. This inertia is the context in which systemic racism grows and festers. Black Catholics repeatedly experience systemic racism and its wounds in a place that should be safe, their parish church.

In order to begin, we must first answer: What does "the Catholic Church" mean? It is a complex answer for a global church that is experienced locally. The church building in which a parish community gathers is a significant part of the answer. "The Catholic Church" is also an institution comprised of other institutions. Besides the bureaucracy made up of diocesan offices and curia, there are the Holy See, the Roman Curia, and the Vatican city-state, as well as schools, churches, hospitals, colleges, universities, monasteries, and retreat centers. These latter institutions include those that are under the direct control of the Catholic hierarchy with a chain of command that extends directly to the Holy See and the Pope. These latter institutions also include those that are independent but affiliated with the hierarchy, such as many, but certainly not all, Catholic colleges and universities. In fact, the United States has only one university that exists within the hierarchical structure of the Holy See, The Catholic University of America in Washington, DC. All of this is often conflated under the umbrella term of "the Catholic Church" by the Catholic populace. This gives the appearance that the church is one and the same to those living both underneath and outside of the Catholic umbrella.

The key institution through which Catholics live out their faith and religious practice is a parish and the local church is where that parish meets. A parish is the local community of the Catholic Church as a global organization. Canon Law has a specific definition of a parish as a community of the faithful. It is also important to understand parishes as semi-autonomous administrative units. Territorial parishes evolve as the surrounding neighborhoods change along with the broader Catholic landscape in the United States, while personal parishes serve a specific constituency, such as a specific racial or ethnic group, or those who desire the Traditional Latin Mass/Tridentine Mass. For many years, parishes have been severely understudied in Catholic discourse. Recent scholarship[2] has highlighted the need for a greater understanding of Roman Catholic parish life in the United States. Even with this increased understanding, there is much that remains sociologically unexplored regarding parish life. This chapter seeks to address that gap in sociological discourse by drawing on interviews conducted with lay African American Catholics mainly, but not exclusively, from the Archdiocese of Philadelphia. Parish life is much more than attending Mass on the weekend. Parish life is also community, relationships, civic engagement, and schools. Parish life holistically influences one's perspective on Catholicism. The lay faithful whose voices are heard in this chapter spoke with me on a variety of issues. For this discussion, we will focus on ways African Americans experience parish life: race and racism, building community through physical and liturgical spaces, organizational processes and their consequences, and how all of this impacts their attitudes toward Catholicism.

Parishioners are not the only people who are in a parish. The perspective of pastors is key to understanding parish life, especially given the theme of organizational processes and their consequences, which parishioners spoke about at length. That is why I also spoke with five priests, four of whom were diocesan priests serving as pastors in the Archdiocese of Philadelphia at the time we spoke. The fifth priest is the only African American priest I spoke with. He belongs to a religious order and was retired at the time we spoke but served as a pastor during his active ministry.[3]

Looking at the themes of race and racism, building community through physical and liturgical spaces, organizational processes, their consequences, and how all of this impacts their attitudes toward Catholicism, from both the perspective of lay faithful and pastors, will allow us to better understand parish life and the perspective of African American Catholics who love a church that does not always love them in return.

RACE AND RACISM IN CHURCHES AND SCHOOLS

While the primary vector of institutional Catholicism is the parish, schools at all educational levels are essential spaces for experiencing Catholicism and the systemic racism that is deeply intertwined with it. In cities such as Philadelphia, Catholic schools are significant spaces for

African Americans, whether Catholic or not, to encounter Catholicism. For African American students, the Catholic Church as an institution is too often a place where they fail to see people who look like them in positions of authority or leadership. The absence of intentionality in creating racially inclusive systems is part of the inertia that prevents significant change.

Repeatedly, a theme that arose in the interviews I conducted about the racism African American Catholics experienced was blatant exclusion. In *American Catholics: Explaining Vocation in Their Own Words*, Ansel Augustine wrote, "At times we [Black Catholics] feel like 'motherless children' fighting for the church we love to love us back."[4] This point is reiterated by theologian, M. Shawn Copeland, who captured Black Catholics' interaction with the church: "Thus, in *our* relationship with *our* Church, more often than not, we Black Catholics feel bereft, orphaned, 'motherless'" [emphasis in the original].[5] Priests and laypeople alike spoke to me about exclusion in Catholic spaces. Theologian Bryan Massingale writes in *Racial Justice in the Catholic Church*, "Many persons of color can tell stories of how they received a rude welcome when visiting a so-called 'white' parish."[6] These moments are called the "n****r Moment" by sociologist Elijah Anderson. He defines these moments pointedly as follows:

> In typically White public settings, White people may view almost any Black person present with some degree of unease or curiosity. This moment of racialized disrespect puts Black people in their "place" and makes them feel excluded on the basis of their Blackness—it gives them and everyone observing the situation the emphatic message that, contrary to what the Black person might have once thought, he or she "does not belong."[7]

Sometimes, these experiences have such an impact that white priests recall them decades later. For priests such as Msgr. Banner,[8] who was the pastor of St. Ambrose parish in Philadelphia at the time we spoke, appreciating that these were the experiences of their parishioners factored deeply in their ministries as pastors. In the early 1970s, Msgr. Banner was a young priest at St. Michael the Archangel, a church in West Philadelphia that has long since closed. Just two blocks from St. Michael's, there was All Saints, a church founded as a national parish for the Italian American community. Msgr. Banner recounted an experience of one of St. Michael's parishioners who was a nurse at a local hospital. She once attended an early Mass at All Saints because she needed to be at work by 7:30 a.m. Msgr. Banner recounted that during Mass, one of the All Saints ushers came up to her and said, "Excuse me, ma'am. Your church is up at Oakmont Street." Anderson could have been describing this incident when he further described the "n****r Moment" thusly: "A White guard may approach the Black person with a disingenuous 'May I help you?' Most Blacks . . . have heard this question time and time again—not really offering help but asking what they're doing there."[9] In this case, the guard is the usher who didn't even bother to inquire what business the woman had at his church. He made clear that no explanation from her was wanted or required. She needed to leave. And that is precisely the purpose of the "n****r Moment"—summoning the power of whiteness to exude racialized disrespect to remind Blacks of "their place" and reinforce the perception of Blacks' lower social standing in a very specific space.

Catholic is derived from the Greek word *katholikos*, meaning "universal." Yet if a church is truly universal, members and visitors alike should be *universally* welcomed. Decades later, the incident invoked strong feelings from Msgr. Banner as he reflected on this disconnect between rhetoric and actions: "That just rivets you to say we're really missing the boat here when we preach Christ's love and acceptance, and we make that kind of distinction without knowing the woman is on her way to work, she's a very faithful Catholic, she's tremendously supportive of the church and teaches in the church. To be requested to leave just by saying, 'Your church is up at Oakmont Street.'" This incident, or "n****r Moment," is one of racialized disrespect. The fact that Anderson says Blacks "don't expect them in spaces perceived to be cosmopolitan canopies"[10] is exactly what makes the Catholic Church in the United States an "ultra-white space"— Black folks *expect* to have such encounters in Catholic spaces. This shouldn't be the case for an institution whose name means "universal."

Msgr. Banner provided a concrete example of exclusion and an African American Catholic being explicitly told she wasn't welcomed in a Catholic Church. I know there are some who will read this and think that perhaps the usher did not know she was Catholic. First, if that were the case, the usher would not have pointed out the exact location of another Catholic church and directed her to go there. The usher assumed she was Catholic or at least intended to be in a Catholic church. Second, if the woman wasn't Catholic and was visiting All Saints because she was interested in learning more about Catholicism, she would have learned that day that she wasn't welcomed at All Saints and, by extension, the Catholic Church. Furthermore, any argument that is a variation on "this is one usher at one church" is an argument that is stuck at the level of personal racism and does not consider how such incidents are part of a larger culture of pervasive systemic racism in the church.

Fr. Dombrowski, who serves as the pastor of what has become a predominantly Black parish as the surrounding neighborhood has changed in recent decades, contextualized Msgr. Banner's example: "Some parishes were notorious for being exclusionary. And so that has worked against us [in efforts to minister to African Americans]. . . . you have to remember that money may have been going in [to evangelize African Americans] but how were the people being treated?" To further contextualize Fr. Dombrowski's point, it is important to note that none of this is new. Black Catholics in Philadelphia were fighting blatant exclusion more than 150 years before the incident Msgr. Banner related and almost eighty years before the founding of St. Peter Claver. In 1817, Black Catholics in Philadelphia petitioned St. Mary's[11] Church, a national parish, where Black Catholics sometimes worshiped before the founding of St. Peter Claver, to have their own children instructed in the parish school.[12] These *Catholic* children were blatantly excluded from receiving the same education that was available to their white counterparts. Exclusion at that level becomes part of a community's collective trauma and the community's collective memory.[13] M. Shawn Copeland encapsulates this point and its consequences: "Such inhospitable and ungenerous recoil renders Black Catholics invisible, strangers, unwelcome in *our* own house. These antiblack reactions are rooted in the equivocations of the US hierarchical and institutional Church regarding its entanglement in the nation's history of transgenerational oppression of Black peoples."[14]

The type of exclusion Fr. Dombrowski spoke of is not limited to being told explicitly that one is not welcomed in a particular space, as

Msgr. Banner recounted, or being told that one's Catholic children aren't welcome in a Catholic school, as happened to the Black Catholics attending St. Mary's in 1817. Exclusion can also be the kind that is rooted in the assumptions and unconscious bias that hang thick in the air when children encounter people in positions of authority who have no insight into their experiences. The resulting hurt lingers, such as it has with William, 60, who recounted his time in elementary school. He said, "I didn't like the way they [teachers and administrators who were exclusively white women religious] talked to me when I came in. They always treated me like I didn't have any money. They didn't ask me, they just assumed."

William's comment speaks to a structural culture rooted in assumptions and the impact of those assumptions. Msgr. Banner offered context and nuance to William's statement:

> There was a tremendous Catholic presence, but when we saw some of the results of our Catholicism in practice, it wasn't all that Christ wants it to be. And certainly, there was prejudice and racism interwoven with some of the statements of church, regular church attending people, and sometimes people in the pulpit, in the preaching and in the interacting, who were consciously or unconsciously prejudiced against people. . . . African Americans . . . were not welcomed as well as they should have been by the Catholic Church.

As the years went by, and as parishes needed to grow their numbers to ensure survival because churches and schools needed to "be filled a little bit more," African Americans were not inclined to join parishes because of this history.

Fr. Dombrowski did not mince words about racism in the Archdiocese of Philadelphia and ministering to African Americans. "In [The Archdiocese of] Philadelphia some parishes were notorious for being exclusionary. If . . . , parishes were welcoming [when African Americans moved into Philadelphia], we wouldn't be sitting here having this conversation." Both of these comments harken back to the work of Fr. John Slattery, the founder of the Josephites. Slattery believed that if the Roman Catholic Church was going to have a major presence in the United States, African Americans needed to be part of its growth, and only African

American priests would sustain this growth. Slattery could not attain widespread buy-in for his vision. One-hundred fifty years later, Msgr. Banner and Fr. Dombrowski are talking about how a lack of welcome for African Americans has had negative consequences for the church. The pervasiveness of the experiences described by those I spoke with are indications that they are not isolated but systemic. We can look at these experiences through the lens of Catholicism as an ultra-white space.

Catholic schools are a key component of the Catholic organizational structure. As a result, they are also places where African American Catholics often have the most consequential and formative experiences of Catholicism. In many cases, these experiences are not positive. This is especially true in places like the Archdiocese of Philadelphia where the experience of Catholicism is already racialized. A number of people I spoke with conveyed this in unflinchingly stark terms. Jackie, sixty, described moving to Philadelphia in the late 1960s. She attended St. Clare's, a Catholic school that had only two Black students in her class of one hundred twenty students spread out over three classes of forty students each. "People would just say, 'Well, you're just from the projects.' 'No, I'm not. What's wrong with the projects?" she told me. She added, "My friends are educated, they're going to school. So I didn't understand what they were saying 'the project mentality.' But this one guy in fifth grade, he called me the N-word. I clocked him. Nobody ever said anything else to me." Like William, Jackie's example is rooted in assumptions of socioeconomic status based on race, which were projected onto African Americans. The resulting messages are meant to question why African Americans were in these Catholic spaces. Jackie's example is in keeping with Anderson's elucidation of the white space. For Jackie, it was a literal n****r moment, not just the metaphorical moments Anderson describes.

Jackie's experiences extended beyond assumptions about where she lived. They included negative assumptions about her appearance, specifically wearing her hair naturally. She told me how the teacher complained about her hair, adding that she wasn't allowed to sit toward the front of the class because her hair "was disturbing the people behind me [her]." She described how her mother showed up at school and stated, "I don't know what your problem is, but that's part of her cultural heritage, and if you need people to sit around her, they will sit around her, but you are not moving my child out of this class." Disappointingly, but not surprisingly, these fights are still being waged today and have moved into state legislatures through the CROWN Act,[15] which seeks to end discrimination against African American women who wear their hair naturally. As of June 2023, the CROWN Act has been enacted in twenty-two states and multiple cities and counties. For Jackie, these struggles persisted into the next generation as she discussed her and her daughter's parallel experiences:

> My guidance counselor [in high school] told me I needed to go to a vocational college because I didn't have what it took to go to a college. Luckily, I didn't listen to her. And that same thing happened to my daughter. She was in eighth grade, and the teacher nun told her that she should go to Francis Tech [a vocational high school]. I said, "What? That's not going to happen. She's going to St. Catherine Sienna [high school] and that's it." She has a master's degree now. I think she did all right in education.

Vincent, thirty-two, converted to Catholicism as a pre-teen after being introduced to Catholicism while attending Catholic school. In fact, he attended the same school and parish I attended until I was twelve years old. While we did not cross paths as co-parishioners, we did have an important shared experience. The church closed in 2005 making it one of many churches in West Philadelphia that are no longer operational. Vincent spoke with me about the high school he attended. Even though the private, Catholic[16] high school for boys is in a rapidly gentrifying but still predominantly African American section of Philadelphia, most of the students are white, and many travel from suburban areas. By Vincent's estimation, approximately 6 percent of the student body were people of color during his time there. He spoke of being tokenized and white classmates believing friendships with Black students gave them permission "to casually say the N-word in a song." Vincent connected experiences in schools and parishes with broader race and class dynamics:

> What we see at Aquinas Academy is not divorced from what we see in mass and how the archdiocese structures church closing. These race and class dynamics, they exist throughout these institutions within the church.

Experiences such as these compelled him, as a teenager, to do the emotional and intellectual labor of setting and enforcing appropriate boundaries not unlike what others have discussed. Here we have African American Catholics recounting instances where it was communicated to them that "their place wasn't in Catholic or educational spaces.

BLACKNESS IN PARISH LIFE

Not unlike other dioceses, Black Catholics in the Archdiocese of Philadelphia have faced numerous obstacles around race, racism, and identity formation. I have touched on several of these, including liturgy as identity work and the struggles of the parishioners of St. Peter Claver parish. Major themes that came out of the interviews I conducted are the importance of Black pastors, the experience of Mass and whether or not spiritual needs are being met, and organizational failure. These themes highlight the parish not only as a community defined in canon law but also as an administrative entity that has problems and challenges just like any other organization. Exploring these themes offers a better sense of the depth of parish life and the problems and struggles within it.

Importance of Black Pastors

The Archdiocese of Philadelphia is not immune from the issues discussed around African Americans having access to the priesthood and religious life. I can count on my fingers the number of Black priests who have been ordained by the Archdiocese of Philadelphia. As of June 2023, there are nine. All of them have been ordained since 1974. Two Black men were ordained for the Archdiocese of Philadelphia in 2023. Before that, the most recent years Black men were ordained in Philadelphia were 2015 and 2000. Including the two priests ordained in 2023, five of these priests are still in active ministry in the archdiocese as of January 2025.[17] Over the course of the conversations for this chapter, I was able to speak with several people who have had two of these priests as their pastors.

During my conversations with Black Catholics who have Black pastors, there was robust discussion around the importance of representation. Being able to see yourself and your experiences reflected back to you from your pastor is something most African American Catholics don't have due to the dearth of Black priests. When comparing going to a church with a white pastor versus a church with a Black pastor, Isaac, whose pastor, Father Cobb, is Black, stated that it is "more fulfilling to have a pastor that cares about me as well as someone who can relate to me personally." He added, "At St. Cyril, it was just the fact that it was just so much more inclusive, and dynamic, and they have African celebrations." Rose, Jackie's daughter, reiterated this point, saying specifically of Father Cobb, "And not saying that just because he's Black he's relatable because that doesn't mean anything, because Blackness is not a monolith. But he's just a relatable person and I feel like he talks, and I understand." Annika, whose parish is led by the other African American pastor explained:

> It's really special because it's so few of them [Black priests in the archdiocese]. Now that I'm older and can start to understand the messages that he is preaching to us, it has more meaning now. Especially coming from a person of color, because I feel like he's speaking from experience and he understands that African Americans or Black people in general go through different struggles as opposed to the white parishioners.

Without the type of connection Isaac, Rose, and Annika describe, it is incredibly difficult to build the type of connection needed to sustain a parish community. It is a type of connection that white Catholics who have always had white priests and Black Protestants who have always had Black ministers, take for granted. This connection, while incredibly important, may be fleeting due to the decline in seminary enrollment and ordinations across racial categories. Annika offered insight into this when she said, "I think our generation, or younger people in general, they don't really see the pleasure in going out for the priesthood. It doesn't seem appealing to them. So they don't go. There is no market for it either. There is nobody saying, 'Here are the sign-ups for it, this is what you have to do.' It's not really talked about in church either."[18]

William, Isaac's father, spoke of both the importance of relatability that comes from African Americans having an African American pastor and the possible consequences when that doesn't happen:

Today, you have pastors of color running churches. I would argue that possibly, they might be more sensitive to things, but when the pastor is not like those members of the parish, they're usually handling things a lot different. And it takes a lot more, a lot more explanation, discussion, and things of that nature, and I think what happened in people that went to school when I went to school, that might've been handled differently. They don't come back. They go find another faith.

African American Catholics who experience the microaggressions discussed in this chapter eventually become so disillusioned that they leave Catholicism altogether. It's like each microaggression is a tiny prick on the body that never heals. After decades of pricks too numerous to count, people begin to realize they have been quietly hemorrhaging for years and painfully admit that the only way to survive is to leave the Catholic Church.

Worshipping While Black

Mass is the principal worship experience for Catholics. As such, Mass most effectively resonates on a spiritual level if it first resonates on a cultural level. Liturgy serves as a form of identity work in predominantly Black parishes through music, preaching, and church aesthetics. Korie Little Edwards has discussed the intersection of religious practice and ethnicity: "Religious space is not just about practicing one's religion; it is also about living out one's ethno-racial identity. People do not quite realize how much of their religious practice is also a way of doing ethnicity—until they have to share their religious space with people who do not share their ethno-racial identity."[19] When that happens, those with power, i.e., whiteness, use their power to gaslight those who are marginalized by asserting that the incorporation of ethnicity and religion is antithetical to religious practice even though they have been doing it themselves for generations. What we see from those I spoke with are the ways African American Catholics have been marginalized in their own parishes when trying to do what white Catholics take for granted.

Miriam belongs to St. Ambrose parish. She is a long-time member of the parish and a founding member of St. Ambrose's African American

Catholics Society. Historically, the parish was dominated by Italian Americans and later by African Americans. Demographic changes in the neighborhood over the last thirty years are reflected in the current makeup of the parish. Presently, the parish has a smattering of Italian Americans with only slightly more African Americans. The parish has significant Indonesian, Vietnamese, and Latinx members and regularly has Mass in Indonesian, Vietnamese, and Spanish. It functions as a shared parish.[20] The African American Catholics Society organizes the 10 a.m. Mass on the third Sunday of the month and invites a Black priest or deacon to celebrate or preach at the Mass. Members of the Society conduct the various ministries for the Mass, including music ministers, lectors, ushers, and people who provide hospitality after Mass. Miriam spoke of the challenges of maintaining a sense of community for the African American Catholics who are scattered across St. Ambrose and other nearby parishes and getting support from the other communities at St. Ambrose. Notably, she pointed out that considerably fewer people attend the African American Catholics Society Mass on the third Sunday of the month. Referring to the other communities at St. Ambrose, she said, "I don't think that they've opened up as much to our style, or the things that we do. The music, the priests coming in, speaking more. They're not really for that." Visibly deterred during our conversation, but filled with resolve, she added, "We keep going. Eventually, something's got to change. We're not going to stop. We're here, this is our parish. We belong here too. And eventually, maybe we'll get some kind of support."

The lack of support from other minority communities within the parish, especially when those communities enjoy support from African Americans, is not unique to St. Ambrose. It serves to further marginalize African Americans who then become a marginalized group within an already marginalized group. This marginalization-within-marginalization is part of the divide-and-conquer function of white supremacy. By first siloing minority groups, then pitting them against each other, while trying to convince them (some more successfully than others) that proximity to whiteness is the key to achieving the benefits of whiteness, white supremacy seeks to keep racial minority groups from seeing the commonalities of experience that they share. If BIPOC Catholics don't see their commonalities of experience, there won't be cooperation and collaboration in the struggle against white supremacy. Acknowledging that anti-Blackness is not limited to whites is essential. There are too many examples to go into here. Anti-Blackness as exhibited by other people of color is also part of the divide-and-conquer function of white supremacy. The seeds of anti-Blackness are sown in an effort to convince those who are minorities but aren't Black that they can build proximity to whiteness through anti-Blackness and that proximity to whiteness will bring the benefits of whiteness. What Black folks know acutely, and what many others still must realize, is that *proximity* to whiteness only results in disappointment because whiteness, and more to the point, white supremacy, will protect itself at all costs even if it means spending centuries convincing generations to believe a lie.

The Need for "A Good Word"

In 2021, the Pew Research Center released a comprehensive study[21] on religion among Blacks in the United States titled "Faith Among Black Americans." I was a consultant on the Pew study, which offers a previously unavailable level of insight into the religiosity of Blacks in the United States. The study includes Afro-Latinx respondents and has a large enough sample size to provide specific analyses of Black Catholics. "Faith Among Black Americans" is the parent study for the 2022 Pew Report, "Black Catholics in America."[22] In 2022, I reflected on the importance of both studies in *National Catholic Reporter*: "'Black Catholics in America' . . . examines Black Catholics within a larger Catholic context and within the context of 'Faith Among Black Americans.' Scholars, practitioners and people of goodwill who are simply interested in learning more haven't had a study that does all of this at once."[23] These two studies provide data and analyses I longed to have while a student. Unfortunately, they simply didn't exist at the time. By consulting for Pew Research Center, I had the opportunity to play a small role in the creation of knowledge I wished I had as a student that will now benefit emerging scholars.

According to the study, only 17 percent of Black Catholics who attend Mass at least a few times a year do so at a predominantly Black church. This is a major difference from Black Protestants, 67 percent of whom report attending a predominantly Black church. Furthermore, while 82 percent of Black Protestants report that religion is important to them, only 58 percent of Black Catholics report the same. These findings are not surprising when viewed in the context of systemic racism provided in this book.

Some of the most interesting findings are around what Blacks hear in sermons or homilies when they attend religious services. The Pew study's results show that 41 percent of Black Catholics had heard a homily on "race relations or racial inequality" in the last year. The study doesn't indicate if that homily was about systemic racism. Given the United States Conference of Catholic Bishops' failure to address systemic racism in its magisterial documents,[24] it is unlikely that systemic racism was mentioned. In this context, we now turn to the insights of those I interviewed about their experiences with parish life.

During the participant observation portion of my research, preaching was a significant part of the identity work being done in liturgy. While I was conducting interviews, it became clear just how much resonant preaching impacts African American Catholics' experience of Mass. For example, Louise is active in St. Ambrose's African American Catholics Society even though she belongs to another nearby parish that is no longer predominantly African American. She spoke of the need for a salient message: "You got to hear the word. You want the word on Sunday." In speaking of the priest at the Society's most recent Third Sunday Mass, she said, "He gave a good word. You're looking for that word." Interestingly, in this case, Louise was speaking of a white priest who is the pastor of a predominantly African American parish in another area of Philadelphia. The pastor is known for his energetic, fiery homilies. Yet, Louise, a convert to Catholicism, also told me that she could easily go back to being a Methodist if there is ever a time she can't find "a good word" in Catholicism.

Debra is a life-long member of St. Ambrose and the founder of its African American Catholics Society. She reiterated Louise's point about the need for a good message when she spoke of her own pastor, Msgr. Banner: "But, nice as he is, don't get that message. You go to church to get a message." Vincent also spoke of the need for depth in preaching: "I also realized the older you get in life, just the more intellectual you get, you start to want deeper diving into the word. A lot of churches just weren't doing that. I think that's what I look for now." Vincent's comment made me wonder if he expects every priest he encounters to be a theologian and thus expects too much from priests. That said, it's never too much to expect Mass to connect with what is happening in society. As discussed in Chapter 3, St. Bernadette Soubirous parish in Philadelphia made intentional efforts to connect the homily content to the lived experiences of parishioners. This is another reason why connecting to a Black priest matters so much. Annika, a former member of St. Ambrose, who currently attends St. Mark's, which at the time we spoke had one of the few African American pastors in the archdiocese, spoke specifically of attending a Black parish that has a Black pastor. She spoke of connecting more with the message because her current pastor incorporates the Black experience into Mass, adding, "I'm listening. I can connect [his sermons] with my Blackness. It just means so much more."

On Music

Music is an incredibly vital part of liturgy at predominantly African American churches and plays a crucial role in the formation of a distinct African American Catholic identity. Annika spoke of music at her church, St. Mark's: "I love that part. And then, I feel like any type of gospel song you would hear on the radio . . . those renditions are what is sung in church." Annika added:

> I've never seen so many instruments fit into one small corner of a church before. After Eucharist, there is usually a song when they're collecting money and donations. There's maybe six songs throughout the service, like full-length songs. I'm just like, "Okay. Well, this is great. This last two hours." It's very interesting, and I think it speaks to our culture too.

Because Mass is Catholics' principal worship experience, having Mass that parishioners can relate to and enjoy is essential to maintaining a stable parish and larger Catholic community. This isn't limited to weekly Mass. A regular feature of Black Christianity, across denominations, is the Revival. A Revival, whether held on one day or multiple days, takes place outside of the regularly scheduled services. Revivals typically have a guest preacher, in this case someone who is known for a captivating and exuberant preaching style. This matters because as the name suggests, the event revives the spiritual life of church members and visitors alike. In reminiscing about revivals, Vincent talked about them as one of the elements of church life that carried over as his original parish went through two painful mergers. He spoke of friends being incredulous at the exuberant display of music and preaching that invoked the Duboisian description of "the Preacher, the Music, and the Frenzy."[25] Vincent reflected on the importance of revivals:

> I think one thing that [St.] Simon does that's been there since the days of [Our Lady of] Grace was the revival. I remember taking friends there to the revival, and they're just like, "What the hell is this?" I'm just like, "Oh yeah. This is how we get down." That's part of engagement. You have to really expose people to what Catholicism really is to particular culture groups versus what you see on TV.

Revivals are a hallmark of Black Christian worship and are rooted in the Great Awakening and the 19th century.[26] C. Eric Lincoln and Lawrence H. Mamiya called the revival "the major form of religious renewal used by protestant churches."[27] There are uniquely Catholic forums of spiritual renewal, such as Novenas and Forty Hours Devotion. These are certainly found in predominantly African American parishes. The fact that revivals have transcended their Protestant origins and are found in Catholic churches demonstrates instances outside of Mass where Black Catholics incorporate the traditions of the Black Church into their practice of Catholicism, interweaving ethnicity and religion in the way Korie Little Edwards described. In doing so, Black Catholics show that their Blackness and their Catholicity are not incompatible and, in keeping with Michele Dillon's work, own their identity as African American Catholics.

FAILURES OF ORGANIZATIONAL PROCESSES

While I was conducting interviews, a topic that came up repeatedly was organizational process, and especially lack of process, in the archdiocese.

This discussion revolved around church closings in three key ways: the church closings and parish reorganizations themselves, the perception of disinterest in the African American Catholic community, and the loss of community when churches close. When churches close, communities inevitably disburse. Everyone who has been displaced does not end up at the same church with some deciding they will no longer attend church. When the faithful see this happening repeatedly in the same area, what results is a perception that leadership is disinterested in the community affected by the church closings.

Church Closings

Losing one's church home is an incredibly painful experience. The pain doesn't get easier if it happens again. The section of West Philadelphia where I grew up had ten Catholic churches during my childhood. This does not include the aforementioned St. Michael the Archangel, which closed two years before I was born. Of the ten churches that were open in my corner of West Philly during my childhood, only two are still open. There are many who have gone through the pain of church closures multiple times. This is just in one part of one section of Philadelphia. There are other sections of the city, as well as other cities, that have had a similar experience.

In the course of my conversations for *Black and Catholic,* participants and I talked about a number of churches that aren't around anymore. In my conversation with Rose alone, we talked about six churches in West Philadelphia that are gone. When the churches are closed, what happens to the people? Where do they go to Mass? Do they go to Mass at all? What happens to the buildings? There are instances where parishes are reorganized and churches are designated as "worship sites" in the short term.[28] In the immediate moment of pain for parishioners who are losing their churches, they are led to believe that their churches will still be available for Mass, weddings, and funerals. Often, they are not. "Worship sites" has become coded language indicative of an established pattern that sees a building deteriorate and fall into such disrepair that the only viable option is to tear it down or sell it to a new owner that will likely raze it.[29] (See also Documents 5.1 and 5.2 in the Appendix.)

This sad reality demands the question, when the buildings are sold, what happens to the money? In a diocese like the Archdiocese of Philadelphia, which has been plagued by scandals related to the sex abuse crisis, a lack of transparency could lead the faithful and general public alike to believe that churches are being sold to pay settlements and court judgments related to the scandal. If that were to happen, it would further traumatize those already harmed by the scandal by repenting for those sins on the backs of others upon whom the church has already greatly sinned.

Fr. Dombrowski served as the pastor of one of these now-shuttered West Philadelphia churches. He mused on whether or not those making the final decision knew anything about the churches and the parishioners that would be impacted: "Did they ever attend Sunday mass? Did they go to the schools? Did they see what the parish does in the life of the neighborhood before they made a decision to close? And I fear to say they probably haven't."

Rose echoed Fr. Dombrowski's point about process, including making a site visit necessary for those charged with decision-making: "Stop closing Black churches and selling them! If you're going to close a church you need to have a plan of what you want to do."

We have to assume that each time a church closes some of its parishioners do not move on to the next church. The decades-long process that led to ten churches becoming two has inevitably resulted in a loss of parishioners in just this one area. Vincent belonged to one of these churches after his conversion to Catholicism as a preteen. He said of the loss of his church, the move to the next nearest church, and the move to a third church once the second closed thusly: "A lot of parishioners came over, but you had a big dip off of how many people from the original [Our Lady of] Grace used to come over. I don't know. I don't know if these communities could deal with another set of closures." Jackie commented on the immense loss: "My parish has gone away. I'm in mourning also, but I'm not going to stop. I still believe. And we all have to go through . . . this is our turbulent, right now, so it's going to be part of our testimony."

Vincent's and Jackie's comments embody the faithfulness and devotion of Black Catholics that was discussed in Chapter 4 and from which this book takes its title. To remain part of an institution that has repeatedly caused hurt and disappointment is the essence of being faithful and devoted. Yet, the church cannot continue to marginalize groups and expect the members of those groups to remain active in the church. We see this in the aforementioned Pew study, which states that 81 percent of Black adults who were raised Protestant identify as such today while only 54 percent of Black adults who were raised Catholic still identify as Catholic.[30]

An issue that stirs up a lot of emotion around the already emotional subject of church closings was the issue of communication and process. William spoke of the parish he grew up in, St. Basil's, and its merger with St. Francis of Assisi. Prior to the merger, the two parishes shared a pastor. Even though St. Basil's Church remained open, William feels strongly, years after the merger, that St. Francis received preferential treatment. "Everything that I saw led me to believe that [the pastor] was advocating to keep Francis of Assisi, and close St. Basil's." William's position on the process that resulted in the closing of St. Basil's underscores the importance of perception. Parishioners' perception of how things are done can influence how they feel about their pastor, their parish, and the church itself.

Fr. Dombrowski passionately reflected on the decision-making processes by archdiocesan officials thusly:

> First and foremost . . . someone has to say "okay, put all your business models away." Let us go see the life of the parish. Let us look at the life [of the parish], not numbers, not reports. . . . Because the first goal of the church is the salvation of the people. So let's see about these people. And then actually come up with a comprehensive plan that says . . . our goal as a church is to maintain the presence of the Catholic Church in this neighborhood!

Ultimately, Fr. Dombrowski's comment reflects seeing the church as an institution that provides services and care, not as a corporate entity. His assertion that using a corporate model for churches doesn't work, and his call for emphasizing caring for people as well as maintaining a presence in the community was reflected by Vincent. After experiencing two church closings, Vincent saw firsthand the way poor communication impacted parish communities. He commented on how better and clearer communication from the archdiocese, and transparency around the realities of churches' financial circumstances, would have eased the difficulty around the church closings. Vincent stated, "I think part of the communication would have been better for a lot of us if it was explained like, 'These things are going on in the church,' and actually being more upfront instead of hiding behind it." Darryl, who grew up as a member of St. Basil's parish and now belongs to St. Cyril's parish, reiterated this point:

> Well, the Archdiocese did not do a good job at implementing the changes. They did a really crappy job. They tried to be transparent about it, but it wasn't transparency. It was more PR. They knew what changes were gonna be made. After the decisions were made, they let people get all their frustrations out, which was, I think the PR. Because at the end of the day, all of the rumors people had been telling you, that's essentially what actually happened.

William said that ultimately, all of these events leave "a bad taste in people's mouths."

Focusing solely on a corporate model is not in keeping with Catholic Social Teaching's call to ensure the common good. It may be the case that closing a church is in keeping with the common good. There certainly are neighborhoods that have a glutton of century-old, underutilized churches, and closing one or two may allow the rest to thrive. However, understanding the spiritual and pastoral needs of the community vis-à-vis the metrics articulated by Fr. Dombrowski, along with clear communication and transparency, is a way to do that while ensuring the church's long-term presence in a community. *That* is promoting the common good.

Yet, as painful as these closures were, the lay people quoted in this section are still practicing Catholics. Vincent, in particular, was adamant that, for him, his view of Catholicism wasn't limited to a building. He stated that his faith was never tied to a "building being here forever" adding that such an attitude is "a dream." This articulation of faith and its importance is another example of the faithfulness and devotion first mentioned by Julia in Chapter 4, reinforced by Vincent's and Jackie's comments. These articulations of faith do not exist behind rose-colored lenses. Rather, they have a level of practicality that has allowed not only their faith but also the practice of their faith to endure.

ATTITUDES TOWARD INSTITUTIONAL CATHOLICISM

So much pain and distrust were expressed in the conversations for both this chapter and the chapter on St. Peter Claver. Therefore, it was important that I asked participants about their attitudes toward Catholicism *as an organization*, namely, what they think Black Catholics need to do about systemic racism in the church and what they thought white Catholics need to do about systemic racism in the church.

While everyone has a role to play, it is essential to keep in mind that it is not the responsibility of African Americans or our Latinx, Asian American, Pacific Islander, and Native American brothers and sisters to end systemic racism. We didn't create this problem, and we don't benefit from its continued existence. However, white people cannot fix this problem without us. We must dictate the terms of our own freedom. As Rev. Dr. Martin Luther King Jr. wrote in "Letter from Birmingham Jail," "We know from painful experience that freedom is never voluntarily given by the oppressor; it must be demanded by the oppressed."[31] We must name our own freedom and how we want our church to be truly authentic, truly safe, and *truly Catholic*. It is then up to those who have denied our freedom—by creating and perpetuating systems of white supremacy that subjugate our humanity—to implement the terms we have put forth. It is essential that the oppressed set the timeline for freedom. Later in the letter, Dr. King goes on to admonish the white moderate who "paternalistically believes he can set the timetable for another [person's] freedom."[32] Dr. King further states that he "hoped that the white moderate would reject the myth concerning time in relation to the struggle for freedom."[33] The work of Black Catholics in achieving freedom is not a gentle accompaniment of white Catholics along a placid path that will not push the limits of white comfort. Rather, it is the exhausting work of setting the terms and establishing the timeline for freedom, then pushing white Catholics beyond their comfort zone to the place where true, lasting change flourishes. As long as white Catholics are able to set the timeline, freedom will never materialize.[34] No one gives up their power freely. As

I say in the title of one of the lectures of my Black Catholics course, "We Won't Wait Any Longer."

William spoke to this point, saying, "The people in the pews have to be willing to talk about the issues that are concerning them, in an open forum. And the church has to provide an open forum for them to share that information." The marginalized must voice their concern and do the exhausting work of lifting their own voice. Otherwise, those in power will be free to dismiss this truly life-or-death issue and claim they didn't know there was a problem. This is not limited to what happens in the church's physical spaces. *Open Wide Our Hearts* does not address systemic racism and limits the discussion to personal racism. In fact, the pastoral letter lauds police officers for the dangers of their work while not acknowledging the dangers unarmed African Americans face simply for being Black in the United States, serving instead as a kind of "copaganda."[35] The USCCB calls for empathy for the dangers of police work but not the dangers of living while Black. *Open Wide Our Hearts* discusses racism as a sin, but by limiting the discussion to the level of personal racism, the USCCB does not discuss the social aspect of the sin of racism. Personal sin is addressed in a personal way through the Sacrament of Reconciliation and penance. Thus, if the USCCB addressed racism as a life-or-death *social sin*, the bishops would be required to rectify this sin in the social sphere. That is, it would need to be rectified publicly. Doing this would require the USCCB to recognize the church's own complicity in systemic racism historically and currently. We won't see any movement on this issue until the USCCB recognizes systemic racism as the pro-life issue that it is and puts as much attention and resources toward systemic racism as it puts toward abortion.

WHAT DO YOU WANT TO SEE FROM WHITE CATHOLICS?

Black Catholics can't do this work on our own. Yet, it can't be done without us. White Catholics who are truly committed to the work of antiracism, not just in a performative way but in an authentic way that makes them uncomfortable, need to bring their fellow white Catholics into that same space. Several participants expressed their thoughts on this matter. Participants talked about accountability and the value of dialogue. Vincent discussed the value of dialogue, in particular: "The biggest thing that, even talking to you in this conversation, is just the engagement. That's the biggest part of the church that I would love to see going at the root." Ann added, "Stand up and be accountable. And stop. I think that what I have seen in Catholic leadership is so many people whose power and position is more important than moral issues." In calling on white Catholics, including episcopal leadership, to be accountable, Ann invokes the need for a public reckoning. Vincent's call for dialogue is another type of public reckoning. Both call on the church to move away from racism as merely a personal sin and toward racism as social, collective sin. While dialogue is essential, it is important to appreciate its limitations. It is not possible to engage in dialogue with someone who isn't open to new ideas and only pretends to want to hear what another person has to say. These are the "unconvinceables." There is no talking *with* someone who is not interested in seeing the world in a new way. There is only talking *to* or *at* them, and it's not the same thing. Dialogue cannot be an end unto itself. If it is to be productive, it must lead to some measurable change. That can't happen if the other party isn't interested in change. Therefore, white Catholics have to do their portion of the work on their own. Then, and only then, can true dialogue happen. Yet, I'm under no illusions that this will definitely happen because the unconvinceables benefit from the three-legged stool of racism, white supremacy, and anti-Blackness, and, consequently, their sense of self depends on the perpetuation of this three-legged stool.

The reality that some will not engage in true dialogue because of their unwillingness to surrender the benefits of white supremacy invokes points made by two of the greatest thinkers the 20th century produced. In *The Souls of Black Folk*, Du Bois famously posed the question that is constantly implied by whites but rarely asked, "How does it feel to be a problem?"[36] Blackness, not racism, is the problem for whites. After all, they benefit from racism, but not from Blackness. This leads us to a comment Toni Morrison made during a television interview in which, with a level of precision worthy of a world-class surgeon, she clearly pointed out how white people benefit not just from racism but also white supremacy and anti-Blackness. She posed to whites the definitive question of what are you without the protections of the three-legged stool of racism, white supremacy, and anti-Blackness: "What *are* you without racism? Are you any good? Are you still strong? Still smart? Do you still like yourself?" As the exchange during the interview continued, Morrison went on to encapsulate the entirety of feelings of white superiority that only exists as a result of racism, white supremacy, and anti-Blackness for centuries: "If you can only be tall because somebody's on their knees, then you have a serious problem. And *my* feeling is, white people have a very, very serious problem. And *they* should start thinking about what *they* can do about it. Take me out of it!"[37] Until that happens, the unconvinceables will remain unconvinced and true dialogue won't happen.

Feelings About the Church

It should be expected that the experiences described in this chapter would have a major impact on African American Catholics' feelings about the church overall. Feelings of exclusion, the pain of church closings, and the loss of community have resulted in attitudes about the church as an institution. Participants expressed a variety of thoughts about what they think about the present and future of the church and their place in it. It is important to note that none of these comments are about their *faith*, i.e., their belief in God and the teachings of the Gospels that are the bedrock of Catholicism. Rather, any wavering that was expressed is related to the *institution* through which they practice that faith and particularly, those who run the institution. If those who run the institution truly want African Americans to be a part of this church, they cannot continue to ignore the sentiment expressed in this chapter. They do so at their own and the church's peril.

When asked what she wants to see from the church, Jackie said, "I want to see that I matter." Let's sit with that. Jackie needs to see from church leadership that she matters because she doesn't believe they think she does. When asked to elaborate, she added, "Not just that I'm tithing, but that my opinion matters, that I'm not just a number." Jackie's statement reflects Fr. Dombrowski's comment regarding the church foregoing a corporate model in favor of providing services and care. Jackie is clearly experiencing the church as an exclusive corporate entity and as an organization that doesn't care whether she stays or goes because she's "just a number." No matter how many Catholics—whether they are Black, Native, Asian American, Pacific Islander, Latinx, LGBTQ+ or another marginalized group—feel this way, it is one too many. Focusing on the impact of racism, Vincent described the exclusive nature of the church, saying, "There's just a lot of ways in which the whole nature of it [experiences of racism in the church] kind of shaped and changed a lot of people's faiths, and they just lost faith in the church."

Yet, there are those who stick with the church and want the church they love to love them back. If they can't find the love they are looking for, they at least want to find a way to have a place in the institution that too often tells them there's no place for them. William expressed, "I don't go [to Mass] because I'm trying to go to heaven. I go because that experience is helping me stay rooted in my faith and be rooted in the world. Okay? So that when I'm doing things, if I think I'm trying to do things the best I can do them, try to be the best I can so that the Lord is saying, 'I'm working with you.' That's what I'm trying to do." Vincent captured succinctly and beautifully what it means to remain faithful and devoted and also be critical and reflective of the Catholic Church. He reflected on whether he would find another church to attend should his church close. "I think I would find another Catholic Church. I think I'm so deeply rooted and there's just like certain things [in Catholicism] that I really identify with and I really value." The points made by William and Vincent, along with the experiences of the people of St. Peter Claver discussed in Chapter 4, show that Black Catholics will find a place in the Catholic Church despite centuries of being told there is no place for African Americans in the U.S. Catholic Church.

WHAT IS THE CHURCH WITHOUT ITS PEOPLE? CONTEXT AND CONSEQUENCES FOR THE CHURCH

When asked what she thinks the church will look like in the future, Jackie replied, "Empty." Jackie's assertion aligns with data from a 2021 study by the Pew Research Center, "Faith Among Black Americans,"[38] which provides some of the most concrete analysis of Black Catholics in recent decades. In the study, Pew found that only 54 percent of Blacks who were raised Catholic continue to practice Catholicism into adulthood, which is a stark contrast to 80 percent of Black adults who were raised and have remained Protestant into adulthood.[39] Furthermore, the Pew report states that only about half (49 percent) of Black Catholics say that "religion is very important to them" while nearly three-quarters (73 percent) of Black Protestants make the same assertion.[40] Additionally, the Pew report shows that 77 percent of the Black Catholics surveyed believe that opposing racism is "essential to being Christian."[41] Yet, only 41 percent of Black Catholics report hearing homilies addressing "race relations or racial inequality" at Mass.[42] Seventy-five percent of Black Catholics say that "opposing sexism or discrimination against women is essential to what it means to be faithful to their religious tradition"[43] but only 27 percent of Black Catholics who attend Mass regularly say they have heard a homily address this point in the year prior to the survey.[44] This is an indicator that church leadership is not reflecting the views of parishioners or providing the spiritual guidance Black Catholics, in particular, desire. In this context, Jackie's comment does not seem pessimistic but rather, prophetic.

If Black Catholics aren't getting "a good word," feel excluded, and believe the church is rife with systemic racism, it makes sense that far fewer Black Catholics than Black Protestants would believe religion is important. It may be more fruitful to look at the 50 percent figure as high rather than low considering the various mitigating factors: 62 percent of Black Catholics said religious leaders should marry same-sex couples, compared with 37 percent of Black Protestants—a staggering figure considering the amount of time, energy, and resources church leaders spend condemning the LGBTQ+ community and same-sex marriage despite Pope Francis' affirming efforts.[45]

During our discussion, Darryl asserted, "for me, the church is its people." In his best-known work, theologian Avery Cardinal Dulles[46] offers Mystical Communion as one of five Models of the Church. In this image, Dulles describes a view of the church as its people and how those people are connected. He states, "With regard to mankind, the Holy Spirit is the divine person who makes us one without our ceasing to be many. The church is one Person (the Holy Spirit) in many persons (Christ and us)."[47] The church is its people connected to each other and to Christ through the Holy Spirit. Dulles' ecclesial imagery aligns with Darryl's perspective because both beg the question: *What is the Church without its people?* Given the perspectives put forth in this chapter, without the people, there isn't much more than empty pews.

A question I am often asked is, "Why do African Americans stay in the church when faced with so much racism?" Frankly, and as I've written elsewhere,[48] it's an illegitimate question that only white people ask. The question itself is predicated on an inability to fathom being in a space that is structured precisely to disparage and traumatize. *Not* being in the center, *not* being the raison d'être of an institution's existence is incomprehensible. Another question I'm often asked, again by white people is some variation of "What can we do about it?" Of course, the "we" in the question is not white people. At least, it's not white people exclusively. That question is really asking what Black people will do. It is a question only asked by those who don't see themselves as both the cause of and solution to racism. Herein lies the difference between African American Catholics and African Americans who worship in the Black Protestant traditions. Catholics don't get a respite from the three-legged stool of racism, white supremacy, and anti-Blackness at church. Despite this, and as seen throughout this book, Black Catholics remain faithful and devoted. As Fr. Dombrowski said, "So, I admire the African Americans . . . who dealt with just terrible bigotry and racism but saw their faith was more important than all this craziness . . . their faith was more than these people."

The perspectives expressed in this chapter convey the message provided by theologian, M. Shawn Copeland: "Black Catholics must so value identity, so value personhood as God's sacred gift, that they will not yield that gift even to the Church and are ready in love to rebuke the Church when it fails to reverence, to protect Black religious, cultural, psychic, intellectual, moral, and physical life: *Black Lives Matter*."[49] Copeland's point encapsulates how Black Catholics will find a way to push through the marginalization imposed by the church and maintain their faith. Our faith as Black Catholics is stronger than our fellow Catholics who can only be tall by forcing Black Catholics on their knees.

SIX

Losing Religion and Gaining Faith

• • • • • • •

Nobel Laureate Toni Morrison once said, "If there's a book that you want to read, but it hasn't been written yet, then you must write it." *Black and Catholic: Racism, Identity, and Religion* is the book I wanted to read in high school, as an undergraduate, and as a graduate student but hadn't been written yet. I decided to write *Black and Catholic* as my effort to fill, but not close, the massive gap in the extant literature on the intersections of U.S. systemic racism, the Catholic Church, and African American Catholic identity. While it does not address every nuance that could possibly come to mind when thinking about systemic racism in the U.S. Catholic Church and its impact on African American Catholics, the book, and all of my work, provides scholars from other marginalized groups in the church a blueprint to look critically at their communities. *Black and Catholic* demonstrates how our identity work is an act of resistance to systemic discrimination—whether it is, racism, homophobia, sexism, or transphobia. I also encourage others to push past the difficulties of creating crucial scholarship on identity work that is centered outside of and rejects the white, Christian, cisgender, heteronormative gaze. The journey to research, write, and also exist as a member of a marginalized group in the Catholic Church is incredibly difficult, deeply painstaking, and heartbreaking. It is also extremely necessary.

This book, and all of my research and public writing and lectures, focuses on centering the *Blackness* of Black Catholics and making clear that Black Catholics don't need the context of whiteness in order to be seen. In multiple interviews, Toni Morrison directly repudiates this insistence that Blackness must be seen through the white gaze. When asked by an Australian reporter in 1998 why her work does not feature whiteness prominently, Morrison stated, "You can't understand how powerfully racist that question is, can you? As you could *never* ask a white author, 'When are you going to write about Black people?'—whether he did or not, or she did or not. Even the inquiry comes from a position of being in center . . . and being *used to* being in the center."[1] Too often, throughout my career, professors, colleagues, and editors have insisted that the only way I could talk about Black Catholics was through the white gaze. Over and over, I rejected their supposition that whiteness must be at the center for anything else to be taken seriously. This is another way whiteness protects itself and ensures everything else remains peripheral. I demonstrate that centering Blackness is both possible and required if the Roman Catholic Church is to be its better self globally. In my efforts to achieve this, there is one particular element that needed to be reconceived.

It is important to elucidate systemic racism in the Catholic Church and its impact on African American Catholic identity by mapping out what racism is and how we can understand it. Racism is woven into the fabric of the Catholic Church in the United States through its practices and official policies. I mapped out this racism through time rather than place. Previous scholarship, such as John T. McGreevy's *Parish Boundaries*[2] and Stephen J. Ochs' *Desegregating the Altar*,[3] focus on place. The framework of place allows systemic racism deniers, also known as "the unconvincibles," to claim that such racism is limited to the places in the specific studies. Therefore, they were the result of individual bad actors or personal racism and not systemic racism. Instead, I use the framework of time to show how the things discussed in previous studies were happening simultaneously and were happening at the direction of the highest leadership in the U.S. church and therefore, were systemic. In the book, I also show how liturgy is a form of identity work in contemporary parish communities through the integration of African American cultural elements and standard practices of Roman Catholicism into a unique identity. I identified three styles of liturgy through participant observation research: Traditionalist, Spirited, and Gospel. These three styles use music, preaching, and aesthetics to create a liturgical experience that is also culturally relevant.

An exemplar of the racism Black Catholics in the United States face can be best understood through the history of St. Peter Claver parish in Philadelphia. St. Peter Claver is the first parish in Philadelphia founded for African Americans, and since its founding, Black parishioners have had to endure ongoing systemic racism and white supremacy from their own church to simply practice their faith. The fight that parishioners have engaged in the decades since St. Peter Claver closed shows the lengths Black Catholics will go out of love and perseverance for a church that too often gives them pain and disappointment in return.

My interviews with Black Catholics, provide them the space to articulate their own thoughts and experiences of parish life and the church more broadly. In a bureaucracy as vast as the Roman Catholic Church, issues of space, place, and community are important. Articulating those issues through the lens of race provides an essential layer of nuance to the conversation. By centering these voices, I also address the void in sociological literature at the intersection of race and religion, helping to fill it by focusing on systemic racism in the context of religion and religious practices. My research treats religion as an organization whose practices are informed by theology and theological values and uses the works of key sociological thinkers in both the sociology of race and the sociology of religion, including Elijah Anderson's discussion of "The White Space"[4] and Joe R. Feagin's analysis of systemic racism alongside Michele Dillon's owning, Lynn Resnick Dufor's sifting, and Nancy T. Ammerman's parish culture production.[5] I use the lenses of Feagin's analysis alongside liturgical designations and the exoticism of Black Catholics to demonstrate the ways race and religion sociologically comingle. Nearly twenty years ago, James D. Davidson and Suzanne C. Fournier articulated the need for studying parishes as distinct from Protestant congregations.[6] In addition to understanding the systemic discrimination mentioned earlier, academic, and particularly sociological discourse, must have an even deeper comprehension of parishes themselves and the churches that house them. *Black and Catholic* joins other notable works[7] in parish studies as a burgeoning subfield of Catholic Studies. *Black and Catholic* adds to this body of emergent literature by rejecting the erasure of Black Catholics in the U.S. Church and by centering data, history, and stories that affirm and uplift the African American Catholic community.

APPROACHES TO PARISH AND CHURCH DATA

As I worked on this book, I realized that it would be beneficial to include data on churches that have closed. I also determined it would be especially useful to look at churches that have closed using census data to examine the propensity of church closings in predominantly BIPOC neighborhoods as well as low-income neighborhoods. I was unable to find the data in the extant literature. After I made inquiries at the Center for Applied Research in the Apostolate (CARA) and the Pew Research Center, it became clear that the data were not available during the time I was gathering research and writing the bulk of this book. I investigated conducting such research as part of this book and quickly realized that collecting the relevant data was a project unto itself.

In March 2023, CARA completed a study entitled, "Parish, Ecclesial and Socioeconomic Statistics for Eleven Dioceses between 1970 and 2020: A Report for the FutureChurch."[8] As the title indicates, the study was commissioned by the Catholic nonprofit organization FutureChurch,[9] which is headquartered in Ohio. The study focuses on eleven dioceses located along the Mississippi River and east of the Mississippi that "were selected to fit the specific needs of FC [Future Church] and they are not meant to constitute a nationally representative sample."[10] The study's methodology appendix does not indicate what the needs of FutureChurch are. Consequently, it is unclear if the dioceses selected are best suited to address the research question. Nevertheless, the study concluded that "the average proportion of people below [the] poverty line, people unemployed, Blacks/African Americans, and Hispanics/Latinos was higher in those neighborhoods where parishes closed/were absorbed than in those neighborhoods where parishes opened/expanded."[11] The study also states, "It appears that poverty rate is a substantially bigger predictor of parish closings than racial composition."[12] Given the intimate connection between race and poverty in the United States and the lack of clarity around FutureChurch's needs, dismissing race as a predictor raises additional concerns about what FutureChurch sought to accomplish with the study's commission.

In the name of full disclosure, in early 2021, FutureChurch's then-co-director contacted me to ask how I would approach a study focusing on the closing of Black parishes and if I would be interested in conducting such a study on behalf of FutureChurch. Despite my interest, I declined, given my workload at the time and knowing that I could not complete such a large project on my own. In early 2021, in the continuing aftermath of George Floyd's murder and the ongoing COVID pandemic, I was swamped. During this time, many institutions, particularly Catholic institutions, had become interested in systemic racism. Consequently, I was giving numerous virtual lectures—sometimes multiple lectures a day to audiences across the country. At that point, I had been researching and writing about systemic racism in the U.S. Catholic Church for just over twenty years. It felt like I had been yelling at a wall for decades only to find that the wall was really a secret door where the people on the other side could hear but had chosen not to listen until that pivotal moment in history.

The Archdiocese of Philadelphia is one of the eleven dioceses featured in the CARA/FutureChurch study. CARA found that the number of parishes in the archdiocese decreased by approximately one-third between 1970 and 2020. During that same time period, other indicators of (arch)diocesan vibrancy dropped precipitously, including the number of Catholic marriages (74 percent decrease), Baptisms (66 percent decrease), number of priests (60 percent decrease), and overall Catholic population (7 percent decrease). These numbers are logical, but they are shocking just the same. These data affirm the empty churches and disaffected Catholics described by those I interviewed for Chapter 5.

The discourse on church closings and parish reorganizations must include an examination of the data without fear or favor or "specific needs." Expertise in digital mapping software can be used to longitudinally analyze church closings in light of the racial demographics of the surrounding neighborhoods. It is my contention that such an analysis in a representative sample of dioceses will provide needed additional insight into church closings. Ultimately, what we see in the CARA/FutureChurch study is that in eleven dioceses, the church's physical presence among African American and Latinx communities and economically distressed neighborhoods has decreased vis-à-vis a reduction in the number of parishes. This reality does not align with the undertaking of a preferential option for the poor as a core value of the church and Pope Francis. Additionally, the final words of Canon 1752, the final canon in the Code of Canon Law, state, "the salvation of souls, which must always be the supreme law in the Church, is to be kept before one's eyes."[13] If the salvation of souls is the church's supreme law, the church must be present.

THE NEED TO SPEAK WITH PRIESTS

I continued gathering data and research, and soon after I began conducting interviews, I realized that I needed to talk to priests about their experiences in Black parishes. Since the Archdiocese of Philadelphia has ordained such a minuscule number of Black priests in its history, I very much wanted to speak with the Black priests about their experiences but determined that for ethical reasons, it would not be possible.

A principle at the bedrock of sociological research is protecting the anonymity of research participants. Therefore, using pseudonyms and masking identifying characteristics is a standard practice. Even with researchers taking the strongest measures possible, there is always a risk that a reader will recognize a place or participant. With the Archdiocese of Philadelphia having ordained so few Black priests, the pool of potential research participants is incredibly small. Thus, it is incredibly difficult to protect a participant's anonymity when there are only a handful of potential interviewees. I considered a type of "herd anonymity" where I would interview all the priests thus making it difficult to pinpoint who I quoted in the text. After giving this possibility much consideration, I determined that a piece of information as seemingly innocuous as the name of the serving archbishop while the priest was in seminary, or the year of his ordination, can reveal a priest's identity. Therefore, "herd anonymity" was not viable. Since I could not provide a reasonable assurance of my ability to protect their anonymity, I could not, in good conscience, ask these priests to talk with me about the racism they experienced while living out their priestly vocations. Ultimately, I decided not to pursue interviews with the African American priests from the Archdiocese of Philadelphia. I was, however, able to speak with an African American priest who was not from Philadelphia.

INVESTIGATING CATHOLIC SLAVEHOLDING

When I first conceived this book, I planned to offer a substantive analysis of Catholic slaveholding, particularly corporate or institutional Catholic slaveholding, in the United States. This analysis would include how the wealth produced through Catholic slaveholding is the foundation on which many Catholic institutions were built as well as showing how the racism that allowed Catholic slaveholding to exist in the first place persisted systemically long after slavery ended via the church's anti-Blackness and discrimination, from prohibiting Black women and men from joining religious life to refusing to authentically confront anti-Black violence following murders of African American people by police in recent years. I quickly realized that the story of Catholic slaveholding must be told on its own. The 1619 Project,[14] the Georgetown Slavery and Reconciliation Project,[15] and other works have shown that untangling the Catholic introduction of slavery to the Americas in 1536[16] and all that it has wrought needs to be tackled on its own. The analysis of Catholic slaveholding was to be another instance of the church as an ultra-white space while purporting itself to be a cosmopolitan canopy. This book has turned out to be more than a sociological treatise. It has been a journey of the discovery of a project, how to carry out that project, and how the project influenced my relationship with the church.

I sat with the data for this book—previous research, archival material, and interviews—as well as my own previous writing and research. Sitting with all of this also meant sitting more deeply with how the Catholic Church benefitted immensely from its participation in the chattel slave industry. I began tracing the money from the Maryland Jesuit province's mass sale of 272 slaves in 1838. I started with information provided by a former colleague who had done preliminary investigating while working with student journalists at the university I was affiliated with at the time. My investigation included tracking down and attempting to access documents related to the sale that are housed at Georgetown University's library but controlled by Jesuit curia in Rome (because they are the property of the Society of Jesus, not the university). I wanted access to these documents to ascertain if Georgetown University was the only institution to benefit from the sale of 272 men, women, and children viewed by the Society of Jesus as farm equipment. My suspicion, then and now, is that other Jesuit institutions, in what was then the Maryland Province, benefited financially from the 1848 transaction. It was not just Georgetown that benefited from the selling of enslaved Black people.

My investigation, as it was, resulted in three major findings. First, the documents I was interested in viewing were undigitized, unorganized, and reportedly housed in a retired Jesuit academic's briefcase, which was in a safe at Georgetown's library. Second, the documents I was especially interested in, letters sent between Jesuits, were in Latin. Knowing that my one year of Latin in high school would not be enough to work with these documents in any meaningful way left me at an impasse. Third, this narrative is much too engrossing and encompassing to be a book *section*.[17] In order to be done properly, it must be a standalone project. While the Maryland Jesuits are the most infamous corporate Catholic slaveholders in the United States, they are not the only U.S. Catholic entity to benefit from human trafficking. Such an investigation must also include the Jesuits' Missouri Mission;[18] the Congregation of the Mission, or the Vincentians, in Missouri;[19] the Society of the Priests of Saint Sulpice, also known as the Sulpicians, in Maryland;[20] the Order of the Visitation of Holy Mary;[21] and the Society of the Sacred Heart.[22] Additionally, dioceses, congregations of priests, and congregations of men and women religious must examine their archives to determine if slaves were included with any property that members brought with them when entering seminary or religious life. If so, they must account for what happened next. That is, did they sell, keep, or emancipate the slaves? Additionally, they must account for any financial windfalls the acquisition of slaves produced.

In March 1861, Alexander Stephens, the vice president of the Confederacy, gave an extemporaneous speech in Savannah, Georgia, where he spoke of the confederate government's foundation: "Its cornerstone rests, upon the great truth that the negro is not equal to the white man; that slavery, subordination to the superior race, is his natural and moral condition."[23] In a quite different context, Psalm 118, verse 22, tells us, "The stone which the builders rejected has become the cornerstone."[24] The builders of Catholicism in the United States, our church's very founders on these lands, rejected the humanity of slaves. Yet, it is slaves, and the labor compelled by their bondage, which provide the foundation—the cornerstone—of Catholicism in the United States. There is no U.S. Roman Catholic Church today without enslaved Black labor. There is no present-day U.S. Church, one that is a major provider of social services and healthcare, education from Pre-K to PhD, and so much more, without the financial largess provided by slavery.[25] I leave this intellectual trail of breadcrumbs for myself as a reminder of the work that must still be done to complete the work I have begun in *Black and Catholic*.

GAINING FAITH

Back in 2019, I wrote an article for *America* magazine.[26] It stated, among other things, that I wanted *Black and Catholic* to end the incredulousness around Black Catholics' existence. I'm confident that has been accomplished. I also wrote that the church could support Black Catholics if it had the will to do so. Now that this book is completed, I am less convinced than ever that the will is there. The murder of George Floyd in 2020 revealed on a large, public scale how deep and widespread systemic racism is in the United States. For many, this public revelation was new information. For African Americans, Catholic and non-Catholic alike, the public revelation brought long-held knowledge and realities into the light. George Floyd's murder brought what African Americans had known for centuries into the broader public discourse. Every institution was called to account, and the Catholic Church was no exception. During that summer, I started titling my public lectures "The Call is Coming from Inside the House" because I wanted to make clear that the Catholic Church is not immune to this long overdue reckoning. This reference to an often-used horror movie trope may have eluded some. Those who understood the reference appreciated that the pain African American Catholics have experienced comes from within the church—the place where, like one's home, we are supposed to feel safe.

The summer of 2020 showed us the depths of performative allyship, in particular, from all those who took a knee in front of cameras but did not use their power, privilege, and platforms to remedy the systemic racism that compels people to take a knee in the first place. We also saw it in all the organizations that hired Inclusion and Diversity experts, either as consultants or for institutional positions. These experts often were not provided with the resources needed to do their jobs or listened to when they proposed concrete ways for doing anti-racist work. Consequently, we saw such positions either reorganized or eliminated in 2023 and 2024.[27] We saw performative allyship in the form of statements from church leaders that called for racial healing while reducing racism to individual sins,[28] did not acknowledge the reality of systemic racism,[29] and, at times, ventured into the realm of a pro-police manifesto,[30] also known as copaganda.[31]

As a consequence of my personal experience and my work, I've spent pretty much every day of my adult life thinking about how difficult it is to be Black and Catholic in the United States. The difficulty that lies in the erasure of Black Catholics, the pain and frustration of racism, the pain of church closures, standing out in an ocean of white faces *all the time*, living with the perception that my race and my religion aren't compatible, and having to explain all of this within my profession again and again. It's too much! Enough! I struggle with being part of an organization that has such a long history of anti-Blackness in the forms of slavery, discrimination, racism, sexism, homophobia, and so many other harms. The ongoing sex abuse crisis still makes my blood boil. So often, I feel like I have nothing more to give to my church. So often I feel that I should turn over this work to someone else. Despite these struggles, I stay. I stay because being at one with my Lord in the most sacred and intimate way through the Eucharist matters to me. It sustains me during times of trial and triumph. I realized that acutely during the pandemic when I didn't attend Mass and receive the Eucharist for over a year. The absence and longing I felt were profound.

I stay because the organizational structure of the church comforts me. There is a clear leadership structure. In referring to Catholicism, when someone says, "They said," I know who "they" are—even if I vehemently disagree with what "they" had to say. The leadership structure of the church, from the Pope to the local parish priest, is clear. I like that. A deep dive into the flaws of the structure or of those who hold positions within it is a discussion for another book. For now, I'll just say that I wish the body of the church were more inclusive. I wish the Catholic hierarchy were more catholic.

I stay because of the witnesses of the pillars of Catholicism in my life. As I said in Chapter 1, I come from a long line of Catholics. My family's Catholicism runs deep through hundreds (and perhaps, thousands) of years and across multiple countries. If it is possible for religion to be in a family's bloodline, Catholicism is in ours. Yet, like so many Black Catholics, including many that are documented in this book, my family struggles with its Catholicism. I've watched as relatives, both immediate family members and close and distant cousins, cease practicing Catholicism and, in some cases, embrace other religious traditions.

Watching this happen makes me think of the family members I consider the pillars of Catholicism in my life—namely, my grandfather, Marcel A. Pratt; his sister, Janet P. Latta; and their uncle, Calvin Aguillard, Sr. As of August 2021, all of them are deceased. My grandfather and Aunt Janet died within less than a year of each other. Their witness, while quite different, has been pivotal to my own development, both as a Catholic and a scholar of Catholicism. My grandfather didn't have much to say about Catholicism or religion generally. It is actions, often far more accurate than words, that are most revelatory. My late grandmother converted to Catholicism when she and my grandfather married. My grandmother was raised in a Christian household, and by her account, the denomination changed frequently as she was growing up. Even though my grandfather was not an avid churchgoer, the Catholicism he brought to his marriage was important enough to both of my grandparents that they decided it was the religion in which they would raise their children. That matters.

My great-aunt, Janet P. Latta, was one of the most faithful and faith-filled Catholics I've ever known. She was a stalwart churchgoer and believer in the rhythms and structures of Catholicism. It is those same rhythms and structures that give me comfort, even when I find them completely vexing! Her witness so impressed and inspired me that I wrote it into the syllabus of my signature course, Sociology of African American Catholicism, later called African American Catholics. When I first began teaching this course, I worked at a university that was less than a mile from my Aunt Janet's church. I decided that I wanted the students to have an outside-of-class experience to engage the class material beyond just the readings for the course. One option was to attend Mass at a predominantly Black church, Aunt Janet's church. To be able to introduce her to some of my students and see her completely in her element as both church elder and quintessential Black Auntie meant the world to me!

My uncle, Calvin Aguillard Sr., my great-grandmother's youngest brother, lived his entire life in New Orleans—a place I love as my spiritual and ancestral home. My Uncle Calvin taught me about our family's history, protested sexual abuse by priests years before members of *The Boston Globe*'s Spotlight Team began publishing their work,[32] and was well-known in New Orleans for his activism and commitment to the church. Along with my Aunt Janet, my Uncle Calvin was one of the most faithful and faith-filled Catholics I've ever known. He showed me how to simultaneously love the church and point out its failings. As I wrote in the foreword to Olga Segura's *Birth of a Movement: Black Lives Matter and the Catholic Church*,[33] I invoke my Uncle Calvin whenever I am asked about how I, or Black people more generally, remain a part of the Catholic Church. When talking about his activism and advocacy in the church, he once said to me, "Baby, this is my church, too. I'm not going to let them mess it up!" I think of that conversation often. I'm strengthened, steeled, by it.

There have been many pillars of Catholicism in my life. Having lost these three in the last few years has made me reflect. I feel the weight of their loss tremendously. Perhaps I feel this weight so acutely because I also feel the weight of stepping into that role and becoming a pillar of Catholicism in my family as I get older. That is incredibly hard considering that I have spent so many years pulling back the curtain of Catholicism and researching, writing, teaching, and speaking about the systemic racism that makes the Roman Catholic Church an ultra-white space instead of a welcome, cosmopolitan canopy.

All of this has put me in constant danger of losing my religion. But it has also deepened my faith. Hearing the stories of those who generously shared their experiences with me showed me how deeply so many Black Catholics love their Catholic faith and love the church that has often treated them poorly. Their faith has enriched my own. As I've written previously,[34] I have faith that the Catholic Church can become its better self, even if it must get there without me. I know there are other Catholic scholars of Catholicism who focus on race, gender, or sexuality who feel the same way. At times, I have been sad, angry, frustrated, and joyful while writing this book. I have also laughed, cried, and wanted to throw my laptop against the wall in a fit of rage. It is fair to say that my emotions have run the gamut. I claim that I lost the capacity for hope as a graduate student. Perhaps I still have a small capacity for hope after all, especially after sitting with the histories and stories of African American Catholics whose faith never waivered, even in the face of parish and church closures. Without me saying anything of the sort, many have told me that they see that my critique of the Roman Catholic Church comes from a place of love and a place of hope that things can be better. I think that is true. I certainly want that to be true. In the end, that is for Jesus to decide—not me.

APPENDIX

Document 4.1. Archdiocese of Philadelphia Decree Transitioning St. Peter Claver Church to Profane but not Sordid Use, 2019

Archdiocese of Philadelphia
Office of the Archbishop
222 North 17th Street
Philadelphia, PA 19103-1299

DECREE
OF THE RELEGATION OF
SAINT PETER CLAVER CHURCH, PHILADELPHIA. PENNSYLVANIA
TO PROFANE BUT NOT SORDID USE

Saint Peter Claver Church, Philadelphia, Pennsylvania was formerly the parish church for Saint Peter Claver Parish and then subsequently the location of the Saint Peter Claver Center for Evangelization as well as the site of the Shrine of Our Lady of Victories. Saint Peter Calver Parish was canonically suppressed in 1985, and the Saint Peter Claver Center for Evangelization was closed on October 31, 2014. Saint Peter Claver Church is no longer needed by the Archdiocesan Office for Black Catholics or the Archdiocese of Philadelphia. Consideration, therefore, must be given as to whether sufficient grave causes exist for the relegation of Saint Peter Claver Church to profane but not sordid use.

The following grave causes suggest that Saint Peter Claver Church be so relegated and no longer be used for divine worship:

1) Saint Peter Claver Church is no longer needed by the Archdiocesan Office for Black Catholics. On October 31, 2014, the Saint Peter Claver Center for Evangelization was closed. Saint Peter Claver Church has not been used as a worship site since that date. Fewer than fifteen members of the Christian faithful had been attending the monthly Mass in the church building at the Center for Evangelization prior to its closure. The Center for Evangelization was itself underutilized prior to October 2014;

2) In response to demographic changes over time, ministry to Black Catholics has been taking place at other parishes throughout the Archdiocese. Since ministerial outreach to the black Catholic community has evolved in this way to meet demographic changes, the closure of Saint Peter Claver Church would not result in undue harm to ministerial outreach to Black Catholics;

3) Besides the church building of Saint Peter Claver Church, there is the former parish rectory building on the property that once was the Saint Peter Claver Center for Evangelization as well as the former parish school

building which is used by Catholic Social Services for the Women of Hope program. While the Women of Hope program is not terminating, it is being discontinued at this location. These buildings are no longer needed for ministry by the Archdiocese of Philadelphia.

4) The deed restrictions on part of the property have been adjusted by a civil court ruling to allow for its sale, provided that a certain amount of the proceeds be used to benefit the Black Catholic Apostolate of the Archdiocese of Philadelphia. The Petition initiating this action was filed with the Court of Common Pleas of Philadelphia Orphans Court Division on October 29, 2015, on behalf of the Archdiocese of Philadelphia. Certain unnamed advocates for preservation of the legacy of the Saint Peter Claver Parish Property objected to the sale of the property by the Archdiocese in a letter written to the judge but never filed an answer to the petition or filed an appearance in the action. The Court then appointed the Honorable Russell M. Nigro (retired PA Supreme Court Justice) to act as *Trustee Ad Litem* on behalf of a group of individuals from the general public who had objected to the sale. Notwithstanding these actions, on December 12, 2017, the Court rendered its decree allowing for the sale of the property free and clear of the recorded restrictions noting "no answers/responses in opposition to the said Petition having been filed of record, nor appearances been entered on behalf of any person(s) alleging an interest in this matter . . . " The Archdiocese of Philadelphia may well wish to sell the entire property in order to support further its ministry to Black Catholics;

5) The Archdiocesan Office for Black Catholics has striven to maintain Saint Peter Claver Church and the other buildings on the property in good repair. However, the costs of maintaining Saint Peter Claver Church have placed a significant strain upon the Archdiocesan Office for Black Catholics and are not conducive to the office's present or future financial stability. The Center for Evangelization formerly headquartered at Saint Peter Claver Church had been able to meet the financial needs for its outreach programs through a grant from the Black and Indian Missions. However, it could not financially meet the costs of the deferred maintenance on the buildings. Further, funds for the needed maintenance cannot be supplied by the Archdiocesan Secretariat for Evangelization, which oversees the Office for Black Catholics, since such an outlay would jeopardize the stability of all ministerial outreach programs entrusted to its pastoral care. The Archdiocese of Philadelphia itself is in the process of stabilizing its own finances, and so cannot bear the additional costs associated with repair to Saint Peter Claver Church.

It should be noted that the Saint Peter Claver Church building does have significant historical value, as it is one of the "mother churches" for Black Philadelphians.

The church building has been historically designated since April 5, 1984, and its façade cannot be altered without the approval of the city historical commission.

Nevertheless, because of the financial strain that would be placed upon not only the Archdiocesan Office for Black Catholics but also other Archdiocesan entities if the required repairs were to be completed at Saint Peter Claver Church and adjacent buildings, in virtue of the prescripts of canon 1212 and canon 1222 §2 of the Code of Canon Law, having judged that sufficient grave causes are present and that the good of souls will not thereby be impaired, and having consulted the Council of Priests on September 17, 2018, I hereby **DECREE** that Saint Peter Claver Church, Philadelphia, Pennsylvania, be relegated to profane but not sordid use.

This Decree is effective as of April 8, 2019, and is to be communicated to the faithful of the Archdiocese in an appropriate manner. Canonical recourse to this Decree is to be sought according to the norms of canon law. All things to the contrary notwithstanding.

Given at the Curia of the Archdiocese of Philadelphia, on the 1st day of March 2019.

[signed]
Most Reverend Charles J. Chaput, O.F.M. Cap.
Archbishop of Philadelphia

SEAL

[signed]
Reverend Sean P. Bransfield
Vice-Chancellor

Document 4.2. Archdiocese of Philadelphia Withdrawal of Decree Regarding St. Peter Claver Church, 2019

Archdiocese of Philadelphia
Office of the Archbishop
222 North 17th Street
Philadelphia, PA 19103-1299

DECREE
WITHDRAWING MARCH 1, 2019 DECREE CONCERNING SAINT PETER CLAVER CHURCH PHILADELPHIA, PENNSYLVANIA

On March 1, 2019, I issue a decree relegating Saint Peter Claver Church, Philadelphia, Pennsylvania to profane but not sordid use effective April 8, 2019. To allow me more time to consider concerns raised relative to the relegation, I issue another decree on April 6, 2019, delaying the date of implication to June 1, 2019.

The causes for relegation listed in my March 1, 2019 decree remain valid. However, in light of the importance of the church, I have determined that additional efforts need to be made to ascertain if it is in fact possible to preserve Saint Peter Claver Church as a place of Divine Worship. Therefore, I hereby withdraw my decree of March 1, 2019, relegating Saint Peter Claver Church to Profane but not sordid use.

Given at the Curia of the Archdiocese of Philadelphia on this 21st day of May 2019.

[signed]
Most Revered Charles J. Chaput, O.F.M. Cap.
Archbishop of Philadelphia

SEAL

[signed]
Reverend Monsignor Gerard C. Mesure
Chancellor

Document 4.3. Sites and Boundaries Report

ARCHDIOCESE OF PHILADELPHIA
COMMISSION FOR PARISH SITES AND BOUNDARIES
222 NORTH SEVENTEENTH STREET • PHILADELPHIA, PENNSYLVANIA 19103 • (215) 587-3566

April 2, 1984

Study of St. Peter Claver Parish according to the directive of His Excellency Bishop Lohmuller on February 3, 1984.

St. Peter Claver
12th and Lombard Streets
Philadelphia, PA. 19147
Founded in 1889
Type of Parish - Negro-Ethnic

Boundaries: South of Market St. to Navy Yard and from Delaware River to Schuylkill River.

Neighboring Parishes: clockwise –

St. John Evangelist   St. Paul
Holy Trinity   St. Mary Magdalen
Old St. Mary   St. Rita
St. Joseph, Willings Alley   St. Charles Borromeo
                               St. Patrick

Number of Families served:

Highest - 1981   184
Lowest - 1970   134
1982   176
Present - 1983   206

Priests: Reverend John McAndrew, Pastor
            Reverend William J. Maguire, Assistant
            Reverend John J. McHugh, Resident

Date of on-site visit: February 17, 1984 - Monsignor Cantrella and Father Cahill

References: Diocesan Map - Page 37
             Catholic Directory - Page 187

BUILDINGS:

Church: Founded as a Presbyterian Church in 1842. Site is historically certified and is subject to provisions of Section 14-2008 of the Philadelphia Code which prohibits the demolishing or altering of the buildings without special permit.

-2-

Capacity of Church is 600 with balcony. The condition is fairly good. A complete report of the buildings by Knowlan, Thoppe and Co. is enclosed. The heating in the church needs work, the skylight is leaking. There are no major repairs with the steam heat and oil furnace.

The Shrine is a section of the church.

Rectory: Room for 8 - four-story house
The condition is good but could use painting and general fix-up. Heating is at times a problem. The pipes need replacement.

School: 1906 - capacity - 240 to 250. 8 Classrooms.
Structure is beautiful (great auditorium) Doors need caulking. There is an asbestos problem. Roof needs replacement; needs burglar alarm; fire tower unsafe; needs insulation; windows need to be replaced.

Hall: Capacity - 160. need refurbishing, and painting.
Structurally it is sound.

COMPOSITION OF PARISH:
Priests: listed above
Sisters: none
Lay Teachers: 6 including principal (only have had a lay faculty for the past two years)
Lay Help: Sexton - 1
Housekeeper - 1
Cook - 1
Janitor - 1
Others - 2 part-time receptionists.

PARISHIONERS:
Year 1982 - 176 - souls 260
1983 - 206 - souls 374
Ethnic background - Negro
Whites are coming into the parish. 50% of the registrations in the last several years were white.
Neighborhood percentage - Catholic 70%
Black 40%

-3-

CHILDREN:	Number of pre-school - unknown
	Attending parochial grade school - 17 catholic
	Attending Catholic High School - 10
	Attending Public High School - ?
	Attending Public grade school - ?
	Attending Parish C.C.D. - none
	Attending other Parish grade schools – none

PARISH SCHOOL:

Parish children	17
Non-Catholics	<u>75</u>
Total	92

Projected for 1984-85   70 children

Tuition - $475.00 - parishioners
         $550.00 - non-parishioners
70% pay tuition.

FINANCIAL STATUS:

INCOME:	1965	1970	LATEST
Church collections	13,180.00	41,729.00	33,137.00
Socials	3,844.00		16,642.00
Diocesan	1,608.00	1,154.00	4,299.00
	9,000.00	4,000.00	121,481.00
TOTAL INCOME:	26,632.00	49,281.00	175,559.00
EXPENSES	26,386.00	49,281.00	182,957.00

PARISH FINANCIALLY VIABLE -

not viable, if the school were closed the Parish would be viable. The Parish is not in debt. There is a subsidy from the Holy Ghost Priests, also of $5,000 per month from February to June only from 2/84 to 6/84. from the Archdiocese.

-4-

PASTOR'S EVALUATION:
    Financially - week day Masses - 12 in attendance.
        Sunday Masses - 175 to 200 in attendance.
        Weekly collection - $500.00
        Shrine keeps the Parish going.
        The enrollment in Shrine and Masses keeps the place going.
        Parish could be viable without the school.

EFFECT OF CLOSING ON:
    A. Older parishioners (half)   - Traumatic (Cardinal Krol and Msgr. Nace)
    B. Younger families (half)   - They would feel it.
    C. School children   - None - 80% non-Catholic

First Parish in Philadelphia for Blacks.

-5-

SITES AND BOUNDARIES RECOMMENDATION:

Although the Commission is aware that the neighboring parishes could absorb St. Peter Claver Parish, nonetheless, the Commission recommends that the Parish should remain as it is especially now that the school has been closed for the following reasons:

1. The Parish would be financially viable now that the school has been closed.

2. St. Peter Claver Parish is within the urban renewal boundaries of Washington Square West which is basically an effort of residential rehabilitation. Furthermore, there are still a number of scattered parcels of ground throughout this project area so the Parish should remain here until these projects are completed.

3. The historical background, in fact the site is historically certified, <u>has a real symbolic significance to the black Catholics of Philadelphia.</u> This factor is considered especially important during these times when the Church is making a concentrated effort toward evangelization of the black community.

-6-

4. There is a possible chance that the blacks might defect feeling that they have been abandoned.

5. Many years ago, the question of Title of St. Peter Claver was subject to a review of legal staff who in turn discussed its findings with the Archdiocese. The Commission does not know whether this question has been resolved or not. Also, in the deciding of the future of St. Peter Claver Parish this fact should be resolved to avoid unpleasant complications.

[signed William A. D[?]lin, Chairman]

Document 4.4. Suppression Letter from Cardinal John Krol to St. Peter Claver

---

Archdiocese of Philadelphia
[???] N. [??]th Street
Philadelphia, Pa 19103 ISC29A-46

Office of the Cardinal

May 26, 1985

To the faithful of Saint Peter Claver Church.

Dearly beloved in Christ:

The spiritual needs of all the faithful of the Archdiocese for whom I am responsible must be a continual concern to me. Where there is life there will be growth, along with decline. As there are occasions for establishing new parishes, so, also, regretfully, there are occasions of the demise of parishes. This process has become a fact of life in the Archdiocese.

The in-migration or population shifts in our large urban areas continue to be a factor in our Archdiocese. We continue to witness the decline of parishes which not too long ago served many people. The small number of families in these declining parishes find it impossible to maintain their parochial facilities. Impossible burdens cannot be placed upon those few families who remain in a parish.

Vatican Council II, which called for adaptation in the changing needs and circumstances of time and place, called specific attention to the needs for changes in parishes:

> "This same concern for souls should be the basis for determining or re-considering the creation or suppression of parishes and any other changes of this kind which the bishop will be able to bring about on his own authority."

(Decree on the Bishop's Pastoral Office, n. 32.)

To insure, within the limits of our personnel and fiscal resources, the highest level of parochial service, our Commission for Parish Sites and Boundaries is continually conducting studies of the changing needs of the faithful in different areas of the Archdiocese. This Commission gathers data which determines the need for new parishes. It also gathers valuable information which indicates the advisability of consolidating, merging or discontinuing some existing parochial facilities.

-2-

According to information obtained from a lengthy series of studies relative to Saint Peter Claver parish, the advisability of changing the canonical status of Saint Peter Claver parish is very much in evidence.

Saint Peter Claver parish was founded on July 29, 1889 as a national parish to serve the needs of Black Catholics in the City of Philadelphia. When the parish was founded the number of Black Catholics in the City of Philadelphia was small and concentrated in the geographic area surrounding the parish. Throughout its existence the parish fulfilled its special mission to the Black Catholic community through the devoted pastoral work of the Holy Ghost Fathers. In more recent times, the Archdiocese of Philadelphia has experienced a growth in the number of Black Catholics whose spiritual needs are being addressed by many territorial parishes throughout this entire city. The phenomenon of gentrification has caused a significant racial change in the very neighborhood where the parish of Saint Peter Claver is located. Due to these facts, it is evident that the reason for the founding and existence of Saint Peter Claver parish no longer exists.

In 1974, Saint Peter Claver parish comprised 680 people in 170 family units. In 1984, Saint Peter Claver parish served 300 people in 50 family units. The parish community could not sustain a parish school thus forcing the closing of Saint Peter Claver school in June of 1984.

After prayerful consideration of the intensive and extensive studies which have been made, I announce the suppression of Saint Peter Claver parish. This decision has been made in consultation with the Archdiocesan Commission for Parish Sites and Boundaries, the Provincial and Council of the Congregation of the Holy Ghost, the Office of Urban Ministry and the Council of Priests. This decision is made in light of the facts which indicate that the existence of a national parish to minister to Black Catholics of the entire City of Philadelphia is no longer demanded or justified.

In making this decision there is no lack of concern for the needs of the Black Catholic community. The expansion and dispersion of Black Catholics in Philadelphia has led to the reality that many territorial, non-national parishes minister to the pastoral needs of this portion of the People of God. This decision does not reflect any lack of pastoral solicitude for the members of Saint Peter Claver parish since their needs can be met by the proper territorial parish where they reside. Our decision is based on the sacred responsibility entrusted to us as Archbishop of Philadelphia to tend to the cares of the entire flock of the Archdiocese of Philadelphia with equity and justice.

Please be advised that Saint Peter Claver parish will cease to function as a parish as of June 30, 1985.

-3-

The Congregation of the Holy Ghost has requested permission to continue the functions of the Shrine of Our Lady of Victories which is located at Saint Peter Claver Church. This permission has been granted in recognition of the devoted service given to the people of Saint Peter Claver parish by the Holy Ghost Fathers. We are pleased that the Holy Ghost Fathers will continue to maintain their religious presence in the Archdiocese of Philadelphia at the Shrine of Our Lady of Victories.

In order to commemorate the historical importance of the parish, the name of the present site will be the Shrine of Our Lady or Victories at Saint Peter Claver Church.

The present parishioners of Saint Peter Claver parish will become members of the territorial parish where they reside effective June 30, 1985. The Reverend John P. McAndrew, C.S.Sp., pastor, Saint Peter Claver Church, will assist the present parishioners in identifying their territorial parish and effecting an orderly transition.

The sacramental records of Saint Peter Claver parish will be kept at Saint John the Evangelist Church.

I am confident that you will be welcomed by your new parishes. I know that through the sincere efforts and prayers of all the faithful this decision will be successful and redound to your spiritual benefit and the glory of God and His Church.

To our faithful parishioners of Saint Peter Claver parish, we pledge our continued concern for their spiritual welfare and our vigorous efforts to provide adequately for their pastoral needs.

Invoking God's blessings upon you, I am

Devotedly in Christ,
[signed] John Cardinal Krol
Archbishop of Philadelphia

Document 4.5. Letter to Bishop Edward Hughes

[line of blacked out text]
[line of blacked out text]
January 9, 1986

Bishop Edward Hughes
[line of blacked out text]
[line of blacked out text]

Dear Bishop Hughes:
As a member of the hierarchy of the Roman Catholic Church in the Archdiocese of Philadelphia, I am writing to you to make you aware of certain shameful occurrences:

St. Peter Claver was "officially suppressed" as a parish in the summer of 1985. This was done against the recommendation of William A. Doolin in his Study of St. Peter Claver Parish according to the directive of His Excellency Bishop Lohmuller on February 3, 1984. St. Peter Claver Church, however, has remained opened with daily Mass and two Sunday Masses.

For many people, St. Peter Claver is their church of choice. Many maintain allegiance to St. Peter Claver because they were not -- and still are not, as witnessed by the racial incidents in southwest Philadelphia recently -- welcomed in many Catholic communities in this area. Because many elderly people are not comfortable in other churches, they have continued to give allegiance to St. Peter Claver Church.

Mrs. Ellis was a woman who was a good and faithful Catholic all her life. She was also an elderly member of St. Peter Claver. Mrs. Ellis became seriously ill and was hospitalized. She asked her son, John, to ask one of the priests from St. Peter Claver to bring her the sacraments. Both priests from St. Peter Claver refused to visit Mrs. Ellis and bring her the sacraments. Mrs. Ellis condition worsened, and as she lay near her death, her son begged these same priests to give his mother the last rites of the church. Again, they refused to be bothered. Mrs. Ellis died. Since St. Peter Claver was the only church Mrs. Ellis had attended, her family requested to have her buried from St. Peter Claver. Father Maguire and Father Neiderberger refused to comply with this request, as well. The relatives, who are of the Baptist religion, then contacted their minister and explained the situation to him. He immediately extended his sympathies to the family and not only offered the use of his Baptist church, but his personal services to the Ellis family.

Allen Stevens, President of the St. Peter Claver Coalition (an organization of former parishioners), heard about the situation. He immediately got in touch with Father Benz and explained the situation. Father Benz contacted the Ellis family and offered the use of Most Precious Blood Church, but by this time, Mr. Ellis was completely devastated. He felt that since the Catholic Church has shown such a lack of compassion, such insensitivity towards him and his family, and a complete lack of respect for his mother, he is renouncing the Catholic religion. He vows to never again set foot in a Catholic church. Needless to say, his relatives and the Baptist minister were quite shocked by the way Mrs. Ellis was treated by everyone except Father Benz. They were not at all impressed with Fathers Maguire and Neiderberger.

Father Benz tried to convince the family that all Catholic priests are not as cold-blooded, rude and insensitive as the two they had been dealing with. The Ellis family is not convinced; however they did agree -- only because they felt Mrs. Ellis would have wanted it -- to allow Father Benz to co-host the funeral services that were held for Mrs. Ellis at a funeral parlor.

A short time after Mrs. Ellis died, Mrs. Rowe became ill. She, too, was an elderly Black lady who was a life-long member of St. Peter Claver. Her family, too, contacted the priests and received the same shameful mistreatment that the Ellis family had experienced. Again, Allen Stevens heard about the situation and was able to find a priest who would help. This time, it was Father McGeown, from St. Frances, who was able to give Mrs. Rowe the sacraments before she died. Mrs. Rowe was buried from a funeral parlor without a Catholic service.

In these two instances, Allen Stevens found out what was occurring and was able to intervene. What happens to those families and situations that he doesn't know about???

I realize the real estate where St. Peter Claver is located is extremely valuable since the gentrification of the area. Blacks are being forced to give up traditional neighborhoods. The priests presently residing at St. Peter Claver are attempting to force Blacks to abandon St. Peter Claver, Our Mother Church, by mistreating our sick and refusing to bury our elderly. It seems that any action, no matter how cruel, insensitive or rude, that will encourage Blacks to leave that church is being pursued by Father Maguire and Father Neiderberger.

I am bringing this to your attention because I hope you will do something about the situation. I have called the Archdiocese but Father Walker and Monsignor Shumaker will not talk to me on the phone and are non-responsive to my letters.

I am personally tired of the general lack of respect I feel the Catholic Church gives its black members. I am encouraging the next family that finds itself in a situation similar to the one described above, to agree to hold the service in the middle of the street, coffin, body, flowers, mourners and all. Block traffic and call attention to the situation. I will then show all the letters that Black people have written that were ignored and tell why this protest is being staged.

A Very Disgusted Catholic,
[signed] Mrs. Adrienne Harris

Document 4.6. Letter to Bishop Eugene Marino

CERTIFIED MAIL – RETURN RECEIPT REQUESTED

ST. PETER CLAVER'S COALITION
[line of blacked out text]
[line of blacked out text]
[line of blacked out text]

April 29, 1986

Bishop Eugene A. Marino
[line of blacked out text]
[line of blacked out text]
[line of blacked out text]

Dear Bishop Marino:

Last Saturday, April 26, 1986, a delegation from St. Peter Claver, Mother Church of Black Catholics, Philadelphia, PA, had the pleasure of attending the Black Catholic Women's Conference in Washington. In fact, several members accepted the hospitality extended by the Josephites, for which we all thank you.

At the conclusion of the conference and prior to Mass, you spoke to us. I listened with great interest and truly share your concerns about what is happening in the Black community. You stated you could not overstate the danger, the peril, the nature of the threat and determination of the enemy. I truly agree that the Black community is under a threat that is more subtle, more destructive and more nefarious than others because this threat is not recognized for what it is and it strikes at the heart and saps the spiritual energies. You asked us to have the courage to be leaders and you said you would give us support and encouragement. We at St. Peter Claver now call on you to be true to your words.

Our church opened in 1892 but our People of St. Peter Claver banded together to worship in 1886 and functioned as a parish community until June of 1985, when Cardinal Krol "officially suppressed" all parish activity. See Attachment 1.

We, the people of St. Peter Claver did not agree with the suppression and were never consulted in the making of this decision. When we requested a copy of the Sites and Boundaries Report, which Cardinal Krol referenced as a basis for his decision to suppress the parish, the Archdiocese refused. God, however, supplied us with a copy of this report, and then we knew why the Cardinal would not, because this document clearly recommends that St. Peter Claver should continue to function as a parish. See Attachment 2.

There is a deep-seated and pernicious pattern of racism within the Archdiocese of Philadelphia. This, along with gentrification has played a major role in Cardinal Krol's closing or suppression of black parish after black parish. This is evidenced by Attachment 3, a letter to Cardinal Krol from Peter Liacouras, President of Temple University, on behalf of Our Lady of Mercy Church, which was also suppressed.

Cardinal Krol's attitude toward the Black Catholics not only of St. Peter Claver, but the entire Archdiocese of Philadelphia, has been one of arrogance and insensitivity. Please read the letters to him from Edith Stevens, Deacon Singleton and myself (Attachments 4, 5 and 6).

We have been and continue to be faithful Catholics. We are seeking justice from Our Church. After investigating the due process procedure in Philadelphia, I find there is none, that although it was recommended that this process should be established -- and that recommendation was made 22 years ago -- Cardinal Krol is still looking into the matter and nothing else exists. I therefore am seeking due process and justice still.

I have written the National Conference of Catholic Bishops and was responded to by Rev. Msgr Daniel F. Hoye. I am attaching copies of that correspondence, for your information.

Bishop Marino, please advise us which channels and which persons to contact in order to obtain a fair hearing, due process within the Catholic Church. We need to hear from you. Prayers are not enough; we need prayers, strategy and action coupled with solid advice from someone such as yourself who has expertise.

If you need more information, please contact me or

Allen and Edith Stevens	Rev. Mr. Albert Singleton
[line of blacked out text]	[line of blacked out text]
[line of blacked out text]	[line of blacked out text]
[line of blacked out text]	[line of blacked out text]

I pray to God that you were not just talking from that alter on Saturday, but mean what you said. I shall await your reply.

A Concerned Black Catholic,

ADRIENNE HARRIS
[line of blacked out text]
[line of blacked out text]
[line of blacked out text]

Encl:
1. Ltr, dtd May 26, 1985 from Cardinal Krol to Faithful
2. Parish Sites and Boundaries Report
3. Ltr, May 9, 1984, from Peter Liacouras to Cardinal Krol
4. Ltr, June 2, 1985, from Rev. Mr. Singleton to Cardinal Krol
5. Ltr, June 27, 1985, from Edith Stevens to Cardinal Krol
6. Ltr, Jan 9, 1986, from Adrienne Harris to Cardinal Krol
7. Ltr, March 15, 1986, from Adrienne Harris to Natl Conf of Cath Bish
8. Ltr, March 24, 1986, from Rev. Msgr Daniel F. Hoye to A. Harris
9. Ltr, March 31, 1986, from Adrienne Harris to Rev. Msgr Hoye
10. Ltr, April 7, 1986, from Rev Msgr Hoye to Adrienne Harris

Document 4.7. Letter from Msgr. Leonard Scott

Re: Fwd: Archdiocese of Philadelphia vs Descendants of St. Peter Claver Parish
Page 1 of 3

From:	Leonard Scott [text blacked out]
To:	Adrienne Harris [text blacked out]
Subject:	Re: Fwd: Archdiocese of Philadelphia vs Descendants of St. Peter Claver Parish
Date:	Wed, Aug 9, 2017 10:19 am
Attachments:	20170404 - Letter to Floretta Caudle re St. Peter Claver Parishioners.doc (40K)

Dear Adrienne,

Thank you for your email of August 3, 2017 and the attachments. As I mentioned to you, Floretta Caudle wrote me regarding this matter on March 29, 2017 and sent me some documents. I am attaching my response of April 4, 2017 to her.

Canonically speaking, the most important attachment you sent was the May 26, 1985 letter of Cardinal John Krol, by which the suppression of Saint Peter Claver Parish was announced. Canon Law (Canons 1734 & 1737) requires that whoever felt aggrieved by that decision had to petition the Archbishop within ten working days to change the decision. Only then - within fifteen days of the Archbishop's response - could the aggrieved person make a recourse to Rome to change the effects of that decision. That opportunity has now been gone for more than 32 years.

This pivotal document of the suppression of Saint Peter Claver Parish has serious effects. Since there is no longer a parish, one cannot speak of parishioners. Those interested and concerned persons can form a group but that group does not have the rights or duties of parishioners. Furthermore, usually when a parish is suppressed, the diocese or archdiocese of that parish takes on the responsibilities of the liabilities and assets. Those responsibilities include the issues arising from deeds pertaining to property of the suppressed parish. Deeds are governed by civil law and not by canon law.

In order that you and your group might have a voice in the civil proceedings regarding the deed for the property of Saint Peter Claver Church, Judge Matthe Carrafiello appointed former PA Supreme Court Russel Nigro as the Trustee *ad litem* to represent the interest of otherwise unrepresented individuals. Judge Nigro

Re: Fwd: Archdiocese of Philadelphia vs Descendants of St. Peter Claver Parish
Page 2 of 3

has met and communicated with representatives of your group. He has tried to work out some agreement between your group and the Archdiocese of Philadelphia. In his email to Dr. Renee Robinson on February 9, 2017 he writes: "My concerns for your group is that if a compromise is not reached, this will become a very costly litigation for your group and it will be an uphill battle to convince the courts that you have standing at this late time to challenge the Archdiocese's agenda."

I think that any canon lawyer would tell you what I have stated regarding the suppression of St. Peter Claver Parish and the effects of that suppression. I think that the advice of Judge Nigro is based on his expertise and experience in civil law. I do not think that it would be helpful to give false hope. I continue to hope that you and your group can come to some agreement with the Archdiocese that will protect the legacy of Black Catholics in the Archdiocese of Philadelphia.

Msgr. Scott

From: Adrienne Harris
Sent: Thursday, August 03, 2017 5:07 PM
To: [text blacked out]
Subject: Fwd: Archdiocese of Philadelphia vs Descendants of St. Peter Claver Parish

Monsignor Scott,
    Thank you for taking the time to listen to my feelings about St. Peter Claver, Mother Church of Black Catholics in Philadelphia.
The attachments below provide detailed information that proves the unfair way this church has been treated.
The last attachment is Archbishop
Pierre's response to my letter with attachments to him and this letter is what prompted me to reach out to you. Per your suggestion, I will
also reach out to the Canon Law Society of America. If you happen to locate a canon lawyer who is interested in this righteous cause, please
provide my contact information to that good person. Thank you for your consideration.

Peace and Blessings!
Adrienne Harris
[text blacked out]
[text blacked out]
[text blacked out]

https://mail.aol.com/webmail-std/en-us/PrintMessage 8/9/2017

Document 4.8. Archdiocese of Philadelphia Decree Transitioning St. Peter Claver Church to Profane but Not Sordid Use, 2022

ARCHDIOCESE OF PHILADELPHIA
222 North Seventeenth Street • Philadelphia, Pennsylvania 19103-1299
Telephone (215) 587-0506 • Fax (215) 587-4545

OFFICE of the ARCHBISHOP

DECREE
OF THE RELEGATION OF
SAINT PETER CLAVER CHURCH, PHILADELPHIA, PENNSYLVANIA
TO PROFANE BUT NOT SORDID USE

Saint Peter Claver Church, Philadelphia, Pennsylvania was formerly the parish church for Saint Peter Claver Parish and then subsequently the location of the Saint Peter Claver Center for Evangelization as well as the site of the Shrine of Our Lady of Victories. Saint Peter Claver Parish was canonically suppressed in 1985, and the Saint Peter Claver Center for Evangelization was closed on October 31, 2014. The Archdiocesan Office for Black Catholics and the Archdiocese of Philadelphia no longer require the use of Saint Peter Claver Church, as the pastoral activities previously based at the Saint Peter Claver Center for Evangelization have since moved to parishes throughout the Archdiocese. Consideration, therefore, must be given as to whether sufficient grave causes exist for the relegation of Saint Peter Claver Church to profane but not sordid use.

The following grave causes suggest that Saint Peter Claver Church be so relegated and no longer used for divine worship:

1) On October 31, 2014, the Saint Peter Claver Center for Evangelization was closed. Prior to the Center for Evangelization's closure, fewer than fifteen members of the Christian faithful had been attending the monthly Mass being held at Saint Peter Claver Church, while the Center for Evangelization was itself underutilized prior to October 2014. Saint Peter Claver Church therefore has not been used for worship since that date, and no situation has arisen during the intervening period that would have required the use of this church;

2) In response to demographic changes over time, ministry to Black Catholics has been taking place at other parishes throughout the Archdiocese. Since ministerial outreach to the Black Catholic community has evolved in this way over time, the closure of Saint Peter Claver Church would not result in undue harm to ministerial outreach to Black Catholics;

3) In addition to the Saint Peter Claver church building, the property contains the former parish rectory building that once was the Saint Peter Claver Center for Evangelization as well as the former parish school building which continues to be used by Catholic Social Services for the "Women of Hope" program. While the Women of Hope program is not terminating, it will be discontinued at this location in the future and moved to another location. These buildings are therefore no longer needed for ministry by the Archdiocese of Philadelphia;

4) Saint Peter Claver Church was previously relegated to profane but not sordid use in a Decree promulgated in March 2019. While that Decree was ultimately revoked by a subsequent Decree issued in May 2019, the reasons that prompted the initial Decree of Relegation not only remain valid, but also have become more pronounced since that time;

5) Deed restrictions on a portion of the property have been removed and stricken by a civil court ruling to allow for the sale of the Saint Peter Claver property, provided that one-third of the proceeds be restricted for the purpose of evangelization to Black Catholics in the Archdiocese of Philadelphia. The Petition initiating this action was filed with the Court of Common Pleas of Philadelphia County, Orphans Court Division on October 29, 2015 on behalf of the Archdiocese of Philadelphia. Certain unnamed advocates for the preservation of the legacy of the Saint Peter Claver Parish property objected to the sale of the property by the Archdiocese in a letter written to the presiding judge, but no answer to the petition or entry of appearance on behalf of these individuals were filed in the action. The Court then appointed the Honorable Russell M. Nigro (retired Pennsylvania Supreme Court Justice) to act as *Trustee at litem* to represent the unidentified individuals from the general public who had objected to the sale. On December 12, 2017 the Court rendered its decree allowing for the sale of the property free and clear of the recorded deed restrictions, noting "no answers/responses in opposition to the said Petition having been filed of record, nor appearance been entered on behalf of any person(s) alleging an interest in this matter…" The Archdiocese of Philadelphia may well wish to sell the entire property on which Saint Peter Claver Church is located. If this were to happen, one-third of the proceeds of any such sale must be restricted for uses that serve as near as possible to the original transferor's charitable intent of benefitting Black Catholics within the Archdiocese of Philadelphia. The Archdiocese intends to propose to the Court that the funds be allocated to evangelization and ministry of the Office for Black Catholics of the Archdiocese of Philadelphia, and the same above-referenced Court must first approve the Archdiocese's proposal of how this one-third of the sale proceeds would be allocated;

6) Saint Peter Claver Church and the former Saint Peter Claver Rectory, which is attached to the church, are in need of significant repair, and the costs of performing these repairs would prove burdensome and detract from resources that could otherwise be applied to pastoral car. An assessment of needed repairs was undertaken by the Archdiocese in August 2022. This process noted that both the interior and exterior of the church and rectory are in poor condition. This assessment estimated that the costs of repairing the buildings so as to render them functional would be upwards of $1,350,000. In addition, since 2010, the Archdiocese has spent over $500,000 to cover necessary ongoing maintenance expenses for the two buildings. These costs have proven significant to the Archdiocese, and the costs of undertaking the repairs needed for the church and rectory, which have been needed for some time now, would impede the Archdiocese from allocating its resources in ways that can more directly impact its current ministries and evangelization efforts. Furthermore, as already noted, with the Court's approval, any future potential sale of the Saint Peter Claver property would directly benefit the Archdiocese of Philadelphia's outreach efforts toward Black Catholics throughout the Archdiocese of Philadelphia.

It should be noted that the Saint Peter Claver Church building does have significant historical value, as it is considered the "mother church for Black Catholics of the Archdiocese of Philadelphia." In fact, it was one of four churches designated for Black Catholics to worship at one time. As an act of pastoral care by the Archbishop of Philadelphia for Black Catholics and addressing the sin of racism, all parishes in the Archdiocese welcome Black people. Furthermore, all of the significant sacred items that were once in Saint Peter Claver Church have been distributed to churches within the Black Apostolate.

The church building has been historically designated since April 5, 1984, and its exterior cannot be altered without the approval of the city historical commission. The historical marker will remain in place as a testimony to the history of the building as many markers are displayed within the City of Philadelphia.

The financial strain that would be placed upon the Archdiocese of Philadelphia if the required upkeep was to be continued and future repairs were to be completed at Saint Peter Claver Church and its adjacent buildings, combined with the loss of potential income that would greatly benefit the Archdiocese's outreach and ministerial efforts towards Black Catholics, render it best to relegate Saint Peter Claver Church to profane but not sordid use. Therefore, in virtue of the prescripts of canon 1212 and canon 1222 §2 of the Code of Canon Law, having judged that sufficient grave causes are present and that the good of souls will not thereby be impaired, and having consulted with the Council of Priests on September 8, 2022, I hereby **DECREE** that Saint Peter Claver Church, Philadelphia, Pennsylvania, be relegated to profane but not sordid use.

This Decree is effective as of January 23, 2023 and is to be communicated to the faithful of the Archdiocese in an appropriate manner. Canonical recourse to this Decree is to be sought according to the norms of canon law. All things to the contrary notwithstanding.

Given at the Curia of the Archdiocese of Philadelphia, on the 9th day of December, in the Year of Our Lord 2022.

[signed]
Most Reverend Nelson J. Pérez, D.D.
Archbishop of Philadelphia

SEAL

[signed]
Reverend Sean P. Bransfield
Chancellor

Document 4.9. Petition for Hierarchical Recourse

Adrienne Harris
[text blacked out]
[text blacked out]
[text blacked out]
March 13, 2019

Petition for Canonical Recourse against the Relegation to Profane but not Sordid Use of St. Peter Claver Church, Philadelphia

Dear Archbishop Chaput,

    In accordance with the provisions of Canon 1734, Section 2, I and the others who have signed this appeal are writing to inform you that we are bringing this petition for canonical recourse against the decree you issued against the Church of St. Peter Claver in Philadelphia on March 1, 2019, relegating the church to profane but not sordid use. Those bringing this petition for canonical recourse have a connection to St. Peter Claver Church, being former parishioners of the church, thus having standing to do so. We bring this petition for canonical recourse within the window of 10 useful days for doing so which exists, with useful time being computed in accordance with the provisions of Canon 201, Section 2. Canon 201, Section 2 makes clear that useful time consists of the time an individual has to take an action and states "§2. Useful time is understood as that which a person has to exercise or to pursue a right, so that it does not run for a person who is unaware or unable to act." Those bringing this petition for canonical recourse state that given the fact that notice of this decree was given in a March 4 article printed in Catholic Philly, this petition for canonical recourse is filed within the window of 10 useful days for doing so which began to run with the publication of this article. Even if it is claimed that the publication of this decree was made prior to March 4, 2019, this petition for canonical recourse has still been filed in a timely manner, in accordance with the provisions of Canon 201, Section 2, and Canon 203, section 1. Two of the days which have run since March 1, 2019, have been Sundays, days on which the offices of the Archdiocese of Philadelphia were closed, preventing delivery of this petition for canonical recourse in person, and also days on which the United States Mail did not run, preventing its transmission through that means. Furthermore, Canon 203, Section 1, states with regard to the computation of time "Can. 203 §1. The initial day (*a quo*) is not computed in the total unless its beginning coincides with the beginning of the day or the law expressly provides otherwise." Thus, given that the decree which was issued to relegate St. Peter Claver Church to profane but not sordid use did not originate at the beginning of March 1, and that neither the decree nor the law nor regulations concerned with the filing of petitions for canonical recourse state that the day on which a decree relegating a church to profane but not sordid use is issued is to be counted as a useful day with regard to the counting of days during which petitions for canonical recourse can be filed against it, this petition for canonical recourse is still filed in a timely manner.

Those bringing this petition for canonical recourse note Archbishop Chaput that you made clear in your decree that St. Peter Claver Church is a "mother church" of the Black community within the city of Philadelphia. Those bringing this petition for canonical recourse would note that it is the "mother church" for Black Catholics both within the city of Philadelphia and the Archdiocese of Philadelphia as a whole. St. Peter Claver was acquired and dedicated in 1892, in order that Black Catholics within the Archdiocese of Philadelphia could finally have a church in which they were welcome and able to practice their Catholic faith without being subjected to racism. It is a documented fact that prior to the acquisition of St. Peter Claver Church, Black Catholics in the Archdiocese of Philadelphia were forced to endure segregated masses, and to receive the sacraments after white congregants. They were not treated as brothers and sisters in Christ, but as second class Catholics. It was within the walls of St. Peter Claver Church, from the time of its dedication in 1892, that Black Catholics were able to have a sacred space in which they were able to freely worship God, and to practice their faith without prejudice. Many financial contributions from Black Catholics made the acquisition of St. Peter Claver Church possible; were it not for the willingness of our ancestors to sacrifice what little they had in order that they might finally be able to bring into being a Roman Catholic sacred space in which they would be welcome, St. Peter Claver Church would not today exist.

Those bringing this petition for canonical recourse state clearly and categorically that we are bringing this petition solely to contest the relegation of St. Peter Claver Church to profane but not sordid use, and act your Excellency has sought to bring about through the issuance of your decree of March 1, 2019. We thus note that this petition for canonical recourse does not address any of the previously contested issues surrounding the elimination of St. Peter Claver "Parish." It is however useful to touch upon one consequence of the elimination of St. Peter Claver Parish which is especially important with regard to the question of the relegation of St. Peter Claver Church to profane but not sordid use, the fact that at no time from the elimination of St. Peter Claver Parish through to the present day has it been the case that those Catholics, especially Black Catholics, who believe that St. Peter Claver Church must remain a Roman Catholic sacred space have been able to work with the archdiocese in accordance with canon law and Vatican jurisprudence to ensure that the future of St. Peter Claver Church as a Roman catholic sacred space could be secured. While it is true that the church and other buildings of the former St. Peter Claver parish campus have been put to various Catholic uses, no plan has been made which would allow for the future of St. Peter Claver Church to be secured in perpetuity as a Roman Catholic sacred space. Even during the pendency of civil proceedings surrounding the future of the property of the former St. Peter Claver Parish, no invitation was made for any Catholics who wished to maintain St. Peter Claver Church at their own expense as a Roman Catholic sacred space, in accordance with the provisions of canon law and Vatican jurisprudence, to do so.

To be clear, those bringing this petition for canonical recourse are not contesting the archdiocese's actions with regard to any other portion of the former property of St. Peter Claver Parish other than the St. Peter Claver Church building itself, as we are aware that canon law does not allow us to contest the alienation of the remainder of the parish property. We do state at this time however that following considerable research, we are aware that the Congregation for the Clergy of the Holy See, the dicastery which addresses among other matters petitions for canonical recourse regarding the relegation of churches to profane but not sordid use if such matters cannot be amicable resolved within the ecclesiastical jurisdiction where they originate, stated in the guidelines it promulgated on the elimination of parishes, the closure of churches and the alienation of church buildings which had been validly relegated to profane but not sordid use, that a church should "retain its sacred character if at all possible." Thus, the congregation made clear that absent a cause of sufficient gravity to justify the permanent closure of a church building, it should remain a Roman Catholic sacred space, regardless of the frequency of when mass is celebrated within it.

Those bringing this petition for canonical recourse are further aware that the only way a church can be validly relegated to profane but not sordid use is for the provisions of Canon 1222 to be satisfied. This requires there to be the presence of a cause of sufficient gravity (a grave cause,) which justifies relegation of a church to profane but not sordid use. We are further aware that there are a very limited number of causes which on their own are of sufficient gravity to justify the relegation of a church building to profane but not sordid use, with two alone being the main causes of sufficient gravity which can justify the taking of such an action. We are aware that one is that a church building has been damaged beyond any point of repair (not that it has damage which is repairable, regardless of how significant that damage may be, but that it has been damaged beyond any possible point of repair.) We are further aware that the other cause of sufficient gravity which can be independently used to justify the relegation of a church building to profane but not sordid use is a lack of funds (from any source,) available to pay the expenses associated with the continued existence of a church building, including utilities for the church, insurance on the structure, and those costs associated with short and long term repairs it may require over time. While it is possible to combine various "just causes" (causes of action which do not in and of themselves rise to a sufficiently grave level to independently justify the relegation of a church to profane but not sordid use) to decree a church's relegation to profane but not sordid use, if the church is not damaged beyond the point of repair and there are funds available from some source to care for it, it is not likely the Congregation for the Clergy would sign off on the relegation of a church to profane but not sordid use under these circumstances, as its statement that a church should "retain its sacred character if at all possible" makes it unlikely it would allow random combinations of various just causes to circumvent this overarching requirement.

In your Excellency's decree, you only cite one cause which on its face is independently sufficiently grave to justify the relegation of St. Peter Claver Church to profane but not sordid use, that being a lack of funds from any source available to care for the church building. Those bringing this petition for canonical recourse state however that the claim that there are in fact no funds available from any source to maintain St. Peter Claver as a Roman Catholic sacred space is not accurate. Aside from the fact that at no time between the elimination of the St. Peter Claver Center for Evangelization and the present day was any request made by the Archdiocese for Catholics who wanted to maintain St. Peter Claver as a Roman Catholic sacred space at their own expense to come forward to do so, no such invitation was made prior to the issuance of the decree which seeks to relegate St. Peter Claver Church to profane but not sordid use. In fact, a group has formed which seeks to take on the care and restoration of St. Peter Claver church as a Roman Catholic sacred space at its own expense.

The Advocates and Descendants of St. Peter Claver, made up of individuals who were parishioners of St. Peter Claver Church and others who are committed to the church remaining a Roman Catholic sacred space has formed. This group wishes to restore the Shrine of Our Lady of Victories within St. Peter Claver Church and maintain the church and shrine at its own expense in accordance with canon law, in order that the church may remain a Roman Catholic sacred space. Those bringing this petition for canonical recourse would note that the Shrine of Our Lady of Victories was the first shrine to be established within the borders of the Archdiocese of Philadelphia. St. Peter Claver Church would not be the first former perish church either within the boundaries of the Archdiocese of Philadelphia or beyond them to become a shrine following the elimination of its parish. Those bringing this petition for canonical recourse are also aware that the Advocates and Descendants of St. Peter Claver would be open to the church serving as a chapel or oratory, other designations under canon law which allow a church to serve as a site of occasional mass and a place in which private worship can occur, if those designations is more agreeable to your Excellency. Any of these designations will allow St. Peter Claver Church to remain a Roman Catholic sacred space, cared for at the expense of those who seek to retain it as such, and available for the celebration of occasional mass and plentiful private worship (private prayer, recitation of the rosary and as a cite of other devotional activities such as the stations of the cross,) in accordance with canon law, Vatican Jurisprudence and the admonition of the Congregation for the Clergy that a church must "retain its sacred character if at all possible.) Other groups are also interested in partnering with the Advocates and Descendants of St. Peter Claver to make the retention of St. Peter Claver Church as a Roman Catholic sacred space possible and to assist with its restoration.

Those bringing this petition for canonical recourse would also note that at no time between October 31, 2014 (the day your Excellency lists as the date on which the final mass affiliated with the ST. Peter Claver Center for Evangelization was celebrated,) and the present day was St. Peter Claver Church open for the two yearly masses which canon law requires to be held within a church that has not been relegated to profane but not sordid use. Through our research, we have become aware that Canons 1167 and 1168 of the Pio Benedictine Code of Canon Law of 1917, incorporated through the provisions of Canon 2 into modern Vatican jurisprudence, require that mass be said in every church both on the anniversary of its dedication and on the feast day of the patron saint to whom it is dedicated, or on the Marian feast day associated with the church if the blessed mother is its patron. We are truly saddened that these masses were not celebrated within the church as canon law and Vatican jurisprudence required.

Archbishop Chaput, too often Black people are told that we ought to pull ourselves up by our bootstraps as White people have done. St. Peter Claver Church is concrete proof of the fact that the Black Catholics of Philadelphia did that before the nineteenth century even drew to a close. Our ancestors brought a Roman Catholic sacred space into being in which they could worship God without restrictions, free from the racism and discrimination they were subjected to in other Roman Catholic churches within the city of Philadelphia. Those bringing this petition for canonical recourse do so, as we believe that this church, the church in which Philadelphia's Black Catholics could finally worship freely, must continue to remain a Roman Catholic sacred space, to serve as a source of spiritual nourishment for us and our descendants, as well as all who may grow closer to Christ while praying within it. It is not sufficient that money which may be gained from a sale of St. Peter Claver Church itself be used for the benefit of the Black Catholic community; we wish to retain St. Peter Claver Church at our own expense as a Roman Catholic sacred space, as canon law permits us to do. In bringing this petition for canonical recourse, we are not demanding that someone make this possible for us; we are asking that our right to do this at our own expense in accordance with canon law be respected. Too often it has been the case that those things the Black community has created have been obliterated. We are determined that St. Peter Claver Church not join that list. We are well aware that many churches in Rome have throughout their history between transferred between religious orders, changed from parish churches to chapels, and remained Roman Catholic churches even after being employed for another canonically valid purpose after such initial transitions of designation. They were not simply closed when the purpose for which they were initially built, or even potentially their second mission concluded. St. Peter Claver Church can continue to exist as a Roman Catholic sacred space, regardless of whether St. Peter Claver Parish or the St. Peter Claver Center for Evangelization exists, and canon law and Vatican jurisprudence make this clear. Those bringing this petition for canonical recourse would ask you or a representative of your choosing to meet with us, in order that we can present our plan to care for St. Peter Claver Church as a Roman Catholic sacred space at our own expense, with the church preferably serving as a restored Shrine of Our Lady of Victories to you. We do not seek a confrontation with you or the archdiocese; we merely seek to ensure that we can retain and care for St. Peter Claver Church as a Roman Catholic sacred space at our own expense. We sincerely hope we do not have to take this petition for canonical recourse to the Congregation for the Clergy and Supreme Tribunal of the Apostolic Signatura of the Holy See. We pray that we hear from you, and we pray you are well.

Sincerely,
[signed]
Adrienne Harris
[signed]
Juanita V Perkins Qui

Document 5.1. Archdiocese of Philadelphia Decree Transitioning St. Laurentius to Profane but not Sordid Use

DECREE
OF THE RELEGATION OF
SAINT LAURENTIUS CHURCH, PHILADELPHIA, PENNSYLVANIA
TO PROFANE BUT NOT SORDID USE

Due to the deteriorating condition of Saint Laurentius Church, Philadelphia and a lack of the funding necessary to repair and maintain the church, consideration must be given as to whether sufficient grave causes exist for the relegation of Saint Laurentius Church to profane but not sordid use.

The following grave causes suggest that the church be so relegated and no longer be used for divine worship:

1) Saint Laurentius Church has been examined by experts who have determined that the building is unsafe for use and in need of extensive repairs. On March 19, 2014 the City of Philadelphia declared the building is "unsafe" and ordered the either repairs be made or the building be demolished. Engineers hired by Holy Name of Jesus Parish, which has ownership of the church, found Saint Laurentius Church "a potential safety hazard to the public."
In summary there are numerous cracks in the façade of the building and the church's towers are in danger of collapsing. The least expensive option, which itself would cost $1 million, is to demolish the entire church. Merely stabilizing or repairing the church would cost anywhere between $1.2 million and $3.4 million. Aside from the needed repairs, the costs of utilities, insurance, and maintenance for the church are approximately $68,000 annually.

2) Holy Name of Jesus Parish, Philadelphia, which has ownership of Saint Laurentius Church, does not have the resources to repair and maintain the Saint Laurentius Church building. The parish already has a debt of approximately $475,000 and has been unable to meet annual operating expenses;

3) there is no other source of funding for the necessary repairs;

4) the financial burden of repairing and maintaining the church would case important pastoral programs of the Holy Name of Jesus Parish, such as outreach to the poor and educational efforts, to suffer due to lack of funds;

5) the church building does not have any special architectural, historical, or artistic significance; and,

6) the people who had been attending Saint Laurentius Church are in reasonably close proximity to Holy Name of Jesus Church.

Accordingly, in virtue of the prescripts of canon 1222, §2 of the Code of Canon Law, having judged that sufficient grave causes are present and that the good of souls will not thereby be impaired, having consulted with the Pastor of Saint Holy Name of Jesus Parish, and having consulted with the Council of Priests on September 12, 2014, I hereby **DECREE** that Saint Laurentius Church, Philadelphia, Pennsylvania, be relegated to profane but not sordid use.

This decree is effective as of October 1, 2014, and is to be communicated to members of Holy Name of Jesus Parish and to the faithful of the Archdiocese in an appropriate manner. All things to the contrary notwithstanding.

Given at the Curia of the Archdiocese of Philadelphia, on the twenty sixth day of September, in the Year of Our Lord 2014.

[signed]
Most Reverend Charles J. Chaput, O.F.M. Cap.
Archbishop of Philadelphia

SEAL
[signed]
Reverend Monsignor Gerard C. Mesure, J.C.D.
Chancellor

Document 5.2. Archdiocese of Philadelphia Decree Transitioning Our Lady of the Blessed Sacrament to Profane but not Sordid Use

---

Archdiocese of Philadelphia
Office of the Archbishop
222 North 17th Street
Philadelphia, PA 19103-1299

DECREE

OF THE RELEGATION OF

OUR LADY OF THE BLESSED SACRAMENT CHURCH, PHILADELPHIA, PENNSYLVANIA

TO PROFANE BUT NOT SORDID USE

Due to the high cost of repairing and maintaining Our Lady of the Blessed Sacrament Church, Philadelphia, and due to a lack of the funding necessary to cover the expenses of the church, consideration must be given as to whether sufficient grave causes exist for the relegation of Our Lady of the Blessed Sacrament Church to profane but not sordid use.

The following grave causes suggest that the church be so relegated and no longer be used for divine worship:

1) Our Lady of the Blessed Sacrament Church has been costing Saint Cyprian Parish approximately $35,000 a year just to maintain. In addition, the church building continues to have problems that necessitate expensive repairs, such as a recent expense of $3500 to repair water damage from a broken pipe;

2) Saint Cyprian Parish, Philadelphia, which has ownership of Our Lady of the Blessed Sacrament Church, does not have the resources to repair and to continue to maintain the Our Lady of the Blessed Sacrament Church building. The Parish has a debt and has difficulty in meeting its operating expenses;

3) there is no other source of funding for the church maintenance and necessary repairs;

4) the financial burden of repairing and maintaining Our Lady of the Blessed Sacrament Church would cause staffing and important pastoral programs of Saint Cyprian Parish, such as outreach to the poor and educational efforts, to suffer due to lack of funds;

5) Our Lady of the Blessed Sacrament Church building does not have any particular architectural, historical, or artistic significance; and,

6) the people who had been attending Our Lady of the Blessed Sacrament Church are in reasonably close proximity to Saint Cyprian Church, so the relegation of Our Lady of the Blessed Sacrament Church would not deprive anyone of the use of a church.

Accordingly, in virtue of the prescripts of canon 1212 and canon 1222, §2 of the Code of Canon Law, having judged that sufficient grave causes are present and that the good of souls will not thereby be impaired, having consulted with the Pastor of Saint Cyprian Parish and having consulted with the Council of Priests, I hereby **DECREE** that Our Lady of the Blessed Sacrament Church, Philadelphia, Pennsylvania, be relegated to profane but not sordid use.

This decree is effective as of August 1, 2014, and is to be communicated to the members of Saint Cyprian Parish and to the faithful of the Archdiocese in an appropriate manner. All things to the contrary notwithstanding.

Given at the Curia of the Archdiocese of Philadelphia, on the eighteenth day of July, in the Year of Our Lord 2014.

[signed]
Most Reverend Charles J. Chaput, O.F.M. Cap.
Archbishop of Philadelphia

SEAL
[signed]
Reverend Monsignor Gerard C. Mesure, J.C.D.
Chancellor

NOTES

Introduction

1. Davis 1990.
2. Davis 1990.
3. Rowe 2019.
4. Bowman 1989.
5. Armstrong 2015.
6. Lorde [1984] 2007, 137.
7. Ammerman 2021.
8. In May 2024, Virginia's Shenandoah County School Board voted to reinstate Confederate eponyms to two schools after having removed them in July 2020. Robertson 2024.
9. Davidson et al. 2006; Adler et al. 2019.
10. Hoover 2014; Cressler 2017; Davis et al. 2017; Adler et al. 2019; Maldonado-Estrada 2020.
11. Emerson et al 2015.
12. Smith et al. 2013; Martí 2014.
13. DiMaggio et al 1983.
14. Mohamed et al. 2021, 22.
15. Emerson et al. 2006.

ONE. Black Faith, White Space

An earlier version of this chapter was published as "Confronting Truths About White Supremacy: Why I'm Writing a Book About Black Catholics and Systemic Racism" *Faithfully*, July 2019.

1. Woodberry et al. 2012; Wright et al. 2015.

2. Massingale 2010.
3. Massingale 2010, 80.
4. Davis 1990.
5. O'Connell 2021; Segura 2021; Massingale 2010.
6. Smith et al. 2014.
7. Dillon 1999.
8. Dolan 1975; McGreevy 1996; Ochs 1990; Shaw 1991.
9. D'Antonio et al. 2013.
10. Phan et al. 2004.
11. Fitzpatrick 1987; Fitzpatrick 1989, 49–86; Hoover 2014.
12. Davidson et al. 2006.
13. Bruce 2017.
14. Hoover 2014.
15. Maldonado-Estrada 2020.
16. Adler et al. 2019.
17. Emerson et al. 2015.
18. Emerson et al. 2015.
19. Emerson et al. 2015.
20. Emerson et al. 2015.
21. Dufour 2000.
22. Dillon 1999.
23. Ammerman 2021; Ammerman 1998.
24. Feagin 2004, 206.
25. Feagin 2004, 203.
26. Feagin 2004, 205–6.
27. Anderson 2022.
28. Anderson 2022, 13.
29. Anderson 2011, xiv.
30. Anderson 2015, 11.
31. Anderson 2015, 10.
32. Anderson 2022.
33. Anderson 2022, 14.
34. Anderson 2022, 15.
35. Anderson 2022, 15.
36. The Biden Administration ushered in the first Black Vice President, the first Black woman elevated to the Supreme Court, and the first Black Secretary of Defense.
37. Anderson 2022, 21.
38. O'Connell 2021.

39. Pratt et al. 2023.
40. Anderson 2015, 10.
41. Pratt 2019a.
42. Cressler 2017; Zech et al. 2017.
43. Torralva 2021.
44. Booker et al. 2021; Oppel et al. 2021.
45. MPRNews 2021b.
46. Barajas et al. 2021.
47. MPRNews 2021a.
48. Associated Press et al. 2018.
49. Caron 2018.
50. Holson 2018.
51. Wootson 2018a; Wootson 2018b.
52. Horton et al. 2018.
53. Schnoor 2006; Thumma 1991; Walton 2006; Yeung et al. 2000; Yeung et al. 2006.
54. Dillon 1999.
55. Dufour 2000.
56. Dillon 1999.
57. Rzeznik 2009.
58. Dillon 1999, 160.
59. Dillon 1999, 123.
60. Dillon 1999, 145.
61. Dillon 1999, 131.
62. Dillon's research was conducted during the 1990s and thus, occurred before Massachusetts legalized same-sex marriage in November 2003 in the Supreme Judicial Court Ruling in *Goodridge vs. Department of Public Health* that went into effect in May 2004.
63. Dillon 1999, 136.
64. Dillon 1999, 142.
65. Dillon 1999, 137, 142.
66. Dufour 2000.
67. Dufour 2000.
68. Dufour 2000, 98.
69. Dufour 2000, 104.
70. Dufour 2000, 94.
71. Dufour 2000, 94–95.
72. Dufour 2000, 98.
73. Dufour 2000, 96.

74. Dufour 2000, 97.
75. Du Bois [1903] 1994.
76. Bernstein 2015.
77. Ammerman 1998, 84.
78. Ammerman 1998, 84.
79. Feagin 2006.
80. Collins 1999.
81. Bonilla-Silva 2018.
82. Du Bois [1903] 1994.
83. Berger 2003, 9.
84. Black Bishops of the United States 1984.
85. Archdiocese of Philadelphia, "About – Archdiocese of Philadelphia."
86. Davis 1990, 177.

TWO. The Numbers Don't Add Up

1. Davis 1990.
2. Pratt 2023.
3. Davis 1990.
4. Davis 1988, 45.
5. Davis 1990, 28–29.
6. This number denotes those who have reported one race. United States Census Bureau.
7. Center for Applied Research in the Apostolate 2021. Those who are self-identified Catholics do not necessarily belong to a parish or participate in the sacraments.
8. United States Conference of Catholic Bishops 2021.
9. Mohamed et al. 2021.
10. Dolan 1975, 2; Day 2020.
11. O'Connell 2021.
12. O'Connell 2021.
13. O'Connell 2021, 66.
14. O'Connell 2021, 73.
15. O'Connell 2021, 73.
16. A reference to Daniel O'Connell, "The Liberator" of Ireland.
17. O'Connell 2021, 73.
18. Dolan 1975, 4.
19. Dolan 1975, 5.

20. Dolan 1975, 20.
21. Dolan 1975, 19–20.
22. Dolan 1975, 22.
23. Dolan 1975, 72.
24. Morris 1997, 164.
25. Edwards 2019.
26. Pirtle et al. 2021.
27. Morris 1997.
28. Morris 1997, 5.
29. Shaw 1991, 9.
30. Shaw 1991, 8.
31. Shaw 1991, 15.
32. Shaw 1991, 22.
33. Steinberg 2007, 31–32.
34. Sanjek 1994, 106.
35. Davis 1990, 28.
36. Heisser et al. 2015.
37. Heisser et al. 2015.
38. Murphy 2001; Ulshafer 2019; Schmidt 2019; Poole et al. 1986.
39. Williams 2017.
40. Williams 2017, 143.
41. Williams 2017, 140.
42. Murphy 2001.
43. Murphy 2001.
44. Finn 1974; Curran 2021 [1983]; Curran 1993.
45. Swarns 2016a.
46. Swarns 2016b.
47. Swarns 2019b; Svrluga 2018; "GU272 Organizations: Who's Who" 2017.
48. Brand 2007.
49. Ochs 1990.
50. Davis and Phelps 2003, 30–31.
51. Dolan 1975, 24.
52. Davis 1990; Ochs. 1990; Williams 2016b; Williams 2017.
53. Ochs 1990, 9.
54. Ochs 1990, 49.
55. Ochs 1990, 49.
56. Ochs 1990, 50.
57. Davis 1990; Davis and Phelps 2003, 47–53.

58. Williams 2016b; Williams 2017.
59. Diaz-Stevens 1993, 61-63.
60. For more on how Archbishop Hughes' attitudes toward Black Catholics impacted the laity, see "A Black Woman's letter to Pius X," in Davis and Phelps 2003, 30.
61. Ochs 1990, 29–30.
62. Davis 1998, 31.
63. Ochs 1990, 30.
64. Davis 1998, 32–33.
65. Davis 1998, 32.
66. Davis 1998, 32.
67. Davis 1998, 32; Davis and Phelps 2003, 59–60.
68. Hemesath 1973, 25.
69. Hemesath 1973, 31.
70. Hemesath 1973, 34.
71. Hemesath 1973, 42.
72. Hemesath 1973, 66.
73. Davis 1998, 33; Hemesath 1973, 186–87.
74. Davis and Phelps 2003, 62.
75. Hemesath 1973, 216.
76. Hemesath 1973, 216.
77. Hemesath 1973, 216.
78. Archdiocese of Chicago.
79. Pratt 2019b.
80. Ochs 1990.
81. Ochs 1990, 65.
82. Ochs 1990, 79.
83. Ochs 1990, 89.
84. Ochs 1990, 89.
85. Ochs 1990, 2.
86. Ochs 1990, 2.
87. Braxton 1988; Lincoln 1999.

THREE. Finding a Place at the Table

An earlier version of this chapter was published as "Black Catholics' Identity Work" in *American Parishes: Remaking Local Catholicism*, eds. Gary Adler, Tricia C. Bruce, and Brian Starks. New York, NY: Fordham University Press, 2019.

1. Mohamed et al. 2021, 97.
2. Dillon 1999.
3. Dillon 1999, 142.
4. Dufour 2000.
5. Dufour 2000, 94.
6. Dufour 2000, 94–95.
7. Dufour 2000, 97.
8. Ammerman 1998, 84.
9. Ammerman 1998, 84.
10. Davis 1988; Eugene 1998; Rivers 1998; Rowe 1994; Whitt 1998.
11. GIA Publications 1987.
12. Mohamed et al. 2021, 44.
13. Massingale 2010.
14. Fraga 2020.
15. Black Bishops of the United States 1984.
16. The names of all parishes, priests, and parishioners are pseudonyms.
17. GIA Publications 1987.
18. Du Bois [1903] 1994.
19. Du Bois [1903] 1994, 116.
20. Grant 1989; Lincoln et al. 1990.
21. Rzeznik 2009.
22. Belluck 2004; Otterman 2014; Pashman 2014; West 2015.
23. Gray et al. 2013.
24. Black Bishops of the United States 1984.
25. Pope Francis 2014.
26. Wendt 1998.

FOUR.   Erasing a Legacy

1. Archdiocese of Philadelphia, "Archdiocese of Philadelphia Announces Closure of Saint Peter Claver Center for Evangelization."
2. Williams 2016b.
3. There are many parallels to the origin of St. Peter Claver and St. Monica Parish in Chicago. St. Monica Parish was the first parish for African American Catholics in the Archdiocese of Chicago. Fr. Augustus Tolton was the founding pastor of St. Monica's Church. More information can be found in Chapter 19 of *From Slave to Priest: The Inspirational Story of Father Augustine Tolton (1854-1897)* by Caroline Hemesath, O.S.F.

4. Pratt 2010.
5. Gans 1979.
6. Archdiocese of Philadelphia, "Parishes—St. Peter Claver."
7. Dolan 1975; Shaw 1991; Pratt 2010; Weisenfeld 2016.
8. Baldwin 2019.
9. Long-García et al. 2013.
10. For detailed information, see Appendix, Document 4.3, the Archdiocese of Philadelphia's Report of the Commission for Parish Sites and Boundaries from 1984.
11. Hahn 2018.
12. See document 4.8, December 9, 2022, Decree from Archbishop Nelson Perez in Archdiocese of Philadelphia, "Decree of the Relegation of Saint Peter Claver Church, Philadelphia, Pennsylvania to Profane but Not Sordid Use."
13. Pratt 2017; Pratt 2020.
14. The Vatican, Code of Canon Law.
15. Long-García et al. 2013.
16. The Vatican, Code of Canon Law.
17. Du Bois [1899] 1996.
18. St. Peter Claver Diamond Jubilee Historical Sketch. Blockson Collection. Temple University.
19. Because of their close proximity to St. Peter Claver, I am using the actual names of these churches.
20. St. Peter Claver Diamond Jubilee Historical Sketch.
21. Anderson 2022, 16.
22. St. Peter Claver Diamond Jubilee Historical Sketch.
23. Presbyterian Historical Society: The National Archives of the PC (USA). 2021.
24. St. Peter Claver. Parish Historical Sketch. Courtesy, Blockson Collection, Temple University.
25. Spalding 1989.
26. "Patrick John Ryan to Congregation of the Holy Ghost and of the Immaculate Heart of Mary," Deed to St. Peter Claver, Courtesy of Adrienne Andrews Harris.
27. "Patrick John Ryan to Congregation of the Holy Ghost and of the Immaculate Heart of Mary," Deed to St. Peter Claver.
28. Letter from Cardinal Krol to the parishioners of St. Peter Claver dated May 26, 1985. Courtesy of Adrienne Andrews Harris.

29. Correspondence between Bishop Terry Steib and Archbishop Eugene Marino. Courtesy of Adrienne Andrews Harris.

30. Email correspondence between Msgr. Leonard Scott and Adrienne Andrews Harris. Courtesy of Adrienne Andrews Harris.

31. See Figure 4.1.

32. Lubano 2016.

33. Hahn 2018.

34. Gambino 2018.

35. Catholic Diocese of Pittsburgh 2020b; Catholic Diocese of Pittsburgh 2020a.

36. Advocates and Descendants of St. Peter Claver Church 2018; Reznik 2019.

37. Horn 2020; Rose-Milavec 2020.

38. Russ 2020.

39. Nortey et al. 2024.

40. "Petition for Hierarchical Recourse." Courtesy of Adrienne Andrews Harris.

41. Bruce 2017.

42. Anderson 2015; Anderson 2022.

43. Anderson 2011.

FIVE.   Race, Community, and Process

1. Facebook post. May 18, 2020. Quoted with permission.

2. Adler 2019; Bruce 2017; Hoover 2014; Davidson et al. 2006.

3. In Chapter 6, I have provided more information about the realities I faced in this regard as a researcher and the subsequent decisions I made.

4. Augustine 2018.

5. Copeland 2023, 482.

6. Massingale 2010, 45.

7. Anderson 2022, 17.

8. In this chapter, I have identified (arch)dioceses by name and used pseudonyms for parishes and the people I interviewed.

9. Anderson 2022, 17.

10. Anderson 2022, 18.

11. Because of its close connection to St. Peter Claver, I am using the actual name of this church.

12. Appleby et al. 2004.

13. Sociologist Janet Jacobs writes about collective trauma and generational harm rooted in the Holocaust in her 2016 book, *The Holocaust Across Generations: Trauma and its Inheritance Among Descendants of Survivors*. A similar examination of collective trauma and generational harm among African Americans is beyond the scope of what I'm doing here. Yet, such an examination—especially one including the additional dimension of membership in a faith tradition steeped in whiteness and white supremacy—would articulate the depth of harm experienced by those founding members of St. Peter Claver and their descendants. It is also important to note that the descendants of St. Peter Claver are both the familial descendants of the founding parishioners as well as the broader Black Catholic community in Philadelphia.

14. Copeland 2023, 482.

15. The CROWN Act stands for Creating a Respectful and Open World for Natural Hair. On March 18, 2022, a federal version of the CROWN Act passed in the House of Representatives. On March 21, 2022, the bill was received in the U.S. Senate and referred to the Judiciary Committee. As of June 1, 2023, there has been no further action. More information can be found at https://www.thecrownact.com/.

16. The high school Vincent attended, while a Catholic school, is not owned or operated by the Archdiocese of Philadelphia. It is categorized as a private, Catholic school.

17. Of the four who are no longer in active ministry in the Archdiocese, one is retired and another asked to be released from the Archdiocese so he could join a religious order of priests. He remains in active ministry with his order. The third was removed from active ministry shortly after his ordination and was later laicized. The fourth died suddenly in December 2024 at the age of 42.

18. Grappling with this issue is beyond the scope of this book. Yet, it is part of the larger conversation I am engaging here.

19. Edwards 2019.

20. Hoover 2014.

21. Mohamed et al. 2021.

22. Diamant et al. 2022.

23. Pratt 2022.

24. Theologian Bryan Massingale discusses this at length in Chapter 2 of his book, *Racial Justice in the Catholic Church*.

25. Du Bois [1903] 1994, 110.
26. Lincoln et al. 1990.
27. Lincoln et al. 1990, 106.
28. Wood 2019a; Wood 2019b; Wigglesworth 2015.
29. Archdiocese of Philadelphia, "Transfiguration of Our Lord (1905-2000)"; Quattlebaum 2009; Christopher 2021; Briggs 2021; McShane 2022; Bond 2022.
30. Mohamed et al. 2021.
31. King 1963.
32. King 1963.
33. King 1963.
34. I elaborated on this point in a chapter that I co-authored with Dr. Maureen O'Connell. See Tia Noelle Pratt and Maureen H. O'Connell. "'Contrary to the Tenets of Christian Social Justice': Racism and Catholic Social Thought in Catholic Higher Education," in *Catholic Higher Education and Catholic Social Thought*, eds. Bernard G. Prusak and Jennifer Reed-Bouley, 47–79 (Mahwah, NJ: Paulist Press, 2023). Also, in Chapter 2 of *Racial Justice and the Catholic Church*, Fr. Bryan Massingale, discusses at length a multi-point plan for liberation articulated by the Federated Colored Catholics at their 1930 convention and how moderate white leaders of the day—notably, Jesuit priest, Fr. John LaFarge, SJ—went to great lengths to thwart the FCC's plan. See Massingale 2010, 47–48.
35. Segura 2021, 58; Makam 2020.
36. Du Bois [1903] 1994, 1.
37. Rose 1993.
38. Mohamed et al. 2021.
39. Diamant et al. 2022, 41.
40. Diamant et al. 2022, 55.
41. Diamant et al. 2022, 43.
42. Mohamed 2021, 4.
43. Diamant et al. 2022, 110.
44. Diamant et al. 2022, 111.
45. Chappell 2013; Bailey 2022; White 2022.
46. Dulles 2002.
47. Dulles 2002, 48.
48. Segura 2021.
49. Copeland 2023, 492. Emphasis in the original.

SIX. Losing Religion and Gaining Faith

1. Wendt 1998.
2. McGreevy 1996.
3. Ochs 1993.
4. Anderson 2022; Anderson 2015.
5. Feagin 2006; Feagin 2004.
6. Davidson et al. 2006.
7. Adler et al. 2019; Bruce 2017; Hoover 2014; Davidson et al. 2006; Maldonado-Estrada 2020; Zech et al. 2017.
8. Kramarek et al. 2023.
9. According to its mission, FutureChurch "seeks changes that will provide all Roman Catholics the opportunity to participate fully in Church life, ministry, and governance." See https://futurechurch.org/mission-vision/. While completed in March 2023, FutureChurch held the study under embargo until January 2024.
10. Kramarek et al. 2023, 747.
11. Kramarek et al. 2023, 6.
12. Kramarek et al. 2023, 7.
13. The Vatican, Code of Canon Law.
14. Hannah-Jones 2021.
15. Georgetown University 2022.
16. Davis, 1990.
17. In the years since I attempted to locate and access these documents, Georgetown University has begun digitizing them and translating them into English. Rothman and Mendoza's edited volume collects a great deal of relevant material in one place, making it much more accessible. See Rothman et al. 2021. Additionally, primary source materials, including the papers of Brother Joseph P. Moberly, SJ, the architect of the 1838 mass sale, can be found via the "Georgetown Reflects on Slavery, Memory, and Reconciliation" website, https://www.georgetown.edu/slavery/
18. Schmidt 2019.
19. Poole et al. 1986.
20. Ulshafer 2019.
21. Swarns 2019a.
22. Society of the Sacred Heart, "Committee on Slavery, Accountability and Reconciliation."
23. Modern History Sourcebook: Alexander H. Stephens (1812–1883).

24. United States Conference of Catholic Bishops, Psalms.
25. All of this is the subject of my next project, *The Cornerstone: Slavery and the Rise of U.S. Catholicism.*
26. Pratt 2019b.
27. Hawkins 2025.
28. United States Conference of Catholic Bishops 2020; Perez 2020.
29. Gomez 2020.
30. Soto 2020.
31. Segura 2021.
32. Boston Globe 2002.
33. Segura 2021.
34. Pratt 2019b.

REFERENCE

Adler, Gary J., Jr., Tricia C. Bruce, and Brian Starks, eds. 2019. *American Parishes: Remaking Local Catholicism.* New York: Fordham University Press.

Advocates and Descendants of St. Peter Claver Church. 2018. *St. Peter Claver, Mother Church of Black Catholics: Let Us PrAy! Let Us PrEy!.* DVD. Philadelphia: Scribe Video Center.

Ammerman, Nancy T. 1998. "Culture and Identity in the Congregation." In *Studying Congregations: A New Handbook,* 78–104. Nashville, TN: Abingdon Press.

Ammerman, Nancy Tatom. 2021. *Studying Lived Religion: Contexts and Practices.* New York: NYU Press.

Anderson, Elijah. 2011. *The Cosmopolitan Canopy: Race and Civility in Everyday Life.* New York: W.W. Norton and Company.

Anderson, Elijah. 2015. "'The White Space.'" *Sociology of Race and Ethnicity* 1(1): 10–21.

Anderson, Elijah. 2022. *Black in White Space: The Enduring Impact of Color in Everyday Life.* Chicago: The University of Chicago Press.

Appleby, Scott R., Patricia Byrne, and William L. Portier, eds. 2004. *Creative Fidelity: American Catholic Intellectual Traditions.* Maryknoll, NY: Orbis Books.

Archambault, Marie Therese, Mark G. Thiel, and Christopher Vecsey, eds. 2003. *The Crossing of Two Roads: Being Catholic and Native in the United States.* Maryknoll, NY: Orbis Books.

Archdiocese of Chicago. "About Fr. Augustus Tolton: Fr. Tolton's Canonization Timeline." Chicago: Archdiocese of Chicago. https://tolton.archchicago.org/about/tolton-canonization-timeline.

Archdiocese of Philadelphia. "About—Archdiocese of Philadelphia." https://archphila.org/about#history.

Archdiocese of Philadelphia. "Archdiocese of Philadelphia Announces Closure of Saint Peter Claver Center for Evangelization." October 9, 2014. https://archphila.org/archdiocese-of-philadelphia-announces-closure-of-saint-peter-claver-center-for-evangelization.

Archdiocese of Philadelphia. "Decree of the Relegation of Saint Peter Claver Church, Philadelphia, Pennsylvania to Profane but Not Sordid Use." December 9, 2022. https://archphila.org/wp-content/uploads/2022/12/Saint-Peter-Claver-Church-Philadelphia-Signed-Decree-of-Relegation.pdf.

Archdiocese of Philadelphia. "St. Peter Claver—Philadelphia." https://archphila.org/parish/st-peter-claver-philadelphia/Archdiocese of Philadelphia.

Archdiocese of Philadelphia. "Transfiguration of Our Lord (1905–2000)." https://archphila.org/parish/transfiguration-of-our-lord-philadelphia.

Armstrong, Jenice. 2015. "Blacks and Catholicism: It's Not an Oxymoron—Philly." Philly.Com.

Associated Press and Elizabeth Chuck. 2018. "Black Men Arrested at Philadelphia Starbucks Say They Feared for Their Lives." *NBC News*, April 19.

Augustine, Ansel. 2018. "Black Catholicism: A Gift to Be Shared." In *Young Adult American Catholics*, ed. Maureen K. Day, 243–48. New York: Paulist Press.

Bailey, Sarah Pulliam. 2022. "Pope Francis Writes to Controversial Nun, Thanking Her for 50 Years of LGBTQ Ministry." *The Washington Post*, January 7. https://www.washingtonpost.com/religion/2022/01/07/pope-francis-writes-controversial-nun-thanking-her-50-years-lgbtq-ministry/.

Baldwin, Lou. 2019. "Long-Time Base for City's Black Catholics Set to Close." CatholicPhilly.com. March 4. https://catholicphilly.com/2019/03/news/local-news/long-time-base-for-citys-black-catholics-set-to-close/.

Barajas, Angela, Martin Savidge, and Christina Maxouris. 2021. CNN.com, October 25.

Barlow, Monique Deal. 2021. "Christian Nationalism Is a Barrier to Mass Vaccination Against COVID-19." *The Conversation*, April 1.

Belluck, Pam. 2004. *New York Times*, May 26.

Berger, Peter L. 2003. "The Craft of Sociology (from *Invitation to Sociology*)." In *Readings for Sociology*, 4th ed, edited by Garth Massey, 3–12. New York: W.W. Norton & Company, Inc.

Bernstein, Jacob. 2015. "Lee Daniels Watches 'Empire'— and Talks Back to the Screen—The New York Times." *The New York Times*. https://www.nytimes.com/2015/04/03/style/lee-daniels-empire.html.

Black Bishops of the United States. 1984. *"What We Have Seen and Heard": A Pastoral Letter on Evangelization from the Black Bishops of the United States.* Cincinnati, OH: St. Anthony Messenger Press.

Bond, Michaelle. 2022. *The Philadelphia Inquirer*, January 5. https://www.inquirer.com/real-estate/housing/st-laurentius-church-fishtown-demolition-apartments-20220105.html.

Bonilla-Silva, Eduardo. 2018. *Racism Without Racists: Color-Blind Racism and the Persistence of Racial Inequality in America*, 5th ed. New York: Rowman & Littlefield.

Booker, Brakkton and Rachel Treisman. 2021. "A Year After Breonna Taylor's Killing, Family Says There's 'No Accountability.'" *NPR*, March 13.

Boorstein, Michelle. 2021. "A Horn-Wearing 'Shaman.' A Cowboy Evangelist. For Some, the Capitol Attack Was a Kind of Christian Revolt." *The Washington Post*, July 6.

Boston Globe. 2002. "Spotlight: Clergy Sex Abuse Crisis." *Boston Globe*, January 6. https://www3.bostonglobe.com/metro/specials/clergy/.

Bowman, FSPA, Thea. 1989. "Address to U.S. Conference of Catholic Bishops." YouTube. June 1989. https://www.youtube.com/watch?v=uOV0nQkjuoA&t=799s.

Brand, Kathryn. 2007. "The Jesuits' Slaves." *The Georgetown Voice*, February 8.

Braxton, Most Rev. Edward K. 1988. "Black Catholics in America: A Challenge to the Church's Catholicity." In *One Lord, One Faith, One Baptism: The Hopes and Experiences of the Black Community in the Archdiocese of New York*, Vol. 2, *Appendices*, 63–82. New York: Archdiocese of New York, Office of Pastoral Research.

Braxton, Bishop Edward K. 2021. *The Church and the Racial Divide: Reflections of an African American Bishop*. Maryknoll, NY: Orbis Books.

Briggs, Ryan. 2021. "West Philly Community Pickets Church Demo by Boys Latin Charter." *Plan Philly*: whyy.org, July 5. https://whyy.org/articles/west-philly-community-pickets-church-demo-by-boys-latin-charter/.

Bruce, Tricia Colleen. 2017. *Parish and Place: Making Room for Diversity in the American Catholic Church*. New York: Oxford University Press.

Caron, Christina. 2018. *The New York Times*, May 9.

Catholic Diocese of Pittsburgh. 2020a. "Bishop David Zubik Accepts Proposal, Establishes Personal Parish for the Black Catholic Community." *Catholic Diocese of Pittsburgh*, June 19. https://diopitt.org/news/bishop-david-zubik-accepts-proposal-establishes-personal-parish-for-the-black-catholic-community.

Catholic Diocese of Pittsburgh. 2020b. "Bishop David Zubik Announces Clergy Assignments for Saint Benedict the Moor Personal Parish." Catholic Diocese of Pittsburgh, June 27. https://diopitt.org/news/bishop-david-zubik-announces-clergy-assignments-for-saint-benedict-the-moor-personal-parish.

Center for Applied Research in the Apostolate. 2021. "Frequently Requested Church Statistics." Washington, DC: Center for Applied Research in the Apostolate.

Chappell, Bill. 2013. "Pope Francis Discusses Gay Catholics: 'Who Am I To Judge?'" *The Two Way*, July 29. https://www.npr.org/sections/thetwo-way/2013/07/29/206622682/pope-francis-discusses-gay-catholics-who-am-i-to-judge.

Christopher, Matthew. 2021. "In Remembrance of Our Lady of the Rosary." *Hidden City: Exploring Philadelphia's Urban Landscape*, December 2. https://hiddencityphila.org/2021/12/in-remembrance-of-our-lady-of-the-rosary/.

Collins, Patricia Hill. 1999. *Black Feminist Thought: Knowledge, Consciousness, and the Politics of Empowerment*. Revised, 10th Anniv., 2nd edition. New York: Routledge.

Copeland, M. Shawn. 2023. "The Radical Transcendence of Black Catholic Life." *Journal of Catholic Social Thought*. Volume 20 (2): 481–96.

Cressler, Matthew J. 2017. *Authentically Black and Truly Catholic: The Rise of Black Catholicism in the Great Migration*. New York: NYU Press.

D'Antonio, William V., Michele Dillon, and Mary L. Gautier. 2013. *American Catholics in Transition*. Lanham, MD: Rowman & Littlefield Publishers.

Davidson, James D., and Suzanne C. Fournier. 2006. "Recent Research on Catholic Parishes: A Research Note." *Review of Religious Research* 48:72–81.

Davis, Cyprian, O.S.B. 1988. "Black Spirituality: A Catholic Perspective." In *One Lord, One Faith, One Baptism: The Hopes and Experiences of the Black Community in the Archdiocese of New York*, Vol. 2, *Appendices*, 37–62. New York: Archdiocese of New York, Office of Pastoral Research.

Davis, Cyprian, O.S.B. 1990. *The History of Black Catholics in the United States*. New York: Crossroad Publishers.

Davis, Cyprian, O.S.B. 1998. "God of Our Weary Years: Black Catholics in American Catholic History." In *Taking Down Our Harps: Black Catholics in the United States*, 17–46. Maryknoll, NY: Orbis Books.

Davis, Cyprian, O.S.B., and Jamie Phelps, O.P., eds. 2003. *Stamped with the Image of God: African Americans as God's Image in Black*. Maryknoll, NY: Orbis Books.

Davis, Darren W. and Donald Pope-Davis. 2017. *Perseverance in the Parish?: Religious Attitudes from a Black Catholic Perspective*. New York: Cambridge University Press.

Day, Maureen K. 2020. *Catholic Activism Today: Individual Transformation and the Struggle for Social Justice*. New York: NYU Press.

Diamant, Jeff, Besheer Mohamed, and Joshua Alvarado. 2022. "Black Catholics in America." Washington, DC: Pew Research Center. https://www.pewresearch.org/religion/2022/03/15/black-catholics-in-america/.

Diaz-Stevens, Ana Maria. 1993. *Oxcart Catholicism on Fifth Avenue: The Impact of the Puerto Rican Migration Upon the Archdiocese of New York.* Notre Dame, IN: University of Notre Dame Press.

DiMaggio, Paul J. and Walter W. Powell. 1983. "The Iron Cage Revisited: Institutional Isomorphism and Collective Rationality in Organizational Fields." *American Sociological Review* 48:147–60.

Dillon, Michele. 1999. *Catholic Identity: Balancing Reason, Faith and Power.* New York: Cambridge University Press.

Dolan, Jay P. 1975. *The Immigrant Church: New York's Irish and German Catholics, 1815–1865.* Baltimore, MD: The Johns Hopkins University.

Du Bois, W. E. B. [1899] 1996. *The Philadelphia Negro.* Philadelphia: University of Pennsylvania Press.

Du Bois, W. E. B. [1903] 1994. *The Souls of Black Folk.* New York: Dover Publications, Inc.

Dufour, Lynn Resnick. 2000. "Sifting Through Tradition: The Creation of Jewish Feminist Identities." *Journal for the Scientific Study of Religion* 39:90–106.

Dulles, S. J., Avery Cardinal. 2002. *Models of the Church.* New York: Image Doubleday Books.

Edwards, Korie L. 2019. "The Bittersweet Reality of Multiracial Churches." *Studying Congregations*, February 5. https://studyingcongregations.org/the-bittersweet-reality-of-multiracial-churches/.

Emerson, Michael O., Elizabeth Korver-Glenn, and Kiara W. Douds. 2015. "Studying Race and Religion: A Critical Assessment." *Sociology of Race and Ethnicity* 1:349–59.

Emerson, Michael O., with Rodney M. Woo. 2006. *People of the Dream: Multiracial Congregations in the United States.* Princeton, NJ: Princeton University Press.

Eugene, Toinette M. 1998. "Between 'Lord Have Mercy!' and 'Thank You, Jesus!': Liturgical Renewal and African American Catholic Assemblies." In *Taking Down Our Harps: Black Catholics in the United States,* 163–75. Maryknoll, NY: Orbis Books.

Feagin, Joe R. 2004. "Toward an Integrated Theory of Systemic Racism." In *The Changing Terrain of Race and Ethnicity,* edited by Maria Krysan and Amanda E. Lewis, 203–23. New York: Russell Sage Foundation.

Feagin, Joe R. 2006. *Systemic Racism: A Theory of Oppression.* New York: Routledge.

Fitzpatrick, Joseph P. 1987. *One Church, Many Cultures: Challenge of Diversity.* Kansas City, MO: Sheed & Ward Press.

Fitzpatrick, Joseph P. 1989. "Cultural Change or Cultural Continuity: Pluralism and Hispanic-Americans." In *Hispanics in New York: Religious, Cultural, and Social Experiences*, 2:49–86. 2nd edition. New York: Archdiocese of New York, Office of Pastoral Research.

Flaccus, Gillian, Janie Har, and Sara Cline. 2021. *The Associated Press*, August 21.

Fraga, Brian. 2020. "Catholic Reporter's Notebook: Black Lives Matter." Patheos, July 21. https://www.patheos.com/blogs/onthecatholicbeat/2020/07/catholic-reporters-notebook-black-lives-matter/.

Gambino, Matthew. 2018. "Latin Mass Enthusiasts to Get New Spiritual Home with 'Quasi-parish.'" CatholicPhilly.com, April 9. http://catholicphilly.com/2018/04/news/local-news/latin-mass-enthusiasts-to-get-new-spiritual-home-with-quasi-parish/.

Gans, Herbert J. 1979. "Symbolic Ethnicity: The Future of Ethnic Groups and Cultures in America." *Ethnic and Racial Studies* 2 (1): 1–20.

Georgetown University. 2022. "Georgetown Reflects on Slavery, Memory, and Reconciliation." https://www.georgetown.edu/slavery/.

GIA Publications. 1987. *Lead Me, Guide Me: The African American Catholic Hymnal.* Chicago: G.I.A. Publications.

Gill, John Freeman. 2021. "These Churches Have Been Closed, but Their Artifacts Live On." *The New York Times*, December 24. https://www.nytimes.com/2021/12/24/realestate/streetscapes-catholic-relics.html.

Gomez, Archbishop Jose. 2020. "Statement of U.S. Bishops' President on George Floyd and the Protests in American Cities." May 31. United States Conference of Catholic Bishops www.usccb.org/news/2020/statement-us-bishops-president-george-floyd-and-protests-american-cities.

Grant, Jacquelyn. 1989. *White Women's Christ and Black Women's Jesus: Feminist Christology and Womanist Response.* Atlanta, GA: Scholars Press.

Gray, Mark, Mary Gautier, and Thomas Gaunt, SJ. 2013. "Cultural Diversity in the Catholic Church in the United States." Washington, DC: Center for Applied Research in the Apostolate.

"GU272 Organizations: Who's Who." 2017. GU272 Memory Project. https://gu272.americanancestors.org/gu272-organizationswhos-who.

Hahn, Ashley. 2018. *WHYY*, March 29. https://whyy.org/segments/saying-goodbye-to-philadelphias-first-black-catholic-church/.

Hannah-Jones, Nikole. 2021. *The 1619 Project: A New Origin Story.* New York: Penguin Random House.

Hawkins, Eleanor. 2025. "Which Companies Are Rolling Back DEI and Which Are Standing Firm." Axios. January 16. https://www.axios.com/2025/01/16/dei-rollback-companies-amazon-meta-mcdonalds.

The Harlem Neighborhood Block Association. 2022. "Shuttered Churches." *The Harlem Neighborhood Block Association Blog*, February 7. https://hnba.nyc/shuttered-churches/.

Heisser, David C. R., and Stephen J. White, Sr. 2015. *Patrick N. Lynch, 1817-1882: Third Catholic Bishop of Charleston.* Columbia, SC: University of South Carolina Press. e-book. no page numbers.

Hemesath, Caroline, O.S.F. 1973. *From Slave to Priest: The Inspirational Story of Father Augustine Tolton (1854–1897).* San Francisco: Ignatius Press.

Holson, Laura M. 2018. *The New York Times*, May 21.

Hoover, Brett C. 2014. *The Shared Parish: Latinos, Anglos, and the Future of U.S. Catholicism.* New York: NYU Press.

Horn, Dan. 2020. "Cincinnati Priest Meets Resistance When He Changes Catholic Parish." *Cincinnati Enquirer*, September 20. https://www.cincinnati.com/story/news/2020/09/14/cincinnati-priest-meets-resistance-when-he-changes-catholic-parish/3456920001.

Horton, Alex and Keith McMillan. 2018. *The Washington Post*, July 8.

Jacobs, Janet. 2016. *The Holocaust Across Generations: Trauma and Its Inheritance among Descendants of Survivors.* New York: NYU Press.

King, Martin Luther, Jr. 1963. "Letter from [a] Birmingham Jail," April 16. African Studies Center—University of Pennsylvania. https://www.africa.upenn.edu/Articles_Gen/Letter_Birmingham.html.

Kramarek, Michal J., Thomas P. Gaunt, SJ, and Mark M. Gray. 2023. "Parish, Ecclesial and Socioeconomic Statistics for Eleven Dioceses between 1970 and 2020: A Report for the FutureChurch." Washington, DC: Center for Applied Research in the Apostolate.

Leege, David C., and Michael R. Welch. 1989. "Catholics in Context: Theoretical and Methodological Issues in Studying American Catholic Parishioners." *Review of Religious Research* 31:132–48.

Lincoln, C. Eric. 1999. *Race, Religion, and the Continuing American Dilemma.* New York: Hill and Wang.

Lincoln, C. Eric, and Lawrence H. Mamiya. 1990. *The Black Church in the African American Experience.* Durham, NC: Duke University Press.

Long-García, J. D. and Kira Dault. 2013. "What's the Difference Between Closing a Parish and a Church?" *U.S. Catholic*, October 22. https://uscatholic.org/articles/201310/whats-the-difference-between-closing-a-parish-and-closing-a-church/.

Lorde, Audre. [1984] 2007. *Sister Outsider: Essays and Speeches*. Berkeley, CA: Crossing Press.

Lubano, Alfred. 2016. *The Philadelphia Inquirer*, June 12. https://www.inquirer.com/philly/news/20160612_Battle_over_proposed_sale_of_first_black_Catholic_church_intensifies.html.

Makam, Palika. 2020. "Copaganda: What It Is and How to Recognize It." *Teen Vogue*, August 5. https://www.teenvogue.com/story/what-is-copaganda-explainer.

Maldonado-Estrada, Alyssa. 2020. *Lifeblood of the Parish: Men and Catholic Devotion in Williamsburg, Brooklyn*. New York: NYU Press.

Martí, Gerardo. 2014. "Editor's Note: Present and Future Scholarship in the Sociology of Religion." *Sociology of Religion* 75:503–10.

Massingale, Bryan N. 2010. *Racial Justice and the Catholic Church*. Maryknoll, NY: Orbis Books.

McGreevy, John T. 1996. *Parish Boundaries: The Catholic Encounter with Race in the Twentieth-Century Urban North*. Chicago: The University of Chicago Press.

McShane, Kyle. 2022. *Rising Real-Estate*, January 5. http://www.rising.realestate/8-story-49-unit-building-to-replace-st-laurentius-church-in-fishtown/.

Mich, Marvin L. Krier. 1998. *Catholic Social Teaching and Movements*. Mystic, CT: Twenty-Third Publications.

MPRNews. 2021a. "The Murder of George Floyd." *MPR News*, Multiple Dates. https://www.mprnews.org/crime-law-and-justice/killing-of-george-floyd

MPRNews. 2021b. "The Death of Philando Castile and the Trial of Jeronimo Yanez." *MPRNews*, Multiple Dates.

Modern History Sourcebook. Alexander H. Stephens (1812–1883): Cornerstone Address, March 21, 1861.

Mohamed, Besheer. 2021. "10 New Findings About Faith Among Black Americans." Washington, DC: Pew Research Center.

Mohamed, Besheer, Kiana Cox, Jeff Diamant, and Claire Gecewicz. 2021. *Faith Among Black Americans*. Washington, DC: Pew Research Center. https://www.pewresearch.org/religion/2021/02/16/faith-among-black-americans/.

Morris, Charles R. 1997. *American Catholic: The Saints and Sinners Who Built America's Most Powerful Church*. New York: Times Books.

Murphy, Thomas J., SJ. 2001. *Jesuit Slaveholding in Maryland, 1717–1838*. New York: Routledge.

Newland, Bryan. 2022. "Federal Indian Boarding School Initiative Investigative Report." Washington, DC: Department of the Interior, Bureau of Indian Affairs. https://www.bia.gov/service/federal-indian-boarding-school-initiative.

Nortey, Justin, Patricia Tevington, and Gregory A. Smith. 2024. "9 Facts About U.S. Catholics." Pew Research Center, April 12. https://www.pewresearch.org/short-reads/2024/04/12/9-facts-about-us-catholics/.

Ochs, Stephen J. 1990. *Desegregating the Altar: The Josephites and the Struggle for Black Priests, 1871–1960.* Baton Rouge, LA: Louisiana University Press.

O'Connell, Maureen H. *Undoing the Knots: Five Generations of American Catholic Anti-Blackness.* Boston: Beacon Press.

Oppel, Richard A., Jr., Derrick Bryson Taylor, and Nicholas Bogel-Burroughs. 2021. "What To Know About Breonna Taylor's Death." *The New York Times,* April 26.

Otterman, Sharon. 2014. "The Murder of George Floyd." *New York Times,* November 2. Multiple articles are listed under this title.

Otterman, Sharon, and Joseph Goldstein. 2021. "New York City's Biggest Police Union Sues over the City's Vaccine Mandate." *The New York Times,* October 25.

Pashman, Manya Brachear. 2014. "Cardinal: Closing 7 Schools Unavoidable in Cash-Strapped District." *Chicago Tribune,* October 29.

Perez, Archbishop Nelson. 2020. "Archbishop Nelson Perez Statement on the Death of George Floyd and Racial and Social Injustice." Archdiocese of Philadelphia. https://stgensparish.com/2020/05/31/archbishop-nelson-perez-statement-on-the-death-of-george-floyd-and-racial-social-injustice/.

Phan, Peter C. and Diana Hayes. 2005. *Many Faces, One Church: Cultural Diversity and the American Catholic Experience.* New York: Rowman & Littlefield Publishers, Inc.

Pirtle, Whitney N., Breanna Brock, Nonzenzele Aldonza, Kaline Leke, and Dallas Edge. 2021. "'I Didn't Know What Anti-Blackness Was Until I Got Here': The Unmet Needs of Black Students at Hispanic-Serving Institutions." *Urban Education* October: 1–28.

Poole, Stafford, CM, and Douglas J. Slawson, CM. 1986. *Church and Slave in Perry County Missouri, 1818–1865.* Lewiston, NY: The Edwin Mellen Press.

Poole, Stafford, CM, and Douglas J. Slawson, CM. 1986. *Church and Slave in Perry County Missouri, 1818–1865.* Lewiston, NY: The Edwin Mellen Press.

Pope Francis. 2014. "Pope Francis: Address to European Parliament." *Vatican Radio,* October 31.

Pratt, Tia Noelle. 2010. *Finding A Place At The Table: Identity Formation Among African-American Catholics.* Doctoral Dissertation. New York: Fordham University.

Pratt, Tia Noelle. 2017. Review of *Parish and Place: Making Room for Diversity in the American Catholic Church,* by Tricia Colleen Bruce. *American Catholic Studies* 129 (1): 56–57.

Pratt, Tia Noelle. 2019a. "Confronting Truths About White Supremacy: Why I'm Writing a Book About Black Catholics and Systemic Racism." *Faithfully*, July.

Pratt, Tia Noelle. 2019b. "There Is Time for the Church to Support Black Catholics—If It Has the Will to Do So." *America*, September 18. https://www.americamagazine.org/faith/2019/09/18/there-time-church-support-black-catholics-if-it-has-will-do-so.

Pratt, Tia Noelle. 2020. "Authentically Black, Truly Catholic: Liturgy and Identity in African-American Parish Life." *Commonweal*, April.

Pratt, Tia Noelle. 2022. "Why Pew's New Study on Black Catholicism Is Critical for US Church Leaders." *National Catholic Reporter*, March 16. https://www.ncronline.org/news/opinion/why-pews-new-study-black-catholicism-critical-us-church-leaders.

Pratt, Tia Noelle. 2023. "Augustine's African Heritage Matters." *U.S. Catholic*, April 28.

Presbyterian Historical Society: The National Archives of the PC(USA). "Philadelphia, Fourth Presbyterian Church." https://www.history.pcusa.org/collections/research-tools/church-record-surveys/pennsylvania/philadelphia-fourth-presbyterian.

Quattlebaum, Jeremy. 2009. *The Necessity for Ruins*, November 23. https://ruins.wordpress.com/2009/11/23/consummatum-est-the-demolition-of-transfiguration/#more-1159.

Reznik, Francesca. 2019. *Losing Faith: The Fight to Save Philadelphia's Historic Catholic Churches*. Senior Thesis. University of Pennsylvania.

Rivers, Clarence Rufus J. 1998. "The Oral African Tradition Versus the Ocular Western Tradition: The Spirit in Worship." In *Taking Down Our Harps: Black Catholics in the United States*, 232–46. Maryknoll, NY: Orbis Books.

Robertson, Campbell. "Schools in One Virginia County to Reinstate Confederate Names." *New York Times*, May 10, 2024. https://www.nytimes.com/2024/05/10/us/virginia-confederate-school-stonewall-jackson-shenandoah.html?smtyp=cur&smid=tw-nytimes.

Rose, Charlie. "Interview with Toni Morrison." *Charlie Rose*. PBS. May 7, 1993. https://charlierose.com/videos/31212.

Rose-Milavec, Deborah. 2020. "God's Dream Deferred: The Dismantling of St. Anthony Parish in Madisonville." FutureChurch Blog, ND. https://myemail.constantcontact.com/God-s-Dream-Deferred---The-Dismantling-of-St--Anthony-s-Parish-in-Madisonville.html?soid=1101674625527&aid=AmQZ9eApES0.

Rothman, Adam and Elsa Barraza Mendoza, eds. 2011. *Facing Georgetown's History: A Reader on Slavery, Memory, and Reconciliation*. Washington, DC: Georgetown University Press.

Rowe, Cyprian Lamar, FMS. 1994. "A Tale of War, A Tale of Woe." *Plenty Good Room* September/October: 10–13.

Rowe, Erin Kathleen. 2019. *Black Saints in Early Modern Global Catholicism*. New York: Cambridge University Press.

Russ, Valerie. 2020. "Black Members of St. Charles Borromeo Church in South Philly Allege Racism and Will Protest to Declare Their 'Parish Lives Matter.'" *The Philadelphia Inquirer*, July 18. https://www.inquirer.com/news/black-parishioners-protest-st-charles-borromeo-church-philadelphia-black-lives-matter-20200718.html#loaded.

Rzeznik, Thomas. 2009. "The Church in the Changing City: Parochial Restructuring in the Archdiocese of Philadelphia in Historical Perspective." *U.S. Catholic Historian* 27:73–90.

Sacred Congregation for the Doctrine of the Faith. 1975. "Persona Humana: Declaration on Certain Questions Concerning Sexual Ethics." Congregation for the Doctrine of the Faith. www.vatican.va/romancuria.html.

Sanjek, Roger. 1994. "Intermarriage and the Future of Races in the United States." In *Race*, edited by Stephen Gregory and Roger Sanjek, 103–30. New Brunswick, NJ: Rutgers University Press.

Schmidt, Kelly. 2019. "Enslaved Faith Communities in the Jesuits' Missouri Mission," *U.S. Catholic Historian* 37 (2): 49–81.

Schnoor, Randal F. 2006. "Being Gay and Jewish: Negotiating Intersecting Identities." *Sociology of Religion* 67:43–60.

Segura, Olga M. 2021. *Birth of a Movement: Black Lives Matter and the Catholic Church*. Maryknoll, NY: Orbis Books.

Shaw, Stephen J. 1991. *The Catholic Parish as a Way-Station of Ethnicity and Americanization: Chicago's Germans and Italians, 1903–1939*. Brooklyn, NY: Carson Publishing, Inc.

Smith, Christian, Brandon Vaidyanathan, Nancy Tatom Ammerman, José Casanova, Hilary Davidson, Elaine Howard Ecklund, John H. Evans, Philip S. Gorski, Mary Ellen Konieczny, Jason A. Springs, Jenny Trinitapoli, and Meredith Whitnah. 2013. "Roundtable on the Sociology of Religion: Twenty-Three Theses on the Status of Religion in American Sociology—A Mellon Working-Group Reflection." *Journal of the American Academy of Religion* 81:903–38.

Smith, Christian, Kyle Longest, Jonathan Hill, and Kari Christoffersen. 2014. *Young Catholic America: Emerging Adults In, Out of, and Gone from the Church.* New York: Oxford University Press.

Society of the Sacred Heart. "Committee on Slavery, Accountability and Reconciliation." https://rscj.org/history-enslavement/the-committee-on-slavery-accountability-and-reconciliation-2016-2020.

Soto, Bishop Jamie. 2020. "Bishop Jaime Soto Calls for Prayer in Wake of George Floyd Death and Civil Unrest." June 1. Diocese of Sacramento. https://www.scd.org/news/bishop-jaime-soto-calls-prayer-wake-george-floyd-death-and-civil-unrest..

Spalding, Thomas W. 1989. *The Premier See: A History of the Archdiocese of Baltimore, 1789–1994.* Baltimore: The Johns Hopkins University Press.

Steinberg, Stephen. 2007. *Race Relations: A Critique.* Stanford, CA: Stanford University Press.

Svrluga, Susan. 2018. "'Make it right': Descendants of Slaves Demand Restitution from Georgetown." *The Washington Post*, January 17. https://www.washingtonpost.com/news/grade-point/wp/2018/01/16/__trashed-2/.

Swarns, Rachel L. 2016a. "272 Slaves Were Sold to Slave Georgetown. What Does It Owe Their Descendants?" *The New York Times*, April 16.

Swarns, Rachel L. 2016b. "Georgetown University Plans Steps to Atone for Slave Past." *The New York Times*, September 1.

Swarns, Rachel. 2019a. "The Nuns Who Bought and Sold Human Beings." *New York Times*, August 2.

Swarns, Rachel L. 2019b. "Is Georgetown's $400,000-a-Year Plan to Aid Slave Descendants Enough?" *The New York Times*, October 30.

Thumma, Scott. 1991. "Negotiating a Religious Identity: The Case of the Gay Evangelical." *Sociological Analysis* 52:333–47.

Torralva, Krista M. 2021. *The Dallas Morning News*, August 5.

Ulshafer, Thomas, P.S.S. 2019. "Slavery and the Early Sulpician Community in Maryland." *U.S. Catholic Historian.* 37 (2): 1–21.

United States Census Bureau. ND. "Quick Facts." *United States Census Bureau.*

United States Conference of Catholic Bishops. 2020. "USCCB and (Arch)-Diocesan Statements on the Death of George Floyd and National Protests." USCCB. www.usccb.org/usccb-and-archdiocesan-statements-death-george-floyd-and-national-protests..

United States Conference of Catholic Bishops. 2021. "African American Affairs Demographics." Washington, DC: United States Conference of Catholic Bishops.. https://www.usccb.org/committees/african-american-affairs/demographics#:~:text=There%20are%203%20million%20African,Coast%20and%20in%20the%20South.

United States Conference of Catholic Bishops. Psalms. https://bible.usccb.org/bible/psalms/0.

The Vatican. Code of Canon Law, Book IV, Function of the Church: Part III: Sacred Places and Times (Cann. 1205–1243). https://www.vatican.va/archive/cod-iuris-canonici/eng/documents/cic_lib4-cann1205-1243_en.html#chapter_I.

The Vatican. "Constitution on the Sacred Liturgy Sacrosanctum Concilium."

Walton, Gerald. 2006. "'Fag Church': Men Who Integrate Gay and Christian Identities." *Journal of Homosexuality* 51:1–17.

Weisenfeld, Judith. 2016. *New World A-Coming: Black Religion and Racial Identity during the Great Migration*. New York: NYU Press.

Wendt, Jana. 1998. "Toni Morrison: Uncensored." Australian Broadcasting Corporation. https://www.youtube.com/watch?v=DQ0mMjII22I&t=207s.

West, Melanie Grayce. 2015. *The Wall Street Journal*, February 10.

White, Christopher. 2022. "Pope Francis Tells Parents Not to Condemn Children with Different Sexual Orientations." *National Catholic Reporter*, January 26. https://www.ncronline.org/news/vatican/pope-francis-tells-parents-not-condemn-children-different-sexual-orientations.

Whitehead, Andrew L. and Samuel L. Perry. 2020. *Taking America Back for God: Christian Nationalism in the United States*. New York: Oxford University Press.

Whitt, O. P. and D. Reginald. 1998. "*Varietates Legitimae* and an African-American Liturgical Tradition." In *Taking Down Our Harps: Black Catholics in the United States*, 24780. Maryknoll, NY: Orbis Books.

Wigglesworth, Alex. 2015. *The Philadelphia Inquirer*, June 14. https://www.inquirer.com/philly/news/breaking/Archdiocese_announces_closure_of_three_Philly-area_churches.html.

Williams, Shannen Dee. 2016a. "Subversive Images and Forgotten Truths: A Selected Visual History of Black Women Religious" in *American Catholic Studies*, 127 (Fall 2016): 93–103.

Williams, Shannen Dee. 2016b. "The Color of Christ's Brides." *American Catholic Studies* 127, no. 4 (Fall): 14–21.

Williams, Shannen Dee. 2017. "'You Could Do the Irish Jig, But Anything African Was Taboo:' Black Nuns, Contested Memories, and the 20th-Century Struggle to Desegregate U.S. Religious Life." *Journal of African American History* 102, no. 2 (Spring): 125–56.

Wood, Sam. 2019a. "4 Archdiocese Parishes in Lower Northeast Philadelphia to Merge Effective July 1." *The Philadelphia Inquirer*, May 19. https://www.inquirer.com/news/archdiocese-philadelphia-four-parishes-merge--20190519.html.

Wood, Sam. 2019b. "3 Roman Catholic Churches to Close in Society Hill, West Philly, and Northeast." *The Philadelphia Inquirer*, July 28. https://www.inquirer.com/news/archdiocese-of-philadelphia-closes-holy-trinity-our-lady-of-ransom-saint-rose-of-lima-20190728.html.

Woodberry, Robert D., Jerry Z. Park, and Lyman A. Kellstedt, with Mark D. Regnerus, Brian Steensland. 2012. "The Measure of American Religious Traditions: Theoretical and Measurement Considerations." *Social Forces* 91: 65–73.

Wootson, Cleve R., Jr. 2018a. "A White Woman Called Police on a Black 12-Year-Old Who Was Mowing Grass." *The Washington Post*, June 30.

Wootson, Cleve R., Jr. 2018b. "An 8-Year-Old Tried Selling Water for a Trip to Disneyland. A White Woman Threatened to Call Police." *The Washington Post*, June 25.

Wright, Bradley R. E., Michael Wallace, Annie Scola Wisnesky, Christopher M. Donnelly, Stacy Missari, and Christine Zozula. 2015. "Religion, Race, and Discrimination: A Field Experiment of How American Churches Welcome Newcomers." *Journal for the Scientific Study of Religion* 54:185–204.

Yeung, King-To and Mindy Stombler. 2000. "Gay and Greek: The Identity Paradox of Gay Fraternities." *Social Problems* 47:134–52.

Yeung, King-To, Mindy Stombler, Reneé Wharton. 2006. "Making Men in Gay Fraternities: Resisting and Reproducing Multiple Dimensions of Hegemonic Masculinity." *Gender & Society* 20:5–31.

Zech, Charles E., Mary L. Gautier, Mark M. Gray, Jonathon L. Wiggins, and Thomas P. Gaunt, S.J. 2017. *Catholic Parishes of the 21st Century*. New York: Oxford University Press.

INDEX

A
Ammerman, Nancy, 6, 24, 70, 133
Archdiocese
  of Chicago, 47
  of New York, 27, 55, 59
Anderson, Elijah, 15, 86, 106, 133
assimilation, 33, 35, 38

B
Bowman, Thea, sister, FSPA, 4

C
canon law, 48, 75, 79, 84, 100, 104, 136
Center for Applied Research in the
  Apostolate (CARA), 32, 134–36
cosmopolitan canopy. *See* Anderson,
  Elijah
Congregation of the Mission. *See*
  Vincentians

D
Dillon, Michele, 22–23
Du Bois, W. E. B., 14, 25, 61, 65, 85, 126
Dufour, Lynn Resnick, 22–24, 70

E
Exoticism of Black Catholics, 19, 133

F
Feagin, Joe R., 14–15, 25, 133

G
gentrification, 81–83, 90

H
Healy Brothers, 46
Hughes, John, archbishop, 36, 44–45

I
institutional isomorphism, 8, 11

J
Jesuits, 41–42, 46, 50, 137-138
Josephites, 43, 45, 47, 49, 109

K
Krol, John, cardinal, 28, 84, 90, 92–93, 98

L
LGBTQ+ Catholics, 82, 128–29
liturgy, styles of, 53–55

M
Massingale, Bryan, 12, 54, 106

O
owning. *See* Dillon, Michele

P
Pew Research Center, 8, 32, 51, 54, 116, 128, 134

S
sifting. *See* Dufour, Lynn Resnick
Slattery, John, 43–44, 47–50, 109–10
slavery, 39–40, 42, 71, 137, 139–40
Society of Jesus. *See* Jesuits
Society of St. Joseph. *See* Josephites

T
Tolton, Augustus, 46–48

U
Uncles, Charles Randolph, 45–46, 49
U.S. Conference of Catholic Bishops (USCCB), 125

V
Vincentians, 40, 138

W
What We Have Seen and Heard, 27, 70

TIA NOELLE PRATT is assistant vice president and director of mission engagement and strategic initiatives in the Office for Mission and Ministry and assistant professor of sociology at Villanova University.

www.ingramcontent.com/pod-product-compliance
Lightning Source LLC
Chambersburg PA
CBHW070358100426
42812CB00005B/1556